PRAISE FOR JUNK FILM:

"Katharine Coldiron dives headfirst into th
and clears a bold new space for thinking ai
sures of cinematic crap... A smart and snea...y .... ,. ...
a cultural critic with a magpie's eye for glittering swill."
—TY BURR, FILM CRITIC ("TY BURR'S WATCH LIST") AND AUTHOR
(*GODS LIKE US: ON MOVIE STARDOM AND MODERN FAME*)

"I've always thought that if art is expression, can it fail? Katharine
Coldiron does a wonderful job of examining this from both sides. She
finds and analyzes a fascinating array of films. It made me laugh many
times, and actually made me want to have a bad movie marathon!"
—GREG SESTERO, ACTOR AND AUTHOR, *THE DISASTER ARTIST*

"Bad movies have been very good to me - I've watched hundreds as
a writer for Mystery Science Theater 3000 and RiffTrax, and even
voluntarily. Katharine Coldiron's examination of such movies names
why I appreciate them so much - it's smart, insightful, and entertaining, and it's for film aficionados and snobs alike."
—MARY JO PEHL, COMEDIENNE (RIFFTRAX, MST3K)
AND WRITER (*DUMB DUMB DUMB*)

"An entertaining ode to cinematic duds. 'Bad movies are
teaching tools for making and studying good movies,' she contends,
exploring what [bad] films and television shows...accidentally
reveal about the techniques of quality filmmaking. Coldiron's
analysis...unearths unexpected wisdom about how movies work.
Cinephiles will enjoy digging into this."
—PUBLISHERS WEEKLY

JUNK FILM

WHY BAD MOVIES MATTER

BY KATHARINE COLDIRON

JUNK FILM: WHY BAD MOVIES MATTER

ISBN: 979-8-9872083-1-1

CASTLE BRIDGE MEDIA
Denver, Colorado, USA
castlebridgemedia.com

Edited by Jason Henderson & In Churl Yo
Designed by In Churl Yo

Cover Composite includes publicity stills from *Best F(r)iends*,
Plan 9 From Outer Space, *Ruby*, *Safe Haven*, *Showgirls*,
Staying Alive, and *Switchblade Sisters*.

For Bill Corbett, Kevin Murphy,
and Mike Nelson

CONTENTS

"There ain't no good! There ain't no bad!"
-THE APPLE, 1980

"Oh, there's bad."
-RIFFTRAX, 2013

INTRODUCTION:

WELCOME TO THE JUNKYARD

I'M SO HAPPY YOU'RE reading this.

I've been studying bad film and other kinds of bad art seriously for about five years, and studying it unseriously for many years longer. This book is the result of all those studies, which means its tone varies between serious and less so. As such, I hope it's informational, but also fun to read. Without a sense of humor, bad art is unstudiable.

The basic operation of this book is discussing bad art: movies, television, and books that are not aesthetically sound. If this were a philosophy text, I would need to define "good" and "bad," relying on Immanuel Kant, or Webster's, or possibly Michael Jackson. But this is not a philosophy text. I've spent years probing art that's "bad," and trying to define this term always seems to be an empty, ambiguous exercise compared to studying the art itself. What goes on in the colossal misfire of *Cop Rock* (1990), or the egocentric exercises of Sean Penn's fiction writing, is much more interesting to me than a collection of unanswerable questions about semiotics and aesthetics. I can already hear one of my grad school mentors calling this lazy thinking, and demanding definitions of "good" and "bad" before I go any further. But what "bad art" means can be an emotional and even moral minefield, as the final essay in this book charts. I'd much rather talk about the art and leave the broader questions to (real) philosophers.

In the course of picking out a title for this collection, an adviser told me he didn't like the word "junk" because it referred to something "discarded and unwanted." He said it's possible to justify loving something *bad*, but junk is "something that someone no longer cares about."

My response was, well, exactly. With exceptions, I'm not interested in defending, reclaiming, or otherwise endorsing these works as good art. I'm not dragging things home from the junkyard to clean them up. I'm going to the junkyard and yelling at the assembled crows about what I see in the piles. That's why I thought *Junk Film* was exactly the right title, because these films and TV and books *are* junk, they *are* discarded and unwanted. Reasonably so; they're terrible. That's the risk you take by picking up this book: that I'm capable of convincing you to visit the junkyard and listen to me.

I did find a few redeemable objects among the refuse. In what follows, I defend Jack Hill's *Switchblade Sisters* (1975) and George Barry's *Death Bed: The Bed that Eats* (1977) as good art, even if they aren't widely accepted as such. They look like bad art, though, which is why they're here. I also write positively about Justin MacGregor's *Best F(r)iends* (2018), but it's here because of its paratextual connections to Tommy Wiseau's infamous *The Room* (2003). It's also here because it has something distinctive in common with a lot of the bad art in this book: it's surprising. I'm a little more dubious about Curtis Harrington's *Ruby* (1977), which is pretty bad, but has some redeeming qualities.

Less dubious are *Cop Rock*, one of the worst ideas for a television show ever to be realized; the Teen Agers films of the 1940s, which demonstrate the problems of digging intentionally disposable art out of the junkyard seven decades later; *After Last Season* (2009), a film so odd it could be considered outsider art; *Attack of the 50 Ft. Woman* (1958), which should be so much better than it is; the films of Neil Breen, universally, unassailably terrible; and *Showgirls* (1995) and *Staying Alive* (1983), dance films with a special commonality that makes them both confusingly awful.

One film, one little film of less than 80 minutes, released 64 years ago, overshadows all these. *Junk Film* opens with its longest essay: a detailed two-part discussion of Edward D. Wood, Jr.'s *Plan 9 from Outer Space* (1959). The first part of the essay, Analysis, explains *Plan 9*'s hallowed place in the pantheon of bad film and speaks generally about what bad film is, how it moves through the world, and its broad categories. The second part, Exegesis, is just that: a scene-by-scene breakdown of *Plan 9* that illuminates its many failures and few successes.

I recognize that introducing the reader to this book with the longest and most detailed essay is a bit demanding, but my work on *Plan 9* sets forth some foundational ideas for the remainder of the book. In it, I offer five basic premises:

(1) Bad movies are unconvincing as movies.
(2) They are, instead, successful records of attempts at making movies. This quality means they give the audience a dual, holographic view: of the successful record and of the failed attempt.
(3) Knowing more about the context of a bad movie is crucial to understanding and analyzing it, but is hardly a license to excuse it.
(4) Bad movies are teaching tools for making and studying good movies.
(5) As such, they are best studied in aggregate.

To explain these ideas in greater detail, I'll refer you to myself, in the essays that follow. I expand upon these points most lucidly in the conclusion to the *Plan 9* essay (pp. 74-78), using specific examples from the film to do so.

For all these movies, I took a pretty typical approach for film studies/criticism: researched them to some degree, watched them multiple times, and took notes, paying attention to camera angles, lighting, mise-en-scène, performance, editing,

PLAN 9 FROM OUTER SPACE PUBLICITY STILL/REYNOLDS PICTURES

shot length, historical context, and aspects of the screenplay (characterization, dialogue). In assessing their quality, I compared them to the generally agreed-upon canon for good film, holding them up to the basic standards established by D.W. Griffith, Cecil B. DeMille, Sergei Eisenstein, *et al* and developed into universality by midcentury Hollywood directors. I'm using obvious and generic examples here because those are the standards by which I'm judging "good" or "bad"—not iconoclasts like Ingmar Bergman or Stanley Kubrick. For those not versed in film history, this process is similar to judging a book's textual quality by how it compares to *Fun with Dick and Jane*, not to *The Sound and the Fury*.[1] Using this process, I progressed through the list of bad or "bad" films about which I had something to say until I had most of a manuscript.

Then I realized, as I was writing about *After Last Season*, that I had been studying the films as texts, and hadn't really turned the mirror to the audience. How films *are* is interesting enough to write about, but how films *affect us* is a murkier and more intriguing set of questions. *Season* affected me strongly, and that reaction, surely, should be part of how I wrote about it.

I had a similar reaction to the prose of Amanda McKittrick Ros. I could break it down and examine why it didn't work, but her effect is more mystical than that. Her sentences broke my brain, temporarily. As Mark O'Connell explains:

> Read a few chapters of one of her books and then pick up a book by, say, Marilynne Robinson…and even Robinson's flawless sentences start to seem slightly contrived. Ros's writing is not just bad, in other words; its badness is so potent that it seems to undermine the very idea of literature, to expose the whole endeavor of making art out of language as essentially and irredeemably fraudulent—and, even worse, silly.

Great prose has infected how I read, too. The sentences in Edna O'Brien's *The Light of Evening* and the skilled fragmentation of Lidia Yuknavitch's *The Chronology of Water* both made perfectly fine writing seem clunky and childish for a little while, until the effect wore off. This is part of why my Ros/Penn essay is in this book, which is otherwise about film and TV: not just because those books are bad, but because they are bad in a way that lit up my brain.

This audience effect seemed as important as pure analysis to understanding bad art generally and these bad works of art particularly. Thus, the final essay in this book undertakes what we like, and what it means that we like it. I examine two films that are bad, in different degrees, and how I have reconciled the fact that I like them anyway.

In brief, *Junk Film* records my thoughts and research about bad art, mostly movies, with some TV and a couple of books thrown in for fun. It doesn't stick to scholarship or to pop analysis, but it endeavors not to bore or to regurgitate staid ideas. It's a book I wrote seriously, but also in the hope that it would be fun for both of us, you and me. You're welcome to read it however you like, whether just the one essay you care about or cover to cover or backwards. All I want is for you to enjoy it. If art, good or bad or otherwise, can't be enjoyed, what's the point of consuming it?

---

1 I recognize that this paragraph is full of argument fodder. This is an introduction, not a dissertation.

A MONOGRAPH ON BAD FILM:

PLAN 9 FROM OUTER SPACE

Author's Note

THE TWO SECTIONS OF this long essay overlap. I wrote it so that you can choose to read just one or the other, rather than both, if you'd like. The central theses exist in both places.

It was difficult to determine how to give names to the characters/actors in *Plan 9 from Outer Space* as I write about them. It would be foolish to call Tor Johnson by his character's name once he is undead, because his bulk and reputation are so clearly the point of his casting; similarly, Bela Lugosi is never given a proper character name. However, other actors are more obscure than these two, so I think of them with the characters' names rather than the actors'. The movie doesn't do a particularly adequate job introducing some of them, though. To save us both a headache, here's a *dramatis personae*:

Jeff Trent (Gregory Walcott) = the husband/pilot
Paula Trent (Mona McKinnon) = the wife
Col. Edwards (Tom Keene) = military guy "in charge of saucer field activity"
Inspector Clay (Tor Johnson) = huge bald dude who becomes ghoul
Eros (Dudley Manlove) = main alien, very smug
Tanna (Joanna Lee) = female alien, not a lot of lines
Ruler (John "Bunny" Breckinridge) = alien in charge; bulging, sleepy eyes
Lt. Harper (Duke Moore) = policeman in the trenchcoat
Larry (Carl Anthony) = low-voiced policeman

"Perhaps none of our films have, so far, been up for awards, but they are **entertaining pictures."**

—EDWARD D. WOOD, JR.,*HOLLYWOOD RAT RACE*

"How much can you say?
He tried, mostly failed, and died."

—TED NEWSOM, *THE CINEMATIC MISADVENTURES OF ED WOOD*

Kelton (Paul Marco) = bumbling policeman
Gen. Roberts (Lyle Talbot) = military guy who assigns Edwards to cemetery
Vampira (Maila Nurmi) = Vampira, wife of the old man, only seen as ghoul
Old Man (Bela Lugosi) = real Lugosi, starts alive and becomes ghoul
Dead Old Man (Tom Mason) = faux-Lugosi, ghoul with cape over face
Criswell (Criswell) = narrator, platinum blond guy who opens and closes movie

The film takes place in a handful of locations: a plane cockpit, the patio of a house, the inside of a spaceship. It's not hard to distinguish these, to refer to them and be understood. However, one major location, a cemetery, is multiple.

CEMETERY (A), THE LOCATION CEMETERY

CEMETERY (C), THE PHOTO CEMETERY

Scenes with Bela Lugosi were evidently shot in a real cemetery in Sacramento (a).[1] Scenes with other characters meant to be at the cemetery were shot somewhere outdoors, not necessarily at a cemetery at all, and almost certainly not in Sacramento (b).[2] One still photograph, used repeatedly for process shots, is likely of a cemetery in Los Angeles, although my research has not uncovered which one (c). Finally, many scenes take place in a "cemetery" setting that's clearly in a studio, as the scenery is unconvincing and the lighting is artificial (d). I refer to (a) and (b) as "the location cemetery," (c) as "the photo cemetery" or similar, and (d) as "the studio cemetery."

It's useful to distinguish these locales when the film cuts back and forth between them. However, the filmmaker clearly intends for them all to be one single location. Since the gap between intention and execution is part of what I'm studying here, we need to understand both, particularly with regard to the cemetery. Thus, each of the locations has a separate nickname, even though they're all meant, per the filmmaker, to be the same place.

If this seems confusing, well, we're on the right track.

---

1 According to Ed Wood in *Nightmare of Ecstasy*. I don't understand how this is possible, as it means he took Lugosi, then quite frail, from Los Angeles all the way to Sacramento, in the cars and on the roads of 1955-6, just to film a few scenes. That seems highly unlikely. I don't think I'm misinterpreting his storytelling in the book, but his wording isn't perfectly clear.
2 Possibly in Sylmar, per *The Cinematic Misadventures of Ed Wood*.

Plan 9 from Outer Space is in the public domain. The quotes from the screenplay are a mix of my own transcription, a transcribed version found on the internet,[3] and the authorized original screenplay edited by Tom Mason and published in 1990 by Malibu Graphics. (A full bibliography is available at the end of this

CEMETERY (D), THE STUDIO CEMETERY

volume.) I mixed these sources in order to make sense of inconsistencies. For example, the neologism "Solaronite" is pronounced differently than it appears in the published script, so I went with the script. Meanwhile, Col. Edwards is named Col. Rance in the script, so I went with the finished film.

As I reviewed the script against the close readings I did on certain scenes, I found that some of the film's smaller and more absurd contradictions did not exist in Wood's words. Some of the word choices that appear in the film were evidently mistakes by the actors, late scene changes, or cuts in the editing room, potentially due to unusable film. It's not my intention to unfairly ridicule Edward D. Wood, Jr. or his work by ignoring any actual logic in his screenplay and instead highlighting the illogic that wound up on the screen. I want to give him credit where it's due. Whenever I analyze a flaw in the film that is not a flaw in the screenplay, I'll footnote it with the written lines. If I don't remark on the differences, either the screenplay matches the film or the difference is irrelevant. I will note this again later, but the point to know now is that I do not wish to be cruel to Wood when he doesn't deserve it.

That said, if an actor makes a mistake that causes a scene to stop making sense, you *reshoot the scene* with the correct line. Wood was famously uninterested in retakes, either for mistakes or for coverage, and so, if his finished scenes fail to make sense, it's still his fault.

The film was shot in 1956 and released in limited runs for a couple of years, until the official run began in 1959. As such, I refer to multiple years in what follows, depending on whether I'm talking about filming or release. It's not sloppy editing. Also, the film was shot in black and white, but a colorized version appeared around 2006.

All emphasis in quoted dialogue is mine.

A monograph—an essay the length of a standalone book—is a weird undertaking. I wrote one about *Plan 9* because I knew I wanted one essay to gather up all my best thoughts about bad movies. Please indulge me if I stray too far off the point.

---

3 From horrorlair.com.

I: Analysis

1. EXTRAORDINARY

As with many films that have changed my life, succored my days, kept me warm when I felt the cold world, I have no memory of the first time I saw *Plan 9 from Outer Space*. One day it was not in my life, and the next day, immutably, it was. I doubt I was fully a child when I saw the movie, and I know it doesn't belong to a situation where I saw it on TV one afternoon in adolescence and let the memory sleep until I needed to waken it. The watching was certainly deliberate, but information on how it took place is not available.

In my late teens, my father started collecting DVDs of all possible quality— everything from *La Dolce Vita* (1960) to *They Saved Hitler's Brain* (1968ish).[4] Certainly *Plan 9* was among them. I doubt that was the first time I'd heard of it, though. Just the most likely occasion for me to run into it.

A memory I can't disconnect from *Plan 9* is advertisements for a record store in Charlottesville, Virginia. I lived there between ages 11 and 13, late 1992 to early 1995, and a very cool record store named Plan 9 operated there. (A small blessing: it still operates as of this writing.) The store used clips from the movie in its TV ads, particularly a duplicated audio bite of Dudley Manlove saying "Plan 9, Plan 9," from the scene where Eros explains his progress to his fey, uninterested boss. From this distance I love that someone named their record store after this movie, and that they elected to use the movie in their ads. But I got it backwards because of my age: I knew about the store before the movie.

Anyway, I don't remember the first time I saw *Plan 9 from Outer Space*, and thus I don't remember my first impressions. Never at any time did I believe I was sitting down to watch a good movie, which means I never gave it a chance to be good, not until I'd come to know it better. I knew the film's reputation going in; I knew I was watching it because it was not good.

Why would anyone do this? It's perverse. At first glance, it doesn't make sense— setting yourself up for a negative experience. At the time, in all likelihood, I was doing it to laugh, to have fun at *Plan 9*'s expense. I learned the practice from my father, who learned it from I know not where. *Mystery Science Theater 3000* (1988-98), possibly, although he was well into adulthood when he found that show. Based on how gleefully he embraced bad movies, I can't believe he didn't have an existing attraction to them when *MST3K* came around.

It's a big question, *why watch bad movies*, and I'm tempted to set it aside for

---

4 Actually an interesting film. It was mostly shot in the early 1960s and then finished by a group of 1970s film students, and you can really tell which scenes were shot when because of the clothes. The Hitler sequences involve the Fuhrer's head in a bottle, just like on *Futurama* (1999-present), and he's as much of a monster to the unlucky characters in the film as any giant bug. The head dies in a fire at the end.

later and get going on *Plan 9*. But, in a way, it's the entire question of this project. If *Plan 9* has any worth at all, it's not because it's any good. It's because it's bad. That badness must have some worthwhile quality, or this project has an empty purpose. The problem could swing philosophical, where I try to define what "good" and "bad" are and what value exists in each. But that seems far afield, when my purpose here is limited to the value, specifically, of *Plan 9 from Outer Space*, of what the film has to show us both literally and figuratively.

Some personalities attract to bad movies because they are bullies and like to laugh at the expense of others. Some enjoy watching what happens when things go wrong. But some—and I've grown into this; I doubt I considered it when I first saw *Plan 9*—want to compare a film going sideways to a film going straight. *Plan 9* is terrible in a rainbow of ways, from conception to completion, from technical to tactical. In picking apart all these flaws and mistakes, I can see and understand why good films work. I'm convinced, in fact, that it's easier to understand good film by examining bad film than by examining good film.

It strikes me, trying to remember how *Plan 9* entered my life, that I watched all those bad movies my dad bought on DVD at around the same time I awakened to film as an art form. I didn't realize how thoroughly my brain was built to analyze film until mid-college, but by then I'd seen dozens of classics, written lengthy emails to friends and mentors about Paul Thomas Anderson and Quentin Tarantino, started building a DVD collection of my own. And all the time I was absorbing Hitchcock and Lynch and the Coens and Bergman and Deren and Buñuel and Dreyer and Keaton, I was watching schlock from the 50s, slashers from the 80s, no-budget garbage from multiple decades.

It all happened at the same time: dizzying heights of fine film, hilarious lows of bad movies. Eventually they became connected in my mind. Eventually I saw that one is not possible without the other, and that a full education in film must include both, possibly in equal abundance.

Such an education might well begin with *Plan 9 from Outer Space*. There exists a canon of bad movies, just as there is of good, and *Plan 9* is as indispensable on one list as *Citizen Kane* (1941) is on the other. It commits every mistake, and fails in every particular.[5] We go to the movies to see something extraordinary, no matter what or when or wherefore. And *Plan 9* most assuredly is extraordinary.

2. CONTEXT

I'm not sure whether I'm writing this with the assumption that you have or haven't seen *Plan 9 from Outer Space*. Do people read essays this long about objects they aren't already familiar with? To learn about them prior to experiencing them? That's valid, but it feels odd. No one writes a monograph-length essay without obsession, and obsession is repellent without a notion of its object.

As a critic I always write somewhere in the middle of the assumption that you have or haven't been here before. I summarize the book or movie as competently

---

5   With minor exceptions. We'll get there.

and briefly as possible, providing what I hope is a reasonable picture to those who don't know the work without boring the folks who do. That's a bit of an art form in itself. The summary must not leave out anything important, nor stuff in too much detail, and it must be lively. If the object under examination is complicated, or bad, or character-driven, the challenge multiplies. I've occasionally cheated by saying my space is too limited to go into a full plot summary, or by pretending I'm writing a trailer script and speaking in taglines. *Will he get the girl? Will she overcome her past? Who's out to get them? It's a race against time to uncover the real truth about this heartfelt confession.* I hope my reader rolls her eyes as she understands that I'm trying to make her roll her eyes.

All that considered, here's a summary of *Plan 9 from Outer Space*. Aliens, unhappy with Earth's irresponsibility with regard to weaponry, hatch a plot to get through to us: reanimate the corpses of the recently deceased,[6] who will then terrify and/or kill citizens, which will cause the leaders of Earth to do what the aliens say. As 1950s movies go, this plot is hardly the stupidest or least likely ever dreamed up. What makes it fall apart like tissues in water is the relationship of the plot to actual scenes appearing in the movie. The plot outlined in this summary isn't really part of the movie until 20 minutes in. Understanding the plot requires understanding that the majority of the movie doesn't necessarily advance the plot much.

The different sequences of *Plan 9* perform like a network of ideas, not all of which connect to each other. These ideas don't proceed logically, one after the other, and do not receive parallel screen time to unfold. I tried to chart the connections between major sequences or plotlines in the film. These charts were so tangled they didn't make sense. That is: all the action in the film attaches to one of nine elements,[7] but some of the elements are only connected to one or two others, while others act more centrally but still don't connect to all nine. All the ideas are in the same movie, but they don't all cross paths on-screen. Here's a list of the major sequences or plotlines, in order of how much they connect to each other:

1.   Jeff and Paula Trent
2.   Criswell
3.   Flying Saucers
4.   Aliens and Plan 9
5.   Cemetery Activity
6.   Colonel Edwards
7.   Bela Lugosi Sequence

---

6   The word "zombie" is never used. The history of zombies in film is available elsewhere, but in short, "zombie" was not so common a word in the genre film of the late 1950s as it would be a decade later, after *Night of the Living Dead* (1968). I have used the words "undead" or "ghouls" throughout this text; the film mostly uses "the dead," which is unnecessarily vague, and later on uses "ghouls."

7   Pure coincidence that there are nine plot elements in *Plan 9 from Outer Space*.

8. Policemen
9. Piloting

"Piloting" only connects to two other elements in the film (the Trents and the flying saucers), and not to the policemen, the cemetery activity, or the sequence early in the film with Bela Lugosi. Meanwhile, the Trents connect to *six* other aspects of the plot (the policemen, the cemetery activity, Col. Edwards, the flying saucers, the Lugosi sequence, and piloting). But Paula and Jeff Trent are not the primary plot of *Plan 9*. The aliens and the plan are, and they only connect directly to five other elements (the Hollywood montage, the cemetery activity, the Lugosi sequence, the Trents, and Col. Edwards).

The film comes off as a disaster on a macro level for the same reason I couldn't visually chart the plot: lack of structure, balance, or connection between sequences. While logical enough when summarized, the plot *seems* not to make any sense. It might have if it was presented in the right way, with the aliens and their plan front and center. Placing them there would mean giving the aliens scenes early and often, connecting the aliens to the ghouls clearly, cutting out some of the pointless scenes with the policemen and with Lugosi, and showing the threads coming together in such a way that the audience can make sense of it slightly before it happens.

However, in the film, some of the sequences don't connect to each other at all, while others connect in illogical ways. Criswell, for instance, opens and closes the film with awkward, vaguely doomsaying speeches, and provides voiceover to (attempt to) tie various scenes together. But he's a strange, clumsy narrator, the stock footage he narrates serves as filler, and his voiceover comes and goes so irregularly that it just forms one more untethered element, a piece of a puzzle that never becomes complete. I can see what the film was trying to do with Criswell's narration, but it fails. Badly.

Already I'm looking behind the camera for an explanation of why *Plan 9* is so bad, instead of making sense of it as a finished product. That's my special gift (or curse): I am ever Toto, pulling back the curtain on the flawed and mortal Wizard of Oz. I get that Bela Lugosi doesn't really exist as part of the same film the other actors are in because the poor man died, and the film was written around existing footage of him.[8] Offscreen context helps a flaw like this to make sense (even if it does not erase the flaw), instead of just existing on the screen for me to pillory. I get that the acting is mostly bad because Wood could not afford decent actors. I get that takes are bad because Wood had to shoot the film on an unimaginably short timeline and wouldn't or couldn't reshoot bad takes. I can perceive the motivations of this film's mistakes even as I note them, laugh at them, refuse to overlook them.

---

8   In *Nightmare of Ecstasy*, Paul Marco says Wood wrote the screenplay around some of the cast members Marco introduced him to. However, it seems much more likely, based on material in the published screenplay and accounts about the productions Wood was trying to mount in 1956, that the screenplay was written primarily to use the footage Wood had shot with Lugosi.

That's what it means to appreciate bad film. Comprehending the cost of good film and the machinery of Hollywood, learning as much context as possible, and picking apart the reasons bad films fall short by understanding *what* they were trying to do, *why* they did what they did instead, and *how* those choices led to failure. *Plan 9*'s ambitions aren't especially distinguished—it played as part of a double feature[9] with a couple of film noirs and *Devil Girl from Mars* (1954)—but the calculated compromises of even those minor ambitions help to elucidate the project's failures.

For example: how running time necessitates stock footage.[10] When Wood was making films, any film's running time had to hit a certain number to be acceptable to distributors and theaters. Using stock footage is much less expensive than shooting new footage, which involves paying actors, renting a studio, using props, and buying film. Using what amounts to public domain material is a cheap way to pad out a movie. Thus, one strategy to increase the running time for any given B movie, so as to make it acceptable to distributors, is incorporating stock footage. Knowing that chain of circumstance helps us understand why there is stock footage in *Plan 9*, and thus makes our ability to empathize with its failures that much stronger.

Why should we empathize with its failures at all? Why not dismiss bad film and go on about our jobs in cinema (creative, critical, scholarly) without seeing and studying the worst of it? If I fail to convince you across this book that bad film is profoundly instructive about the art and craft of cinema, here's another reason: all art exists on a spectrum, and it's difficult to appreciate the furthest end of the good side if you lack full familiarity with the furthest end of the bad side. A good, musical sentence may be pleasing, but if all you ever read and hear are good, musical sentences, how can you grasp the work and talent that go into them? How will you ever gain perspective about which end of the spectrum the art you absorb lives in? How will you ever understand how much further to the other side that spectrum goes? Surrounding oneself only with good art is how critics become isolated from the range of creative work that exists, how they become ever more specialized, how they find themselves in tiny, rarefied biospheres of good art of only a particular variety.

I am hardly the first to say this, but it bears repeating: growing as an artist or critic can only occur through an omnivorous diet for art. As an example from my own diet, I've read barely any horror outside of Stephen King, so I have no sense of whether he's one of the best writers in the genre or one of the worst. I can guess,

---

9 http://movieline.com/2009/09/08/plan-9-from-outer-space-the-original-bad-movie-we-love-turns-50/

10 Stock footage is film that can be reused without attendant rights issues. Generally it's footage of crowds, landmarks, or otherwise generic material. A modern example is shots of unidentifiable people (heads cut off or faces indistinct) that appear on the news when the reporters are talking in voiceover about a perennial health issue like smoking or obesity.

based on his reputation, but I can't trust that guess any further than I can trust the whims of the marketplace.

Reading and watching in multiple genres is essential, but that's about breadth of diet, and true omnivores attain depth, as well. Without bad poetry, we cannot recognize good poetry. As long as absorbing bad art doesn't lead to complacency,[11] that absorption can only increase our capacity to understand what we create. And although analyzing good art leads us to a strong understanding of why it works as it does—indeed, it's the entire model of arts education—analyzing bad art is faster, and can even be more fun.

3. AUTEUR

At some point we must talk about the filmmaker, Edward D. Wood, Jr., whose reputation may precede him into these pages. Johnny Depp memorably portrayed him in Tim Burton's *Ed Wood* (1994), which concludes with the first screening of *Plan 9*. It's a very good and interesting film, one that makes an optimistic but misguided hero out of Wood. Yet I think it would be a mistake to assume that film does more than sketch the real human being Edward D. Wood, Jr. was. It hardly accounts for his many depressing years drinking through scummy films like *Necromania* and *Drop-Out Wife*.

It also doesn't explain the peculiar condition shared by Wood, Tommy Wiseau, Claudio Fragasso, James Nguyen, and many others: the conviction that the movies they make have genuine quality. It's a unique delusion, this incapacity to see what divides their films from, say, Alfred Hitchcock's or Dario Argento's. And it's not as if these filmmakers think they're just doing something different, but valid; they genuinely do not understand why the wider public rewards other directors with Oscars and boffo box office and not them. Wiseau submitted *The Room* (2003) to the Academy Awards in all seriousness. In *Best Worst Movie* (2009), Fragasso repeatedly defends *Troll 2* (1990) as if it is a perfectly fine and normal horror movie instead of the surreal trainwreck it truly is. And, well, here's James Nguyen on the special effects in *Birdemic: Shock and Terror* (2010):

> From a distance, I think those eagles and vultures look pretty shocking and terrifying. And they come a little closer, maybe more shocking and terrifying. And when you get close up to them, they look different. It's something new, something you haven't seen before. Maybe it's art.[12]

I can't make sense of this condition. James Nguyen and I both watch *The Birds* (1963), and we both watch *Birdemic*, and yet what he sees in each film and what I see in each film are radically different conceptions of the same material. How

---

11 Avoid the tempting shortcut of "at least I'm a better poet than William McGonagall" if you ever want to improve.

12 https://bloody-disgusting.com/interviews/23593/special-interview-birdemic-shock-and-terror-director-james-nguyen/. Not one word of this quote is objectively true.

he can sense that the one is good, and fail to sense that the other is bad, I do not understand. Interpretation of a film, and a judgment of its quality by degrees— these are subjective critical comparisons. But I see that Nguyen's framing is lousy, his timing is inhumanly poor, his visual style is amateurish at best and nonexistent at worst, and his actor guidance is meaningless. And I see that Hitchcock is an expert of all these qualities. Nguyen does not see any of this. He sees no distinction. In both films he sees good movies.

It's like that old philosophical problem of never *really* knowing that I'm seeing the same color as you are when we both call something blue, because maybe I've just learned to call blue what you call red. Are we seeing different movies, somehow? Are our two brains processing them differently?

Wood's angle on this condition has to do with "good enough," if Burton's portrait of him is to be believed. Or possibly "the audience won't notice." But how can the audience not notice? How can this work be good enough? In some of the shots of Col. Edwards alone in a white abyss with a pair of binoculars, you can see the material of the dropcloth behind him slightly bunch along the bottom third of the screen, an indication that he isn't standing in front of, uh, the sky . Maybe drive-in audiences wouldn't notice that. But a gravestone that waggles like cardboard when an ambulance attendant kicks it? Blatant cuts between day and night shots within mere moments of story time? A momentum-draining cut trying to hide the fact that Tor Johnson couldn't struggle out of a grave on his own? Come on. The audience is not blind. If they don't notice these things, they are not watching this inherently visual medium.

COL. EDWARDS IN FRONT OF THE WHITE ABYSS

And how can Wood, with his metatextual knowledge of how films are made, forgive such obvious flaws? Or is that metatextual knowledge the reason he believes the audience doesn't see them? Because he has fallen in love with the way a rectangular frame transforms a set into a universe, does he believe he can fool an audience into accepting *anything* inside that frame?

Viewers with no experience in bad film sometimes think that makers of bad movies must dislike, or disrespect, the art form. How could they, why would they, besmirch it so if they loved it? Don't they see the mockery they make of cinema? But that isn't how it works. Edward D. Wood, Jr. *loved* movies. He loved the wonder of them, the out-of-body of them, the way a good movie makes itself a wide-open possibility space and invites you inside. These are qualities *Plan 9 from Outer Space* attempts, almost bravely, and totally fails to convey. It's a bad movie because, at bottom, *it is unconvincing as a movie*.

Where *Plan 9* succeeds valiantly is as *a record of an attempt at making a movie*. This is the secret of bad movies that are good to watch. They have a kind of holographic quality, showing you the attempt at a thing as well as the thing itself, because the thing itself is so transparent that it cannot hide the attempt. In any film, an especially savvy audience member can perceive the attempt—can guess at the mechanisms Stanley Kubrick used to create his signature tracking shots, can understand that some of Terry Gilliam's genius lies in how well he uses a fisheye lens. But even *semi*-savvy viewers of bad film can perceive a failed attempt at a movie, can see what Wood or Wiseau or Bert I. Gordon were going for, the nature of their endeavor and how it compares to others' successes, and can follow the record of their failure.

The most enjoyable bad movies fail not just due to general incompetence but because of obvious peccadilloes: James Nguyen's fixation on Hitchcock (*Birdemic*, *Replica* [2005]), David Prior's fetish for not-quite-military stories (*Deadly Prey* [1987], *Killzone* [1985]), Neil Breen's messiah complex (any of them). Wood's oeuvre was mostly lurid and exploitative, but *Plan 9* was a love letter to the movies he most adored. Repeated viewings show that love through the *record* of his *attempt* to do them justice. His peccadilloes charm and satisfy even as the execution of his ideas pratfalls. It's part of why *Plan 9* remains so watchable when other bad movies of its era bore and annoy. Wood wanted to succeed with a product he loved, where so many B-picture makers in the 1950s just wanted to churn out the product.

Wood's affection does not make *Plan 9 from Outer Space* good. No force on earth could accomplish such a task. It's a good record, but not a good film. And the reasons why are abundant.

4. CATEGORY

The qualities that make a good movie have been catalogued and debated exhaustively elsewhere. Whole libraries exist to explain how movies are good. But what makes a bad movie, how and why a film goes wrong—that's not studied so often. *Plan 9 from Outer Space* winds up being a useful exemplar for this question, and could be, perhaps, *the* exemplar from which a lesson plan for bad film can arise.

Tolstoy claimed that every unhappy family is unhappy in its own way. By the same logic, bad movies could go wrong in a thousand unique ways. But, after study, I've determined that Tolstoy does not apply here. Bad movies generally move in one of a handful of tracks:

1) **Cynical trash.** These movies are made entirely for profit, and bear no interest in art. Some big movies like *Battleship* (2012) lie here, but the similarities bear out all the way down to straight-to-video nonsense like *Samurai Cop II* (2015). The main quality that distinguishes these movies is how obvious it is that *no one*, no actor, crewman, or creator, cares whether there's anything artistically sound about the film. *Everyone* is there for a paycheck. You might think of Michael Bay movies, but they demonstrate

real craft;[13] his many imitators are closer to the mark.

2) **Missing link.** Movies are a team effort, generally requiring the work of dozens or hundreds. If just one of those cogs is out of alignment, the movie will be less-than. If the cog is large enough, the whole movie falls apart. Kevin Spacey is grossly miscast in *The Shipping News* (2001), which makes the movie fail to cohere, since it's nearly a character study. The Russos don't direct anything but action particularly well, so a good deal of *Captain America: The Winter Soldier* (2014) feels impersonal and dim. The acting, writing, and production values are all there, but the angles and the proliferation of shakycam make the movie annoying to watch.

3) **Movies that ought to work but don't.** Attempted blockbusters go here to die. The biggest and best example is *Waterworld* (1995), which had all the money it could possibly have needed, plenty of star power, and an interesting premise. But it's an awful movie, as thin and weak as a seedling. Baz Luhrmann's *Australia* (2008) should have been a sweeping epic, a generous slice of awesome, and instead, no one has any fun, especially not the audience.

4) **Poor photocopies.** There's a species of straight-to-video movies called "mockbusters" that capitalize on looking similar to contemporary hits in the DVD rack. *Transmorphers* (2007) (*Transformers* [2007]), *Atlantic Rim* (2013) (*Pacific Rim* [2013]), *Android Cop* (2014) (…), you get the idea. Some filmmakers do this a little less blatantly and cynically, gathering up a few ideas in vogue and slapping a movie together, whether due to lack of imagination or the desire to be part of a zeitgeist. It never works. Inspiration and originality are always better than deliberate cribbing.

5) **Auteur incompetence.** This category has a very distinct pattern: a single filmmaker takes on every aspect of production, writing/producing/directing/starring/distributing/etc., and winds up in over his head to such a degree that the movie is a complete wreck. The photo negative of Orson Welles' achievement with *Citizen Kane*. Kings of bad film (Tommy Wiseau, Neil Breen) live here.

These categories can overlap. The Golan-Globus producing team made a lot of cynical trash, but plenty of it ought to have worked: they threw money, time, and talent at their projects, if not always in correct proportions, and every so often their ideas were actually good. Missing-link movies and movies that ought to work often overlap in the saddest ways. A great cast can be given terrible direction (the Star Wars prequels), or a good script can be edited to death. Kids' movies like *Boss Baby* (2017) are both cynical trash and poor photocopies.

Wood shows all the signs of no. 5: sheer, unshared incompetence. In his

---

13 Tony Zhou of Every Frame a Painting proved this to me in 2014, and since then, I've gone about proving it to as many others as possible. Watch his video about "Bayhem" on YouTube and you just might be convinced, too.

early work, he is enthusiastically in charge of everything about the movie, and everything about the movie goes wrong. His later work leans closer to cynical trash, but *Plan 9* is not a photocopy of anything, it doesn't have just one missing link, and there's not a single molecule of coulda-been-a-contender within it. It's all Wood's work, earnestly done, and it's all bad.

In *Plan 9*, Wood assembles a set of attributes for bad movies just as emergent as the common attributes of good movies: bad takes, cheap sets and props, terrible acting, witless writing, discontinuity, poor editing, inexpert framing, inappropriate lighting, illogical structure, and unintentional comedy. Many or most of these elements exist in all bad movies, although the last is possibly the most essential.

5. MECHANISM

My very favorite thing in *Plan 9* is a line of Paula's:

```
                    PAULA
  The saucers are up there. And the cemetery's out
        there. But I'll be locked up in there.
```

Free of context, this line communicates no more or less information than it does in the film. I think Paula's trying to say that despite nearby dangers, there (↑) and there (→), she'll be safe there (←), in the house. But the line is *so* badly written, from its broader intention of contributing to the screenplay and thus the story of *Plan 9 from Outer Space*, down to its nuts and bolts, the words it uses, that I cannot be sure. It's so badly written that it leaps out of the television at me every time I watch the film. It's so badly written that I cannot conceive of taking seriously, even for one moment, the film that contains a line like this. I always expect someone—Peter Bogdanovich, maybe—to stride onto the set in front of Paula and Jeff bellowing "Cut, cut cut—can't we tweak that a little?" Someone, anyone, please interfere with the existence of this line spoken onto celluloid in the Year of Our Lord 1956. Undo it. Unmake it. Otherwise the very endeavor of cinema is in question, shaken at its foundations, because a crew full of living human beings could allow this line to be uttered and not simply walk away in resignation; because Wood could write this line, hear it delivered, and think "yes" rather than "no, no, a thousand times no." The existence of this line casts doubt on the artistic endeavors of all of us, like a vast and terrifying umbrella *de* bad art, shading our dreams from the sun.

Why is this my favorite part, this nadir of badness? Why is this terribly written and not-wonderfully-delivered line a source of delight rather than despair?

The mechanism inside me that loves bad movies is responsible, but I do not know how that mechanism functions, when it was built, nor what it does to transform bad art into joy. Paula's "there" line makes me sit up and notice, and even rewind to hear it again. I do the same thing for particularly well-said lines in *good* movies, for moments when an actor's craft shines brightly. Does it make any sense that I enjoy very good and very bad art in almost the same way—with delight, engagement, analysis, and repeat viewings?

No more than it makes sense to enjoy bad movies in the first place, I guess. Especially if I'm enjoying them without condescension in my heart.[14]

Anyway, this awful line may be my favorite part of *Plan 9* for its extraordinary vapidity, but it's hardly the only terrible moment in the film. I'll talk about many more individual moments in Part II, but for now, let's look at a scene that simply contradicts itself.

After a montage that juxtaposes stock footage of the military with the actions of Col. Edwards and voiceover from Criswell explaining what's (meant to be) going on, Edwards has a conversation with an Army captain. It purports to be about firing missiles at the UFOs both men have just seen. The majority of the conversation only makes sense if both men acknowledge that their target is real UFOs.

                    CAPTAIN
        Quite a sight, wasn't it, sir?

                    EDWARDS
        A sight I'd rather not be seeing.

                    CAPTAIN
        Are you worried about them, sir?

                    EDWARDS
    Well, they must have a reason for their visits.
                    CAPTAIN
    Visits? Well, that would indicate visitors! Are
    big guns the usual way of welcoming visitors?

                    EDWARDS
        We haven't always fired at them.

                    CAPTAIN
                     Oh?

But at the tail end of the scene:

                    CAPTAIN
    Oh, this is a training maneuver, sir. We only did
        a little practice firing at the clouds.

The line invalidates the entire scene, and Col. Edwards's stated role as the

---

14 More on this later.

man "in charge of saucer field activities," and even the montage and voiceover that preceded. It's been suggested[15] that the captain says the line sarcastically, knowing that he has to play along with the omerta laid down by the "upper echelon." But if it is sarcasm, it's amazingly subtle, in a film that does not otherwise acknowledge the existence of subtlety as a concept. The actor's performance does not suggest sarcasm to me. Instead, it seems like he relieves his own anxiety about these uncertain "visitors" by repeating that he was only participating in a training maneuver.

Why on earth was the scene written this way?[16]

The captain's last line belongs to a scene in which Edwards knows the UFOs are real and the captain does not, but that isn't the scene we just witnessed. Most of the dialogue belongs to a scene in which Edwards and the captain candidly discuss something they're not supposed to admit they saw, but the conclusion to that scene isn't the one in the film. The result is a Moebius strip of a scene, one in

---

15 By Rob Craig in *Ed Wood, Mad Genius.*

16 Remember what I said in my author's note about the differences between the screenplay and the finished film? Well, this scene is written very differently than the filmed version. It's a lot shorter, so the back-and-forth about the saucers doesn't have the chance to contradict itself quite so much.

> CAPTAIN
> Do you suppose Washington will also deny this "rumor"?
>
> COLONEL
> It was Washington that gave this fire order.
>
> CAPTAIN
> Ten to one the files read "Training maneuvers."
> [pace change]
> Looks like we beat them off again, sir.
>
> COLONEL
> What are they? What do they want? Where do they come
> from? Where do they go?
>
> CAPTAIN
> They, sir? Who? Why this is a training maneuver, sir.
> We only did a little practice firing at the clouds.
>
> COLONEL
> Wonder what their next move'll be.

All punctuation Wood's. The scene still doesn't make sense, because it's *still* unclear when and whether the captain is being sarcastic, while Col. Edwards mostly speaks as if the captain isn't even there. Also, Criswell's voiceover is not written into the screenplay at all. But this version is a little less crazymaking than the final film.

which two approaches do not cohere into one meaning. This move would almost ascend into an intellectual puzzle, except that it's the result of idiotic screenwriting rather than a genuine intention of unsettling the audience.

Often, for exactly the opposite of this reason, experimental art reads as bad art, especially for mainstream audiences.[17] Inconsistency reads as error, rather than a purposeful disruption of audience expectations. Consistency is safe and clean and easy to digest, and experimentalists do not prize these qualities.

When I read or see something experimental and avant-garde, it's my job as a critic to work out whether the artist's ambitions make sense, not whether the end result makes sense *to me*. (It's a hair's breadth away from considering artist intent, but an important hair.) Sometimes I can't understand what the art is doing, but I'm aware that it has consistency and internal logic. "She's clearly up to something," is my best praise for experimental art I can't penetrate. An inner integrity to the art conveys meaning, even without a message I can interpret.

One of my favorite tales to tell in the classroom is itself a teaching story. My mother, a professor specializing in early modern poetry and translation, sometimes taught Shakespeare to college sophomores. Sometimes she assigned *Coriolanus*, which is rarely taught or performed, being a bit weird, and violent, and stark, and Roman. My mother assigned the play knowing her students would hate it, because they always do. She told them ahead of time to try and read with an open mind. The next class, she asked them to tell her the reasons they hated *Coriolanus* (again, they always did; there were always answers to this question), and she wrote them on the board. Then she went through these reasons and demonstrated that nearly all of them arose not from flaws in the play, but from unmet expectations on the part of the student. The student expected X, Y, and Z from a Shakespeare play, and instead got H, Q, and M. The play was not bad; the student was annoyed that the play didn't do what he thought it would.

The average reader[18] dislikes almost nothing more than having his expectations upended. It makes him hostile, because all of a sudden, the world is no longer well-ordered and easily understood. Possibilities open up, and he hasn't thought of them, and that means he's unsafe, out of control, a rube in the big city, lost in the forest.

After this exercise, few of my mother's students liked *Coriolanus* much better, but most of them respected it more. She had to demonstrate what the play was

---

17　The most interesting book I read about Wood was Rob Craig's *Ed Wood, Mad Genius*. He claims that Wood was a brilliant outsider artist whose films rely on Brechtian and Absurdist theatre ideas. I think he is dead wrong, because Occam's razor applies (either Wood was secretly one of the most thoughtful and best-read filmmakers in Hollywood at the time, forging a unique vision during the worst decade of the century to do so, *or* he was simply short on money and talent), and because theatre and cinema theories are more incompatible than they seem. But Craig does shore up my point here, that if you are *very* determined to read bad art as experimental art or vice versa, it's possible to do so.

18　Emphasis on "average," whether widely read or not. Many readers, of all stripes, enjoy having their expectations upended. But a hell of a lot of people read cozy mysteries.

actually doing, within its own little parabola, and how those actions were off-target only in light of the reader's expectations, not in light of what the play meant and messaged. Its violation of audience expectations is part of its genius, part of its experimentalism: a feature, not a bug.

Seeing any violation of expectations as a bug is how audiences close their minds. It's how we get homogenous art. It's how work that dares gets written off as work that fails.[19]

This cluster of ideas brings me back to bad film again and again. Few good movies have the capacity to surprise me, particularly in contemporary American cinema, but bad movies are *bottomlessly* surprising. They violate my expectations over and over. They fail to conform to standards so rigidly established they might as well be law. They *fail*, generally; this is unfortunate, but it doesn't deter the pleasure I take in them. I delight in how carelessly a Z film tosses off the shackles of linear storytelling, three-act structure, rational casting, and a coherent visual style. *Plan 9* does all of this, which is part of what makes it so much fun to watch. What will happen in the next 10 minutes? No idea. A stock footage montage, for no reason? Sure, okay. Recast one of the most distinctive actors of the 20th century midway through? All righty. Guy in a cowboy hat appears out of nowhere to save Paula from the monster? I can get on board with that. Didn't see it coming, but whatever. At least it's not another Dark Night of the Soul.[20]

In a good film, broadly predicting the next 10 or 30 or 50 minutes is like predicting the weather in southern California. *It'll be sunny.* There are variations, but mostly, trust me, it's gonna look like this. I find joy in the chaos of bad movies. Others find greater joy in the comfort of predictable character arcs and sound plot resolutions. This is fine; but you can't talk me out of the *uses* of bad art, the ways in which it illuminates good art, keeps it honest.

6. ENTHUSIASM

I've chosen to write at such great length about bad movies in part because of the above: the wonder of their unpredictability, my belief in them as teaching tools, the scale and spectrum they help to define between their efforts and movies that are excellent or just mediocre. I know, too, that I have a high tolerance for the otherwise painful parts of bad movies. My reaction to discontinuity, visible boom mikes, and inept screenwriting is usually mirth, not annoyance.

However, some things do get to me. There are few examples in *Plan 9* of issues I can't tolerate,[21] but here's a pretty well-known one from another movie: in *Over*

---

19 This is not to say that work that fails should be regarded generously as work that dares (as Rob Craig does, bless him). Bad art should not be excused with a flippant "oh, it's experimental." Sometimes this is case-by-case. For now, restrict my conclusion to: meritorious experimental art is often mistaken for bad art, and it is not.

20 Here, narrowly, Craig and I agree: "Unconventional film tends to distance an audience expecting generic, predictable entertainment, even as it attracts those who seek something challenging and different." From *Ed Wood, Mad Genius.*

21 See p. 41-42 for one.

the Top (1987), the main character is inconsistently referred to as either "Hawk" or "Hawks." There is no excuse for this kind of mistake. A director or an assistant director or a script supervisor or even the actor who played Hawk(s) should have stopped the scene to correct the mistake, every single time. That they didn't means no one cared enough about such basic filmmaking integrity as *the main character's correct name* to solve the problem, neither then and there nor later, in editing, in ADR, ever. Other things about *Over the Top* crack me up (that it's structured like a romantic comedy, except the meet-cute is between a man and his estranged son; that it's wall-to-wall arm-wrestling for the final half-hour), but that mistake just pisses me off. It indicates that no one gave a damn. On a film set, someone, anyone, should always give a damn.

When a movie is cynical, when the filmmakers have whoomped up this product and put everyone to work to make something meaningless, not for pleasure or ambition but solely for profit, I never have a good time. A huge swath of direct-to-video movies qualifies, with titles like *Oblivion* (1994) and *Merlin: The Return* (2000). Charles Band made piles of them, mostly as producer. These movies are insulting. They wasted the time of everyone involved in production and they waste the audience's time, too. They exist on the premise that it's easier to make and sell meaningless crap than meaningful crap, and I cannot withstand this idea. It's wasteful. Good unproduced screenplays are inexpensive and plentiful! You have the resources to make something with costumes and special effects and actors, and you make *this*? To hell with you.

But a lack of cynicism—this element makes watchable so many awful films, including *Plan 9 from Outer Space*. Wood loved movies, he loved Hollywood, he loved monsters and aliens, and he put everything he had into this single project. That it came out the way it did reflects one critic's assessment of the film as "a triumph of will over talent."[22] It's a lousy movie because Wood was a lousy writer and director. But he *loved* what he was doing, and that enthusiasm oozes from every frame of *Plan 9*, for better or worse. Earnest efforts at filmmaking are almost never a waste of time.

The naïveté *Plan 9* displays about its own flaws and faults presses its audience to feel a kind of incredulous affection. *It really believes it's good*, the audience thinks. *It really believes it's doing well*. This is sweet, like tiny kids playing soccer is sweet, as they trip over each other and bumble vaguely in the direction of the gently rolling ball and sometimes wander off to the edges of the field. Wood not knowing that he could be doing any better lets us love him and his creation. If he *elected* not to do any better—choosing to cheap out, when he had available the option of a better script and fewer gaffes—that would make the film unenjoyable. I would be angry at him for wasting resources, rather than feeling endeared to his incompetence.

---

22 This phrase was spoken by a male voice in the early minutes of *Flying Saucers Over Hollywood: The Plan 9 Companion*. I don't know who it was—presumably one of the many interviewees in the film.

Again, viewing *Plan 9* as a successful record of the *attempt* to make a film is much more emotionally profitable than viewing it as a failed film. As a record, *Plan 9* reflects a dedicated filmmaker with unique ideas, one unconstrained by genre boundaries or typical narrative arcs. This filmmaker surrounded himself with flash-in-the-pan weirdos and unlikely patrons, and from those ingredients, cooked up a stew of inadequate flavor but unusual complexity. Such an attempt may be gently ribbed, but never dismissed as meaningless. Making things we love is perhaps the deepest human endeavor, only one notch above storytelling as the most powerful way to keep ourselves from the void. Wood genuinely loved *Plan 9*, and so do I.

I love the airplane cockpit scenes, filmed in a set that would have to vastly improve to meet the condition "bare minimum." I love that the police lieutenant explains that many UFO sightings don't include "a glow" by saying "well, haven't you heard?" as if UFO sightings are changing hemlines or developments in a showy trial. I love that there is no sensible universe in which Bela Lugosi's character's wife looks like Vampira, in death or in life, and yet there she lurks. I love the proliferant fog in the cemetery set, which exists to no purpose. I love with all my heart the actress who comments on Lugosi's character's death, "First his wife, then he." There may never be an actress with worse line delivery, though we search high and low. She has no conviction, no confidence, and no interest in what she says. She is awful, failing even at *trying* to act, and for this reason I love her dearly.

In a good film, she would have been replaced. (But then, in a good film, she wouldn't have asked a deeply pointless question about the virtue of burial vs. crypt.) Someone would have recast either Vampira or Lugosi to make their marriage more plausible. The cockpit set would have actual equipment in it. The film's plot would be comprehensible from early on, and there would be no sequences of stock footage. Characters wouldn't run in circles and scenes wouldn't contradict themselves. A good film would give us so much less.

7. EYE

The list of flaws in *Plan 9* can go on at enormous length. My point is not to ridicule the film—I love it too much to do that with genuine disdain in my heart—but to demonstrate how easy it is to locate and name *easily fixable* flaws in the film. It's a movie that brazenly shows what not to do at every decision point, from casting all the way to editing. And its flaws are so evident, so apparent, that the viewer doesn't need a film degree to see what's going wrong.

While drafting this section I watched *Birds of Prey*, a 2020 film about the DC Comics character Harley Quinn et al. It was so seriously flawed that I didn't enjoy it. A handful of my friends had seen it earlier in the year and lauded it to me. This has happened repeatedly in my adult life, but I was particularly surprised when it happened with *Birds of Prey*.

I *do* have a film degree, which honed and lent experience to a native talent for film analysis. What I saw in *Birds* was:

- Flamboyant voiceover tying together unconventional plot sequencing, which should have worked but made the film lose momentum repeatedly
- A screenwriter who didn't understand that the meatiest part of an ensemble film is when the ensemble is assembled, not the lead-up to that event
- Action sequences that cribbed from copies of copies of interesting action sequences
- Music choices that started out unique and devolved into cliché
- Art direction so immoderate that, in the climax, the set read like a set instead of a genuine environment of any kind
- A miscast Ewan MacGregor

I'm certain that most of my friends did not see most of this. For some, the action scenes felt comfortable instead of tired. The sequencing reminded them favorably of *Pulp Fiction* (1994) instead of reading as pointless, and it distracted them from the thin plot. Margot Robbie's extraordinary talent hid the weaknesses of the film she carried.

These failures are not me being picky, nor my friends being blind. They're hidden in plain sight. Movies in this decade click along so rapidly and appealingly, with a plethora of pleasing textures and interesting colors and distracting motion, that the untrained audience member is too dazzled to perceive that they are often watching crap. I loved *Birds of Prey*'s costumes and it was plainly a well-financed film; the aroma of studio money disguises the reek of studio shit pretty well. But not perfectly. I have a very good nose.

The point: it takes effort and training to perceive the failures of the average studio film. It takes a ton of hours in a dark room watching shadows. It is *hard*. Studios do everything possible to disguise these failures. But filmmakers like Edward D. Wood, Jr. make undisguisably bad movies. Their flaws are visible to anyone with one eye and half a brain (except, evidently, Wood himself).

The more obvious the failure, the more valuable the film to cinema students of all kinds—makers, critics, buffs. If they can pick out poor transitions as they happen, and notice the difference between film stocks when stock footage appears, they might be able to spot more subtle flaws in more legitimate movies. If I hadn't seen *Gigli* (2003)[23] fail completely at flamboyant voiceover, I might not have noticed that *Birds of Prey*'s doesn't hit the mark. If I hadn't suffered through Jason Beghe as Hank Rearden in the second installment of *Atlas Shrugged* (2011-2014),[24] I wouldn't have understood why MacGregor's performance was irritating instead of quirky.

As I watch bad film, my eye for film improves. I can discern so much more about what's in the frame of a good film, for example, by observing what's in the

---

23 Not recommended. Painful in how it fails.

24 Also not recommended. I usually love vanity projects, and the first one (2011) was kind of an interesting mess, but *Atlas Shrugged II* (2012) is negative fun.

frame of a bad film. There's a yawning gulf between bad framing and unimaginative framing, but you can't really see it until you see enough of the former. If you've ever gone from an average American film to a good French film, you know what I mean. The gulf there is between unimaginative framing and innovative framing, and it yawns just as widely.

Bad film is much more plentiful than film objectively good enough to be taught, and I posit that bad film has even more to teach. *Plan 9*'s flaws are a decent sampling of how film can go wrong, but there are scores more flaws out there that other movies have explored. In the films of Coleman Francis, nothing happens. Neil Breen's work has unignorable tics—objects dropping to the ground, shots of feet—that fail to create meaning through repetition. Some films are poorly lit, others have painful musical numbers, others are weird patchworks of popular ideas. But every item in this paragraph is a useful point of reference for an aspiring filmmaker or critic. *This is what could go wrong. This is how to recognize what isn't working. This problem crops up in mediocre film, too, but here it's big enough to see.* It's hard to show someone what the work of a good boom operator looks like. It's incredibly easy to point out a bad one.

Bad film also fascinates with the *range* of its flaws. Why is it that Wood can light a scene, but can't block one? Why do so many bad directors get eyelines right, but framing wrong? How can Coleman Francis so consistently forget to have anything *happen* in his movies? "What were they thinking?" is not the most useful question about bad movies. Far from it.

The more I pick apart bad film, the more there is to study and understand. Everything in them grants me insight on the labor of moviemaking—the risk of it, the scads of individual vibrating electrons that have to unite in purpose to create a usable molecule.

Since bad movies like *Plan 9* are so often successful records of an attempt to make a good movie, they contain valuable archival information. Like the notebooks of a novelist. Except the novelist in this case is not a single creator, but the conglomerate artistic endeavor of filmmaking. Bad film is a long, entertaining, wearying record of that endeavor's failed sorties. The only way to properly admire the success is to witness the failure.

8. RIFF

On my right bicep is a colorful tattoo of Tom Servo, one of the robot characters from the television show *Mystery Science Theater 3000*, which ran on various networks from 1988 to 1999. The premise of the show was an elaborate frame for a pretty simple idea: let's make fun of bad movies. Tom Servo, along with another robot named Crow and a human companion, Joel (1988-1993) or Mike (1993-1999), are forced by bad bosses to watch these stinkers, and they avoid despair by cracking jokes, or "riffing," on the movies' risible qualities. The creators of *MST3K* mostly continue to do this work in new formats, whether Michael J. Nelson's RiffTrax, Joel Hodgson's two Netflix seasons of a revived *MST3K* starring Jonah Ray, or Trace Beaulieu and Frank Conniff's live touring show, The Mads.

I don't know for sure, but I think part of the reason these men keep doing the same weird job 20+ years after the original show ended is because of how specialized it is, which leads to audience demand (no matter how niche) that can't be met by very many people. Riffing seems a lot easier than it is. The concentration of jokes has to be high, one every seven to 10 seconds, and that energy has to keep up for a movie's running time, around 5,400 seconds. That's more than 500 jokes. Decent jokes.

Beyond the per capita problem, there's a special breed of integrity in what *MST3K* did with its films that's even harder to duplicate. Very rarely did the riffers condescend to the film at issue, or take cheap shots at it, or insult it. Sometimes this did happen; comments about Joe Don Baker's weight,[25] for instance, or about a female actor's annoying voice.[26] But most often, the *MST3K* writers made jokes that met the movie where it lived, that engaged with the movie instead of punching down at it. Imitators have tried to do it the other way, just hurling insults for 90 minutes, and it does not work. Joking about a movie's plot (or lack thereof),[27] or about ideas presented in its dialogue, gives the viewer some *substance* to laugh about, a hook to hang humor on, as opposed to just, say, mocking bad special effects. The latter is obvious and represents shallow, fleeting engagement with the film. *MST3K*'s work with film shows almost universal respect for the endeavor of filmmaking, even if that respect drops to minimal levels for certain movies.

An example: in *Outlaw of Gor* (1988, riffed 1993), characters often say "Where the hell am I?" and the riffers always respond "You're the hell here." The joke is simple, but repetition makes it funnier, and points out ably that the script is repetitive. They could have made fun of the sidekick's dorky glasses, but that's a bully move. Digging into what the screenplay does wrong is an *analytical* move.

Many fans of *MST3K* go on to be fans of bad movies, your author included. The danger in going gaily from the satire to the real thing lies in failing to understand the mechanism of *MST3K*'s engagement with film, and perceiving only that it's fun to laugh at bad movies. Make no mistake: the writers of *MST3K* know as much about film as scholars, as historians, as producers and directors. They know what it is and isn't to make a movie. Sometimes the riffs gesture toward this thesis of mine, that bad film is profoundly instructive in the ways of good film: noting the use of the grip truck as a stunt vehicle in *Werewolf* (1995 / 1998) or a very pointed continuity problem in *Space Mutiny* (1988 / 1997). Of course, sometimes they just play word games and build extended jokes about Ron Howard's *Willow* (1988).

Irresponsible and meanhearted entertainers have used the *MST3K* model to fling mud at movies without the depth of understanding the original riffers held.

---

25 Evidently Baker made a rude public statement about how *Mitchell* (1975 / 1993) got riffed, so the crew did not hold back when they riffed *Final Justice* (1984 / 1999).
26 They're not very nice to Kathy Ireland in *Alien from L.A.* (1988 / 1993), but, even with my most feminist hat on, her voice is *awful* in that movie. A minor character in *Tormented* (1960 / 1992) also gets this treatment, which I excuse a little less.
27 Cf *The Castle of Fu Manchu* (1969 / 1992).

They think the value of *MST3K* lies in tearing down the failed work of incompetent filmmakers—in shaming them. No. The value is in analysis. Comedy is best when it analyzes, not when it skims and pokes along the surface of something. Jerry Seinfeld's observational humor does not have the intellectual durability of George Carlin's excoriation of societal mores. *MST3K* must analyze the badness of a film before riffing it, and that's why the concept works without relying on cruelty (for the most part). Their process *opens* the film, where mocking *closes* it.

But because the riffs are breezy and the show is an inexpensive Midwestern creation, it looks like easy work, making fun of movies so bad the jokes seem to happen of their own accord. So folks who fancy themselves cultural critics begin ridiculing, in the model but not the spirit of *MST3K*, and the whole discourse of cinema studies suffers. It's too bad. The legacy of *MST3K* could be its commitment to sorting through the sludge at the bottom of the barrel, surfacing with phenomenal examples of the weirdest and worst of what cinema has to offer.[28] I would not trade the hours I've spent watching *MST3K* for an afternoon with Ingmar Bergman or Alfred Hitchcock. I'm positive I learned more from the riffs.

Where the rubber meets the road: there exists a RiffTrax for *Plan 9 from Outer Space*. It's funny. Conveniently, there's a good example of unkind ridicule in it: a running joke about Bela Lugosi's morphine addiction. It's beneath them, and it stings badly, especially when held against Tim Burton's compassionate portrayal of the same issue in *Ed Wood*. Otherwise, it's a solid riff, pointing out Lt. Harper's hilariously unsafe gestures with his prop gun, the evocative shape of the aliens' mother ship, and multiple ways in which Wood cheaped out on production, like the "police car" outside the "station" and the bad cockpit set. If you missed how ungracefully Wood switches between studio shots and day-for-night location shots, RiffTrax has your back. And they expose some of the illogic in the script, like the "Solaronite" speech and Criswell's opening monologue.

RiffTrax does not get the last word on *Plan 9*. Edward D. Wood, Jr. does. The movie has stuck around not because it's hated or mocked, but because it's loved—because of its flaws, I wager, not in spite of them.

9. AGGREGATE

What I've learned from bad movies, I've learned from the preponderance of them. Patterns appear, like the degree to which they lean on inflated stakes and exploitation, or the amount of time spent on driving and parking. Lumps and bumps appear in all kinds of movies; the other day I spotted a mid-scene cut in the Coens' *True Grit* (2010), a masterpiece. But the lessons of bad movies exist most usefully in aggregate. That means examining a single bad film or a small handful of them is not necessarily the best way to learn the lessons within them.

---

28 Some films, like *Manos: The Hands of Fate* (1966 / 1993), might have been permanently lost if not for the *MST3K* treatment. A dubious reward.

This is true for good film, too. You can't learn everything you need to know about filmmaking just from *Citizen Kane*. Again, you have to be an omnivore, absorbing as much as you can from as many different levels and styles of artwork as you can. You have to go everywhere, and you have to remember where you've been every time you sit down to work.

That said, if you were to select just one bad movie to try and learn from, *Plan 9 from Outer Space* is a top choice. It's unofficially considered the *Citizen Kane* of bad movies, after all. Although I'm not sure the reason for that is especially well-grounded, I'd posit that it's a kind of direct oppositional force to *Citizen Kane*. Everything *Kane* does right, *Plan 9* does wrong. It has a very deep bench, in terms of the flaws it offers up and how plainly they appear. I have learned from so many bad movies—well into the hundreds—but *Plan 9* is the granddaddy of them all.

The only way to assess a single bad movie thoroughly enough to learn from it is to perform an exegesis: an exhaustive analysis, scene by scene. So that is what I shall do.

II: *Exegesis*

We open on CRISWELL PREDICTS, a title card that likely visually echoes Criswell's regular TV show.[29] The speech Criswell, whose record of untrue predictions has been well-covered elsewhere, gives, is so extraordinary that I must reproduce it in full.[30]

> CRISWELL
> Greetings, my friend. We are all interested in
> the future, for that is where you and I are going
> to spend the rest of our lives. And remember, my
> friend, future events such as these will affect
> you in the future. You are interested in the
> unknown, the mysterious, the unexplainable. That
> is why you are here. And now, for the first time,
> we are bringing to you the full story of what
> happened on that fateful day. We are giving you all
> the evidence, based only on the secret testimonies
> of the miserable souls who survived this terrifying
> ordeal. The incidents, the places--my friend,
> we cannot keep this a secret any longer. Let us
> punish the guilty. Let us reward the innocent. My
> friend, can your heart stand the shocking facts
> about grave robbers from outer space?

It's an excellent blend of inane, circular, and alarmist, very clearly read from a script out of frame (you can see Criswell's eyes move), with delivery as unique and risible as William Shatner's. Aspects of the speech do not cohere to the film that follows; for instance, "what happened on that fateful day," when the fateful events took place over a series of days or potentially weeks, and "punish the guilty…reward the innocent," when the guilty are all dead, aliens, or dead aliens. Not a stellar beginning, to demonstrate inconsistency before the movie even begins.

---

29 Criswell's daily (!) show ran from 1953 to 1961. All episodes have been lost.
30 Per Mason (1990), Criswell wrote this himself. I'm skeptical, because it reads so much like Wood, and there are other errors in Mason's editorial work in that book. However, none of Criswell's lines appear in the screenplay. Could he have written his entire voiceover? Most likely to me is that Wood wrote it in post-production, but my research doesn't say. One source indicated that Criswell's show always opened with those three lines: "Greetings, my friend […] in the future." I don't quite believe this, because the lines are so often quoted as an example of Wood's bad writing, and surely someone with a memory of Criswell's show would have corrected this misapprehension.

Next come the credits, which vary between words "carved" on a gravestone and words projected against a photo of a cemetery. The variation has no logic. The theme music for *Plan 9 from Outer Space* is sort of dumb, thudding and dramatic and simplistic, but it's also immediately recognizable and sets the tone well.[31] Wood's credit arrives in a clap of thunder and is styled as "Written-Produced-Directed" against a black sky full of stars.

The next six minutes compose most of Bela Lugosi's work in the film. Criswell narrates as a small collection of mourners, including Lugosi, stands around an open grave. It appears to be midday. No diegetic[32] dialogue. The "old man" (Lugosi) has lost his wife. Her death came "suddenly and without warning" despite Lugosi's obvious age. We cut, thrice, to a pair of gravediggers sitting on the ground doing nothing in approximately the same kind of landscape and lighting.

> CRISWELL
> It was when the gravediggers started their task
> that strange things began to take place.

Yet instead of showing these strange things, we cut to a plane in the sky. Screenwriting lesson: do not set up something you don't knock down. The audience has a short memory. If you say something as anticipatory as Criswell's line, you have to follow it up, preferably then and there.

The plane, as it turns out, provides an establishing shot. Cut to the apparent inside of a cockpit, which has no equipment at all. Just a clipboard tacked to one wall and a circular chart, likely a flight computer, tacked to the other. Two men, dressed in pilots' uniforms, sit in a two-shot. The man on the left has a microphone for a two-way radio strapped to his chest. Both men have

PLAN 9 FROM OUTER SPACE PUBLICITY STILL/REYNOLDS PICTURES

in front of them half-circles of plywood attached to poles, intended, somehow, to be steering devices for the "plane." The pilot, on the right, is Jeff; the copilot, with the radio, is Danny.

---

31 The music from *Plan 9* is all library music, the auditory equivalent to stock footage. *Nightmare of Ecstasy* claims the main title is Alexander Mosolov's *Iron Foundry*, but it is not. Music writer Paul Mandell traced the full story of the film's music for *Film Score Monthly* in 1996: https://web.archive.org/web/20101013003604/http://sammel-surium. heimat.eu/soundtracks/P9FSM.html

32 "Diegetic" means it originates and exists within the world of the film, where "non-diegetic" means the opposite. Diegetic music would be music that comes from a visible radio or performer, where non-diegetic music is, for instance, the Imperial March in *The Empire Strikes Back*.

A little unconvincing, uninteresting dialogue passes between the men, and then a commotion of light and sound interrupts them. Outside the window floats a flying saucer, on visible piano wire,[33] before a background of painted clouds. Nothing about it looks remotely convincing as a special effect.

A female flight attendant, Edith, joins them. The saucer moves away, out of frame.

                         EDITH
              What in the world...

                         DANNY
              That's nothing from this world.

The copilot communicates a mayday into the radio. My understanding goes that "mayday" should be reserved for extreme emergencies, not for unthreatening appearances of UFOs, but he says it anyway. The saucer flings from left to right across a couple of shots with different drawn backgrounds, and then, in a process shot, sinks into the photograph of the Los Angeles cemetery that appeared in the credits. Again, none of this is convincing. The saucer wobbles like a toy.

Cut to the gravediggers. Aha! This must be a strange thing beginning to take place! Except the background of the gravediggers doesn't match the cemetery from the process shot where the UFO landed, and the cockpit scene was long enough to disconnect the viewer from the funeral, the gravediggers, and the supposed strange things. Wood attempts to make the connection through editing—juxtaposing the saucer, the cemetery, and the gravediggers. But editing fails to provide continuity when the shots contain no inherent similarities.

Throughout *Plan 9 from Outer Space*, Wood tries to depend on parataxis to connect one thing to another. Parataxis is a literary strategy that forces meaningful connections between disparate phrases or ideas merely by setting them next to each other. Samuel Beckett used it in *Not I*, stringing together many short, disconnected phrases to cast the spell of an idea rather than stating it outright. David Markson uses parataxis boldly; some of his books are long lists of facts that only connect to each other cumulatively, over the course of many pages. He makes few traditional narrative connections, and instead leaves it up to the reader to determine what the small, disconnected units of meaning have in common with each other.

If Wood were being this obtuse on purpose, I'd call him a surrealist, lining up a series of shots that have little in common in order to make an artistic impression rather than tell a linear story. But that is not what's going on. Wood means for the two cemeteries he has put on screen thus far—the one with Lugosi and the one in the still photograph—to be just one. He means for the gravediggers to appear to be in the same place; the threefold cuts between the funeral scene and the gravediggers indicate that they're supposed to be nearby, watching the funeral.

---

33 Probably, per *Nightmare of Ecstasy*.

Shortly Wood will introduce a third cemetery, in a studio, and it, too, is meant to be the same place. The saucer that appeared near the plane cockpit connects to the omnicemetery, which connects to the gravediggers, who connect to the funeral. Supposedly.

Where Beckett and Markson are graceful with parataxis, Wood is clumsy. Mere juxtaposition doesn't provide enough consistency to help the audience understand the connections Wood attempts. The reason is wrapped up with the acceptable grammar of cinema, which was established a hundred years ago and has only been refined—not dramatically changed—since.

Three main elements establish consistency between shots in the audience's mind: *lighting*, *location*, and *landmarks*. Cutting from a scene with dim lighting to a scene with strong lighting leads an audience to believe you're cutting to a different *time* (night to day). Cutting from a location shot to a studio shot leads the audience to believe you're cutting to a different *place* (outside to inside). Cutting between places that have no recognizably similar landmarks makes the audience lose track of the characters' *movement*. The average moviegoer might not be able to explain this if asked, but editing consistency depends upon these three elements as basic premises. Keep your lighting consistent between shots that are meant to take place at the same time; keep the appearance of your location consistent between shots meant to occur in the same place; keep the landmarks clear in frame if you want the audience to know where the characters are and where they're going.

Many, many examples will come up between now and the end of this essay of Wood misusing this basic grammar of consistency in *Plan 9 from Outer Space*. In each circumstance, it's useful to remember the three Ls.

The gravediggers think they hear something "sorta spooky-like" in, I remind you, a cemetery, and decide to leave without finishing their task, which is, I remind you, burying the old man's wife. Cut to mist rising against a black backdrop, with a dead tree and a portion of a structure in the foreground. It's unmistakably a studio shot, while the gravediggers are on location outdoors. Vampira emerges from the edge of the structure—cue dramatic violins—and, the editing suggests, advances on the gravediggers. The implication of danger exists based on nothing but editing proximity. The gravediggers and Vampira never appear in the same shot, and the locations and lighting are completely different.

PLAN 9 FROM OUTER SPACE PUBLICITY STILL/REYNOLDS PICTURES

Also, here's the first evidence of Wood's inability to block scenes logically: the gravediggers are walking *away* from supposedly covering *her* grave. Unless they walk in a circle, or she rose from the grave without them seeing her (??) and waited a little distance away to attack them, it makes no sense that they would meet her *approaching* them.

The gravediggers scream off-camera as

Vampira raises her arms (in a medium shot, which is not as effective as a close-up would have been). Fade to black.

Later we learn that Vampira is meant to be the old man (Lugosi)'s recently deceased wife. This is not intuitive. She is clearly not of an age with him, and her appearance is extreme. "Wife" is no part of what that appearance communicates—not in 1959. The implication may be that her costume and makeup result from her ghoul-ness, from her zombified nature, rather than depicting how she appeared in life. We cannot know, as we have no basis for comparison, because we never saw her when she was alive. The appearance of the other ghouls is inconclusive in this regard; Tor looks the same except for white contact lenses, and with Lugosi it's difficult to draw a comparison given that he's played by two different actors once he's a ghoul. The fact that Vampira had to be recognizable as Vampira in order to be an attraction for film audiences familiar with her TV show is certainly a piece of this puzzle, and it's one example of the film's backstage motivations resulting in onscreen confusion.

A lot of this information is to come. We in the audience don't even know she's a ghoul yet, and certainly we can't connect the existence of ghouls with the saucers. But that's my point: we see a scary woman, we see the gravediggers being put in jeopardy? maybe?, and we have no context for any of it. Just the editing, which juxtaposes all this without imparting much information and without making physical sense. I can put the pieces together after watching *Plan 9* multiple times, but the idea that the audience could have seen past all these leaps in logic to connect Vampira with Lugosi, and with the flying saucers, on the basis of *editing*, staggers me.

Cut to Lugosi leaving a small, unattractive ranch house while Criswell narrates about his grief. It's a pretty silly speech, and it makes Lugosi's tender acting seem overbaked. Also, he's wearing a caped coat in this scene, which sort of connects to Vampira's costume, but really just reminds the viewer of the actor's fame as Dracula rather than offering a sense of his character in *Plan 9 from Outer Space*.[34] (The fact that he never gets a name doesn't help.) He walks left, offscreen, and the film freezes. You can tell because the spindly tree in the center of the shot, previously tossed by the wind, stops moving, and because Lugosi's shadow remains on the lawn even as the sound effects of squealing brakes and a scream materialize, indicating that the owner of the shadow has come to some great harm.

Cut to stock footage of, apparently, an ambulance; a siren wails over the footage, but the writing on the back of the car is indistinct. Fade to black.

Fade up on a crypt the size of a child's playhouse, against the same stark backdrop as Vampira's "attack." Four people emerge from the playhouse crypt. Criswell reveals that this is the old man's funeral (at night?) and his...DEAD WIFE

---

34 Perhaps Wood meant to offer dual resonance—to connect to Vampira *and* to remind the audience of Dracula. But one of these references is in-film and the other is metatextual, and using one piece of costume to imply both is just confusing rather than efficient and/or winking.

(cut to Vampira) is watching. Ah! Vampira is the dead wife! Wait, really?

The mourners are not the same mourners as at the wife's funeral. Two linger for a bad, expository conversation:

> WOMAN MOURNER
> Tell me something. Why was his wife buried in the ground, and he sealed in a crypt?
>
> MAN MOURNER
> Something to do with family tradition. A superstition of some sort.
>
> WOMAN MOURNER
> Oh.

I do not have a satisfactory answer for why this matters. Maybe Wood thought the gravediggers on location vs. the playhouse crypt in a studio needed some kind of diegetic explanation. It really does not, or at least no more than any of the other inconsistencies apparent in this record of the film so far, and yet here is this dialogue, delivered by a not-that-bad actor and the Worst Actress in the World.[35] The Worst Actress in the World discovers the dead gravediggers, or really two mannequins dressed like the dead gravediggers, and screams.

We need to talk about time frame for a moment. Let's assume that the old man's funeral could have been put together in a week. Let's further assume that only a week passed between Vampira's death and the old man's walk into traffic. That would still mean the dead gravediggers had been lying there for two entire weeks without anyone a) noticing they were missing or b) noticing their rotting corpses. I think the idea is that these events happened right on top of each other, in a matter of days.[36] But that is even more unrealistic than the plot has been thus far. And it's a *logical* inconsistency, not a fantasy-based run of the imagination. Funerals take more than a day to plan. Despair like the old man's doesn't develop overnight. It's just not credible.

I write those words and then laugh at myself, laying out a reasonable argument for why something in *Plan 9 from Outer Space* is not credible. But it matters that Wood handwaved his way through real-world logic even as he ignored bad framing and terrible performances and silly plot contrivances. Movies breathe and expire on the confidence viewers have in them, and ignoring the timeline of funerals and body decomposition erodes that confidence just as ably as a crummy UFO model on a visible bit of piano wire. What frustrates me about bad movies is not the

---

35   See p. 30 for further thoughts on this gal.

36   In the screenplay, Larry the policeman says of the bodies, "Looks like they've been here a coupla days." So Wood did *attempt* to give us a time frame, but it didn't end up in the film. And it's still illogical.

cheapness of a film or the incompetence of its crew or actors, but choices like this timeline thing. Wood could have implemented any of a dozen solutions for this inconsistency if he'd thought about it longer than a minute. It's his responsibility to be at least *that* careful, if not much more. But he didn't. He wasn't. And it annoys me, when other flaws please and delight me.

Cut to three men piling out of a "police station" into a "police car." One of these men is Tor Johnson, instantly recognizable from his bulk. The car does a pretty sloppy job of leaving the station, and the maneuver reveals a small, harsh cone of lighting projected onto the dark sidewalk and street for the shot. The car speeds along a dirt road somewhere in Los Angeles in lighting that could generously be called day for night.[37] It pulls to a stop half out of frame in an absolutely terrible shot. The camera tries to pan left to catch the characters leaving the car but doesn't quite make it. Back to the studio cemetery, and Criswell's narration, for the police arrival. Tor is identified as Inspector Daniel Clay. They meet another policeman already on the scene (Larry) and pass some lines about the situation.

Tor Johnson's delivery is not great, but it's not worth unkindness. Besides, Wood's dialogue is, was, and always will be the most incomprehensible part of any of his scenes.

Tor walks through heavy mist. He takes out his gun. The music is apprehensive. Near the gravediggers' bodies, a policeman in a trenchcoat (Lt. Harper) comments, "Looks like a bobcat tore into 'em." At the sound of a siren, he identifies it as the "morgue wagon."

Cut to the Trent patio, in the sole graceful bit of filmmaking in all 78 minutes of *Plan 9 from Outer Space*, where Paula Trent says, "That's the fifth siren in the last hour." This transition, unlike every other, draws a genuine connection between what we just saw and what we're seeing now. This patio must be close to the cemetery, or these characters would not have heard the same siren as the policemen. But they did, unmistakably. The sound bridge across the cut, plus comments by two characters on either side of the cut, told us so. This is good work by Wood, and I credit him for it.

An inept, unfortunate conversation follows between Jeff and Paula. Jeff reveals that he saw "a flying *saucer*" "shaped like a huge *cigar*," an inconsistency we might

---

37 "Day for night" is when cinematographers adjust camera settings and/or editors adjust exposure techniques so that a scene filmed in daylight is dim enough to appear to be night. This phenomenon is visible everywhere in movies of all budgets and calibers across the 20th century, from *Attack of the Giant Leeches* (1959) to *Psycho* (1960). It can occasionally be successful, in black and white, with the right conditions, but it usually isn't (and in color, it isn't even passable). Daylight looks like daylight, with sharp shadows and ambient illumination—especially in bright, sunny southern California, where so much 20th century American film was shot—whereas nighttime just doesn't look like that. With the technology available during the classical Hollywood period, it was expensive and difficult to film on location at night, and the footage often looked bad. The previous shot of this very film, when the three men leave the police station, indicates fairly well the limitations of night shooting.

have been able to forgive because "flying saucer" was vernacular for UFOs at the time, but we saw it too, out the window of Jeff's cockpit, and it was not shaped like a cigar at all. Jeff explains that "big Army brass" swooped down on him after his plane landed and had him swear not to tell anyone about what he'd seen, which is of course why he's telling his wife.[38] He also seems irate that despite it being "a fact" that UFOs "have been seen for years," he can't tell anyone about it (again, aside from Paula).

The dialogue does something frustrating here: it doubles back on itself.

```
                    PAULA
     There must be something more you can
              do about it.

                    JEFF
     Only there isn't. Oh, but what's the use of
     making a fuss. But last night I saw a flying
   object that couldn't possibly have been from this
     planet. But I can't say a word! I'm muzzled by
                    army brass!
```

Jeff's speech shows him waffling between convictions: *I can't do anything about this situation, and I see no point in speaking up, but I'm angry and I want to speak up.* It's reasonable that in real life a person might think and feel all this simultaneously, but in fiction, one "but" after another makes a character look foolish and indecisive.

Of course, indecisiveness *can* be displayed in fiction. It's not illegal. But it takes time and care to show a character genuinely struggling,[39] rather than making the character seem like kind of an idiot. In this scene, the screenwriter appears to be wasting our time, as Jeff cycles through one idea after another too rapidly to make us believe he's truly considering them.

A flying saucer passes overhead just then. Jeff and Paula fall down awkwardly. Cut to the cemetery, and two men carrying a stretcher. The policemen fall down, a corpse tumbles into some hay (??), and a falling ambulance attendant kicks a tombstone, which wobbles. Tor sees the saucer too, and so do we. It lands in the cemetery still photo again. Tor, gun drawn, passes the playhouse crypt, from which emerges a man with a Dracula cape drawn over his nose.

This man is definitely not Bela Lugosi, but it is so plainly meant to be Lugosi that I won't waste many more words on it. Somehow this flaw is less egregious to me than Vampira being set up as Lugosi's wife. Actors die; recasting happens. Wood's solution, to cast a man who doesn't resemble Lugosi in *any* way except hairline, and to have that man just cover most of his face every time he's on camera, is pretty stupid. But it's far from the stupidest thing in the film.

---

38 I stole this joke from the RiffTrax of *Plan 9 from Outer Space*.
39 Cf *Hamlet*, a very long play.

The music intensifies as Tor wanders around the set, until, oh no! Vampira appears. She and faux-Lugosi tag-team Tor (in separate shots), with offscreen results. The useful information in this sequence is that the ghouls are not affected by bullets.

The policemen hear Tor's gunshots andfind him dead. Lt. Harper says very dumb dialogue ("Inspector Clay's dead—murdered—and *somebody's* responsible"), and gestures with his gun as if it's a mere prop rather than a deadly weapon.

Cut to funeral no. 3 within 20 minutes. The editing suggests that Vampira is one of Tor's mourners.

Cut to flying saucers (3), and so begins a baffling montage. Criswell narrates, mostly in the style of a newsreel.

1) Footage of the 101 freeway in Hollywood: from the highway looking south, and then of a car with people pointing out of it.
2) A printing press runs.
3) Man unfolds newspaper: SAUCERS SEEN OVER HOLLYWOOD.
4) CBS building with badly processed saucer overlay effect.
5) Lady looking out of phone booth.
6) NBC building with saucer overlay.
7) Phone booth lady again, making a call. Criswell tries to connect this footage to the flying saucers.
8) Newspaper near coffee paraphernalia, same headline as no. 3.
9) Saucer over darker sky than before.
10) Drunken-stumbling man picks up newspaper near garbage can, same headline as nos. 3 and 8.
11) Probable Hollywood street at night (lots of neon) with saucer overlay. Two shots.
12) Guy outside bar in daytime looks up, rubs eyes, glances at booze bottle in hand. Back to night shot as in no. 11; back to man, who puts bottle down.
13) UFOs against outer space-type sky-with-stars backdrop. They appear drunk as well.
14) Passenger plane above Pentagon, Washington Monument in background.
15) Some kind of spinning radar dish. Saucer. Dish.
16) Military jeeps filled with helmeted men drive down a dirt road. Saucer (visible shadow on backdrop). Jeep with missiles, clearly in the desert, nowhere near Washington (or Hollywood, for that matter). Saucers.
17) Men loading large missiles into something. Houses in background. Man looks into eyepiece of some kind of large weapon.
18) Col. Edwards, in front of the blankest backdrop in the film, lifts binoculars to his eyes.

From here, we move into a second, more explicitly military montage, which alternates between no. 18, shots of the saucers, and various military footage.

The first montage lasts about two minutes. If I squint, I can see what Wood was trying to do: demonstrate that the saucers are a national issue, not one local to the cemetery near the Trents' house; and transition between the UFOs in Hollywood[40] (the previous bit of the film) to the military operation of which Col. Edwards is a part (the next bit of the film).

It's hard to imagine how, on his budget, Wood could perform these moves more directly, rather than using the indirect methods of Criswell's voiceover and the assembled stock footage. That sentence is me being fair to Wood's external limitations. But the solution of this montage is no solution at all. It introduces a bunch of new settings and faces we'll never see again, and inserts footage we absolutely do not need (no. 2, no. 12, no. 16). It's possible that Wood thought the audience would believe *he* had shot the footage of Hollywood—the CBS and NBC buildings, for instance—and be impressed. But that is beside the point, which is that no audience can follow and squeeze meaning from a sequence of two dozen shots that barely connect to each other and have hardly anything to do with what came before.

And this brings us back to the single biggest problem with *Plan 9 from Outer Space*: its networked-but-disconnected jumble of ideas, the failure of its plot summary to convey a sense of what happens on screen. (See p. 17-18.) A good montage should connect with some or all of what came before it and prepare us for the next sequence of the film.[41] I can see Wood straining toward this goal, but he completely misses it. The montage connects to earlier scenes only by virtue of the UFOs (no Lugosi, no Vampira; other characters *see* the saucers, but the significance of this seeing has yet to be revealed). It prepares us for the sequences involving Col. Edwards, in a way, but the military footage (nos. 16 and 17) is, of all the shots in the montage, most plainly stock footage. Col. Edwards standing in front of nothing at all immediately follows rough, well-used shots of men in front of a landscape with actual houses on it, which makes clear the distinction between what was filmed by Wood and what was not.

So little that happens in this montage connects to what comes before and after, and so little of it matters to the film as a whole. I can summarize the purpose of the montage (as above), but that summary does not include the lady in the phone booth or the two drunks, because those characters add no significance to the summary, or, consequently, to the film as a whole. They may as well not be in

---

40 The movie implies somewhat successfully that the Trents live in or near Hollywood. Jeff's copilot reports to Burbank Tower on his radio, and refers to "the old San Fernando Valley" as a visible landmark in his first line. Also, the still photograph of the cemetery has palm trees in it. A later scene more directly indicates that the Trents live in San Fernando, but at this point in the movie it's all implication.

41 Cf, for instance, every athletic training montage in every 1980s movie. They reflect back on the character's journey to this point and prepare him, and us, for what he will have to do next. Their main purpose is to show time passing and/or a slow change occurring in a compressed amount of screen time, but it's key that they connect to scenes and elements before and after.

the film for all they add to it. Similarly, the two scenes to come with Col. Edwards before he travels to Hollywood have only expository significance to the plot of *Plan 9* as summarized (aliens reanimate the dead in order to get Earthlings to understand the threat they pose to the universe). He's present at the confrontation that closes the film, and he's relevant to the supposed national issue of the saucers, but his screen time is disproportionate to his importance to the main plot of the film. He does not drive the plot nor contribute to it; he's just…nearby. And he gets a lot of scenes for someone who's just nearby.

Wood has a hard time sticking to the plot, as this montage shows. It demonstrates the problems with *Plan 9* in miniature: trying to use editing to solve problems editing cannot solve, cheap/inadequate props and sets and visual strategies, filler that makes viewers lose the thread.

Confusion of the kind in this montage halts us in our tracks and keeps us from going with the flow of the movie. We notice all of a sudden that we're watching a movie, one that isn't making any sense to us, instead of living a little bit inside the movie. Further, because we're trying to figure out what's going on, we tend not to remember what we're seeing.   Little of what we see sticks in our minds until the movie starts to make sense again. It's a major problem with confusing movies (those not confusing because of deliberate artistic intent, that is): the way our memories erase what doesn't make sense until almost the whole movie vanishes.[42]

On into the second montage. Criswell's voiceover identifies Edwards as "Colonel Tom Edwards in charge of saucer field activities." I do not have an adequate quip for that job description, especially considering that its existence renders two later scenes totally inconsistent. Col. Edwards "fires" on the saucers, which leads to a series of interspersed shots: stock footage of military men firing large-caliber missile-type weapons, bottle rockets popping near saucers dangling before the cloudy-sky backdrop, and Col. Edwards in his solitary void. He lifts his binoculars and lowers them a few times. The music suggests something very exciting is happening.

The film stock of the military footage is so distinct from the stock of the saucer/Edwards footage that they don't even cut together especially well, forming a jarring sequence that fails to communicate an intention passing from Col. Edwards to the missiles to the saucers. Also, the tiny explosions by the saucers try to communicate scale, but they don't, because the saucers are so clearly props.

This montage hangs together a little better than the one preceding it, but exactly because of that montage's confusion, this Edwards-related sequence doesn't really sink in or matter to the audience. We stopped trying to parse this movie during the prior two minutes. Edwards seems as much like a character we need to remember as the lady in the telephone booth.

Which is why it's a bit surprising when a helmeted Army captain with a giant walkie-talkie joins Col. Edwards in his void, and then speaks dialogue to him. We've heard only Criswell for a few chaotic minutes, and here we are in an

---

42   More about this in the essay on *After Last Season* (2009).

actual scene!

It's a pretty poor scene, one which contradicts itself almost surreally (see p. 25-27 for a full explanation), and it includes this line:

EDWARDS

```
For a time we tried to contact them by radio, but
  no response. Then they attacked a town. A small
   town, I'll admit. But nevertheless a town of
                people. People who died.
```

This line, *so* badly written, produces nothing but questions. Is he talking about where the Trents live? If so, who died in the Trents' town? Why didn't we see a scene of that happening? Or hear any reference to it until now? If it's another town, which town? And why haven't we heard any reference to *that*? Is this movie meant to be a record of all UFO contact with Earth? If so, why leave this fatal conflict out? Or is it a record of some other sequence of events? By what logic does this movie portray them?

Edwards asks a few questions of his own, the captain offers up his nonsensical, contradictory last line, and then, to finish the scene, Edwards says "I wonder what their next move will be."

Cut to "space," where tiny saucers hover around a mother ship roughly shaped like the planet Saturn[43] and crowned with a nipple.

CRISWELL

```
What will their next move be?
```

Dissolve to a curtained set containing two desks with a bunch of sciencey equipment piled on top. For once, this shot makes sense. Criswell's voiceover plus the space shot have served as setup, establishing that the men in this room are aliens and we're about to learn what their next move will be. But it took a twice-repeated line and a longish establishing shot to set that down. The sciencey equipment helps, along with the costume of the man who enters through the curtains. He wears leggings and a satin tunic, adorned with a lightning bolt on the left breast, with a gun at his waist. It signals "uniform," and, if you've watched enough 1950s sci-fi flicks, "alien."

The man at the desk does not get a name. The other characters call him "Excellency," the credits call him "Leader," and the script calls him "Ruler." For simplicity's sake I will call him Bunny, which was the nickname of the actor.

Soon, Eros and Tanna enter in the same uniforms. The scene that follows is largely expository, and not terrible on its face, except that the ideas presented are so laughable. Here we learn the meaning of "Plan 9"—it is the strategy (such as it

---

43 To me, it most closely resembles an 1980s toy called a Pogo Ball. But you, reader, are likely more familiar with Saturn.

is) the aliens have chosen to implement on Earth.[44]

Eros tells Bunny that they have already begun to implement Plan 9, which "deals with the resurrection of the dead," by "rising" two of the "recent dead." If the audience can remember back before the montage, we will be able to connect what Eros says to the gradual menace of Vampira and faux-Lugosi. Big if. Eros explains that they had to kill a policeman (Tor), but that the Earthlings suspect nothing. What they *could* suspect, based on what has occurred, is unclear.

Tanna gets a medium shot, but no dialogue until they leave Bunny's room.[45] Outside, she and Eros chat a bit, to reinforce the scene we've just watched, and attempt to speculate about what's coming next.

```
                        TANNA
    What do you think will be the next obstacle the
            Earth people will put in our way?


                        EROS
    Well, as long as they can think, we'll have our
      problems. But those whom we're using cannot
    think. They are the dead. Brought to a simulated
      life by our electrode guns. You know, it's an
      interesting thing when you consider...the Earth
    people, who can think, are so frightened by those
                who cannot: the dead.
```

If this scene were any good, Eros would answer Tanna's question so as to set up the next morsel of the plot. That is what good scenes do: they are individual vertebrae, providing continuity and structure to the whole. Tanna's question is a good start to a decent scene, because—like Criswell's "What will their next move be?"—it's a question that the audience may also be asking, and the film can answer. But Eros does not answer her question at all. He reveals common knowledge (the dead cannot think) and ruminates shallowly on something that doesn't bear on the plot.

Asking and answering too baldly in a screenplay is no good, either, as the movie begins to feel like a puppet show. But in this instance, either Tanna should not have asked this question, or Eros should have answered it, if the scene was meant to convey any kind of audience satisfaction. Eros's answer connects to hardly anything of substance we've already seen or will see. Without reaching backward and looking forward, scenes are just filler.

Filler scenes waste the audience's time on "shoe-leather," a term which

---

44 I enjoy the idea of a little file cabinet full of plans from which the aliens make a choice every time they find a new planet.

45 Though "Bunny's room" is a strange thing to call a set, I cannot see my way to calling it an office.

unfortunately means two totally disparate things in creative writing. In journalism, it means an old-fashioned, active method of information-gathering: going to multiple places and talking to sources rather than sitting glued to a computer. In other forms of creative writing, it means expending space and time on moves that can easily be inferred rather than described. If, in a short story, an author describes a man getting up from the couch and going to the door to answer a ringing doorbell, the man has used up some of his shoe-leather walking from one place to another, and the author has wasted the words to describe it when she could have jumped to the important part. "The doorbell rang. Sheryl stood on the doorstep," is better than "The doorbell rang. He stood up from the couch, walked across the room, and answered the door. Sheryl stood on the doorstep." That middle sentence purports to offer information about how a character gets from point A to point B, but such detail about a journey from the couch to the door is almost always unnecessary.

In movies, shoe-leather scenes come in several varieties. Bad movies generally have many more scenes of cars driving and parking than good movies. [46] Brainless filmmakers include these scenes because they presume the audience will not comprehend how a character traveled from home to office without a driving-and-parking scene to explain it. (We will.) Filmmakers with woes related to running time include these scenes to pad a thin film to feature length. In another variation on shoe-leather, characters might do chores or have domestic conversations that have no bearing on the plot and are too mundane to genuinely build character. In *Silent Rage* (1982), a character who appears and then dies within ten minutes of screen time learns across a page or two of dialogue that her homemade cinnamon cake is bad; in *Deadly Prey*, the main character and his wife banter about him getting up late in the morning. In any manifestation, shoe-leather scenes are a sign that a filmmaker has minimal respect for his audience.

This scene with Eros and Tanna outside Bunny's room isn't a shoe-leather scene, but a scene that wandered away from its purpose at some point during drafting and was never reexamined to give it focus. That's why Eros's final lines *feel* like shoe-leather. If Eros had given Tanna an answer, we would know where we were going, narratively, and the movie would imply it has some confidence. But he doesn't, because there is no answer to her question. No obstacles against Plan 9 ever materialize. The rest of the movie involves the human characters confronting the plan's outcome (the ghouls) and then…Eros talking to them. That's it. There is no conflict, or at least not a conflict with organic stakes and consequences like the one Tanna's question posits.

In this one scene, this one line of Tanna's, not even halfway through, the film collapses—shows itself as a jumble of half-baked ideas rather than a story. If Eros had an answer, the movie would have something like a plot. But he doesn't, and it doesn't.

---

46 I owe a debt of gratitude to the writers at RiffTrax for this insight, which they note in *many* movies.

EROS
Well, our ship should be regenerated.
We better get started.

Off the saucers go. They leave the mother ship and hover in a darkened cloud-backdrop shot. Cut to the Trent patio, Paula with a magazine and Jeff leaving the house dressed in his pilot's uniform. They have a vacuous conversation, sort of about Paula's safety in light of the flying saucers and the weird events at the cemetery, which evidently still register as two separate threats. She goes inside and Jeff leaves, getting into a convertible (on the passenger side) parked against a black backdrop as stark as Col. Edwards's void.

Dissolve to an establishing shot of a passenger plane in flight. Cut to the cockpit set. The scene that follows accomplishes very little, aside from straightfacedly using the phrase "balling it up in Albuquerque." Jeff worries over Paula's safety. Edie the flight attendant performs some wordplay that isn't really a joke and then apologizes: "I'm sorry, Jeff, that was a bad joke." Also, she encourages Jeff to use the plane's radio to request a check-in on Paula.

Lightning crashes, somewhere. Cut to Bela Lugosi, the real one, in full Dracula costume, tramping through the location cemetery from the first funeral scene. Criswell identifies him as "THE DEAD OLD MAN!" He spreads his cape wide and walks off. Dissolve to Lugosi almost entering the side door of a house, a rapid shot which offers us no useful information, as we have not seen this side door before. Cut to a fairly well-composed high-angle shot of Paula, asleep in bed with an open book near her elbow. The telephone rings. She rouses and answers it. She speaks to "Mac," who is, multiple viewings have helped me to understand, the radio operator at Burbank Tower. Although the previous scene set up that Jeff was going to radio in and ask for a call like this, "Mac" is not well-established as the radio operator's name, vs. a nickname like "bud" or "buster." Plus, the chain of plausibility has weak links along the way: that Paula would know Mac's name, that Mac would have nothing better to do (as an *air traffic controller*) than call Paula to check on her.[47]

Quick cut to Lugosi entering the side door, then back to Paula's bedroom for a wider shot. The bedroom door opens, and in comes faux-Lugosi, covering his face so aggressively that I doubt the actor could see where he was going. Paula screams and runs, and he pursues her at a gentle mosey. She runs through the studio cemetery, a white flash in the darkness; cut to real Lugosi leaving the side door.

This series of shots communicates adequately, if not perfectly, that the man in the bedroom is supposed to be Bela Lugosi, THE DEAD OLD MAN. For once, the editing explains across the obvious continuity problem of faux-Lugosi, rather than just confusing us. It is still laughable that the two men are meant to be one, but the mechanics of what Wood means to communicate are, on this occasion, not too

---

47 A line cut from the screenplay indicates that Mac "thrives on doing favors for the pilots." Still.

sloppy. We do have to connect the side door Lugosi enters with Paula's bedroom, but since the side door is a night shot, it's possible. It would have been better to see Paula entering or exiting the same side door at some point.

Paula runs through an indistinct landscape and trips. Vampira peers through some dead branches. Cut back to Paula, in a fully lit shot, getting to her feet in the studio cemetery. She runs left. Cut to real Lugosi walking into the location cemetery again. Shot of a grave headed by a tiny gravestone, the shape of a pencil eraser . The soil over the grave moves and shifts as if something's underneath it. This shot would be creepy if it weren't surrounded by so much incompetence.

Vampira walks away from the camera, evidently through crunchy dead leaves. She half-turns and gives something out of frame an assessing look, then continues. Faux-Lugosi moves through the studio cemetery. In a lightning-fast shot, Paula runs through the same portion of the cemetery she's already run through. Grave soil moves in a much lengthier shot. Paula runs from a different angle, away from the camera. Grave soil tumbles into the grave, a very nice effect. Vampira walks, arms out in zombie stance, right to left across the frame. Grave soil collapses completely. Paula runs (well, jogs), screaming.

Then, a wonderful shot: Tor Johnson rises out of a grave, lit from beneath, eyes blank, shadow looming. It's great, except he only gets a third of the way up before he begins to struggle and rock against the side of the grave. He wiggles like a fish. It's unfortunate. (Also, the stone behind him doesn't match the pencil-eraser gravestone, so it doesn't really follow that the grave with the collapsing soil is the same one he's coming out of.) Cut to a different angle of Tor, in a different position, standing up. The two shots and actions do not match at all, and the cut and blocking drain some of the menace from the initial creepy shot of Tor.

Paula runs. Now that Tor's out of the ground, each of the ghouls gets their own shot, but the shot length isn't quite parallel. The rhythm is choppy and fails to ratchet up the tension. None of the ghouls looks that fearsome, perhaps because we haven't seen them do anything too scary. Between Tor and Vampira, a shot of the pencil-eraser gravestone falling into the pile of loose dirt. Although what occurs in that shot will be important later, right now it doesn't connect to Tor. There is no visually consistent indication that he rose from *that* soil, rather than a second location with a larger gravestone. The landmarks don't match.

Paula runs again, downstage to upstage. Tor moves left to right. Faux-Lugosi stalks downstage to upstage. The breeze from his cape sets a-wobble a grave marker shaped like a cross.

Then, suddenly, we're on location, in day-for-night, and a car drives into frame on the right. On the left, a woman in a diaphanous nightgown like Paula's emerges from the grass at the side of the road and runs along the shoulder. I cannot emphasize enough how bad the framing is here. The idea, I think, is for the car to encounter Paula as she runs out of the cemetery and takes a comical nosedive at the side of the road. But the camera keeps panning with tentative, halting motions, trying to get the movements of both subjects in the same frame as they both move left. The effect is amateurish.

A shot of the driver (Farmer), [48] a husky guy in a white cowboy hat, is interrupted by a shot of faux-Lugosi, I believe to indicate that these two characters are in approximately the same location in spacetime, but the lighting and locations are completely different and it doesn't come off. Shots alternate between the ghouls and Farmer, who apparently knows Paula.

FARMER
Mrs. Trent! Mrs. Trent! What's wrong?

She seems to have fainted. Farmer picks her up and carries her into his car. The editing suggests that the three ghouls (actually four—there's a shot of real Lugosi in there) are closing in on Farmer and Paula, despite all other evidence that they are nowhere nearby. After the car drives off, faux-Lugosi walks patiently after it, then breaks off, back to the field that the editing has indicated is the cemetery, based on where Paula came running into the road. Vampira and Tor also walk…away, although there is no kind of implied "to" or "from" in the geography of this sequence. They are each in their own shots, and they each turn and go the other way from where they were going, and that is all.

Where to begin. This is meant to be one of the scary sequences of *Plan 9*, this attack on Paula by the ghouls, but it is almost entirely unscary. Part of the reason is the movie's general shoddiness, but there's also a mild failure of stakes and a geography problem.

Although the film has told us that the two gravediggers were torn apart, as if a bobcat had been at them, we have likely forgotten that, with all we've been through since then. It's not immediately clear, in this sequence, what will happen to Paula if the ghouls catch her. What kind of danger is she in? We know via dialogue only, not visuals. Also, we can't believe the danger is that exigent, since we only see Paula in the same shot as any of the ghouls a few times, and they walk in no particular hurry as she runs. Are they really so close on her heels? [49]

Further, the editing implies—not terribly, but not well—that all these characters are in near proximity. But we simply cannot know where they are in relation to each other without a) two-shots, [50] where the distance between two characters is evident, or b) landmarks, where two characters move past the same object or structure so we know approximately where they each are. In so many of the shots in this sequence—almost all of them—a character stands in or moves through his or her surroundings totally alone, and those surroundings do not have landmarks that match those in the other characters' solo shots. That is, Paula runs

---

48 He's called "Farmer" in the credits, but I have no idea what's supposed to communicate that. He's driving a convertible. Still, it's the name Wood gave him, so I'll use it.
49 This is common enough to be a horror trope—the shambling monster and the sprinting victim. But it hardly helps.
50 Moviemaking term for "shot with two people in it."

through a field with no identifying landmarks, so when faux-Lugosi walks through a field with no identifying landmarks, how do we know it's the same field? Vampira stands near some dead tree branches, and Tor walks by some, too, but they are so indistinguishable that it would take an overlay to tell if they're in the same place.

When a landscape is indistinct, and characters have too many separate shots, the audience cannot connect the movements of individual characters to each other. (Remember those three Ls.) A distinct landscape helps us draw a rudimentary map of the action in our minds and comprehend the danger our characters are in. *Alien* (1979) illustrates this concept in the computer tracking scene, where Ripley watches the alien dot and the Dallas dot move closer to each other, until one dot blinks no more. Most action scenes don't literally map out like this, but they do usually offer visual landmarks to help us understand how the characters are moving through space and how close they are to each other.

A related problem is when limited sets lead to contradictory geography. Paula runs through the same shot of the studio cemetery in two different directions: first toward the camera, and then away. Then, Faux-Lugosi, supposedly pursuing her, walks through the set away from the camera. He's following her most recent move, but with the chaotic editing and repeated solo shots, there's no way the audience can be sure of that. The set is so small that there's no sense of pursuit, just of two characters going in circles. The film tries to use right-to-left and left-to-right blocking tricks to indicate that the characters are moving through the same landscape, or that one is pursuing the other, but Wood doesn't have the attention to detail and consistency required to make maneuvers like this work.

After the action scene is over (we can tell because the theme music ends), a police car wails along the same road Farmer drove along to find Paula, and possibly the same road the police car came along to get to the cemetery earlier in the film. It drives right to left, implying that it's following Farmer's car. But then we cut to the police car pulling up at the studio cemetery, from which Farmer drove *away*. I could excuse this in isolation by saying, well, it's all in the same neighborhood, whatever. But the truth is that Wood doesn't know how to block a series of scenes, or possibly doesn't know that such blocking is required for a movie to make spatial sense. This is just the latest example of it.

Four policemen get out of the car. One last shot of real Lugosi in the location cemetery, and then he flings his cape around his shoulder in a practiced gesture and heads offscreen.

The policemen wander through the cemetery, looking for something, although what it could be we do not know. How the police knew to come to the cemetery when Paula was in danger (if their arrival is even related to her) is also a mystery; we don't see evidence that anyone called the police, and too little time seems to have passed between Farmer driving away with her and the police arriving.

At last, Vampira and Tor appear in the same shot, and as monsters go, they rank as "strong attempts at scary." If we could have taken any of the film seriously up to now, they might look scarier. They walk from left to right.

Cut to a new set: the inside of Eros's ship. He and Tanna gaze out the window, to the left of frame. This, that the ghouls walk right and the aliens look left, plus the music overlap, plus Eros's next line, "They'll be at the hatch in a moment," combine to form a good indication that Eros and Tanna are looking at Vampira and Tor. Yet there is still no *geographical* indication that these two shots occur in physical proximity. (Plus, we brought in the police for a second only to drop them.)

Finally, here *Plan 9* connects Vampira and Tor with the aliens. The film has not succeeded in doing this so far, despite trying.[51] The scene in Bunny's room doesn't even really manage it; we can understand the plan, but the ghouls (especially Vampira) are so blank, so hard to read, that it's far easier to consider them motivation-free monsters without a past or future than elements of the plan the aliens discussed. Plus, the connections between the aliens and the cemetery where the ghouls stalk are weakly made. We can't immediately believe that the cemetery photograph in which the saucer lands is the same place as the studio cemetery, nor that the toy saucer which lands in that photo is the same place as the room in which Eros and Tanna now stand. It takes a lot of leaps to get where Wood wants us to go, and we are short on springboards.

These connections could have been made, or made stronger, in a variety of ways. Showing Eros and Tanna leaving the saucer in the studio cemetery earlier on in the running time might have done it. Or a line in the scene with Bunny about Eros's landing location. Or a shot of Vampira or Tor in the same frame as the saucer. Or some kind of recurrent musical motif. Or a conversation between some of the other characters about seeing something specific in the cemetery, rather than just lights and sounds. Naming the cemetery, to show that all the various landscapes are meant to be the same location, would have helped. There are many solutions to the jagged continuity of location and event in this movie, and Wood implemented none of them.

Vampira and Tor enter the ship. Tanna demonstrates that the aliens have physical control over the ghouls. Cut to faux-Lugosi, approaching a structure that is meant to be the outside of Eros's ship. We can tell because the door that opens for him makes the same sound and motion as the one that opened inside the ship for Vampira and Tor. (*That's* continuity that grounds us with a landmark. See how easy it is?) Visually, the structure faux-Lugosi enters bears no resemblance to the round, silvery saucer we've seen so frequently. This isn't an easy problem to solve without money, but building a structure with squared-off sides and a ladder, and claiming it's a disc-shaped UFO, is a poor effort.[52]

---

51 After multiple viewings, I suspect that Wood wanted us to make this connection much earlier in the film, maybe as early as the gravediggers' death. But he also purposely writes the characters *not* making the connection. Sophisticated stories can allow the audience to know more than the characters, but this is just chaos.

52 After this essay was published, I learned something amazing about this "poor effort" from a collector: someone on the prop team for *Plan 9* glued square shapes to the bases of the toy saucers used in filming to make them match the squared-off set in this scene. The size of the toys and the angles by which they're shot means you can't see this in the movie

Behind Eros and Tanna are two windows, one a black square and the other a daytime cloudscape. Since the two windows are *right next to each other*, and thus should be showing approximately the same view, this mistake is particularly silly. It exists in all the scenes that occur in this room.

Two cops enter the studio cemetery and exchange bad dialogue.

> POLICEMAN
> It's tough to find something when you don't know
> what you're looking for.

Comforting to know he's as confused as we are.

The saucer takes off from the cemetery photo. Lt. Harper and Larry hear it but don't seem to see it.

> LARRY
> What do you suppose that noise was?

> LT. HARPER
> Whatever it was, it's no more strange than the
> other things happening around this cemetery.

There's a bad, bad cut in this scene, simply switching from one angle on a two-shot of Lt. Harper and Larry to another angle on the same pair. It's the kind of cut that low-quality filmmakers use to conceal poor or incomplete takes, and it's disorienting, like blinking and finding you've magically switched seats in your living room.

Larry affirms that they've come to the cemetery based on a report from Farmer and Paula, although based on the editing, the timing doesn't really work. If Wood had *dissolved* from the ghouls moving away (individually) through the cemetery to the police car pulling up, it would have indicated the passage of time. But he simply *cut*, which makes it seem like the two events happened in immediate sequence. Which is illogical.

The other two cops come rushing up, and the four of them talk about the noise of the saucer taking off. Lt. Harper seems confident that the noise is/was a saucer, when not even 60 seconds ago he wouldn't speculate ("Whatever it was…").

The writing in this scene demonstrates that, at least when he wrote it, Wood wanted to keep balancing the characters' apprehension of strange goings-on in the cemetery between the ghouls and the flying saucers, without the characters understanding that the two phenomena are related. The way the characters assess the threat in the film swings between these two phenomena almost at random.

---

at all—you can only tell in looking at the props themselves. Having done so, I stand by my statement here.

The police seek answers for first one phenomenon, and then the other. Lt. Harper and Larry, on their own, talked about the ghouls, while the foursome talks about saucers. There's no consistency across the two conversations.

Here's the scene between the four cops in full.

KELTON
Lieutenant, Lieutenant! Did you hear that?

LARRY
How could we help it?

POLICEMAN
It sure was strange.

KELTON
Know what it was?

LARRY
No more than you do.

POLICEMAN
If it weren't for orders I'd get out of here
right now.

LT. HARPER
It was a saucer.

POLICEMAN
A flying saucer?

LARRY
What makes you say that?

LT. HARPER
You remember the noise we heard the other night?

LARRY
We were knocked to the ground!
How could I forget?

LT. HARPER
Exactly, but you're not remembering that sound.

> LARRY
> There you're wrong, Lieutenant. I'm with the fact
> the sound is similar, but what about
> the blinding light?

> LT. HARPER
> Well, haven't you heard? Many times a saucer
> hasn't had a glow, or a light of any kind,
> for that matter.

> LARRY
> That proves it. What next, Lieutenant?

The inconsistency and stiltedness of this dialogue speaks for itself. Each line rushes into the last uncomfortably (especially "Exactly" and "That proves it"). I don't even know what to say about "Haven't you heard?" Sometimes analysis fails me.

In the screenplay, this scene and its purpose are clearer. Sometimes the saucer that lands in the cemetery makes both sound and light, and sometimes it does not. This scene tries to point out that it can still be a saucer whether it makes both sound and light or not, and tries to get these policemen to all agree that they heard and saw a saucer the other night and, this evening, have heard it but not seen it, *and yet* it was probably the same saucer. Believe me that the screenplay does not make it *much* clearer, and that Wood should have implemented better, more consistent special effects and done at least one rewrite if he really wanted to get this across.

The conversation turns back to the ghouls—again, the ghouls and the saucers have been patched together here and there across the screenplay, rather than interwoven. Kelton and Unnamed Cop[53] have discovered a grave with freshly upturned dirt. Lt. Harper puts his foot up on the side of the grave, but we don't see what the cops are seeing. The grave is just offscreen. That means we can't compare it to either the grave from the moving-soil shots (with the pencil-eraser gravestone) or the grave from the Tor-gets-stuck shots. No wide shots encompass the disturbed grave or Kelton going into it. We just see medium shots of the policemen. This is not helpful in connecting the location of their conversation to where Tor rose from the dead.

The policemen expend some dialogue about the disturbed grave, including one of the two major self-contradictions in the film.

> LARRY
> Do we have the right to look down there,
> Lieutenant?

---

53   I think his name is Jamie, but I wouldn't put money on it. The script doesn't specify.

                              LT. HARPER
                         Ah, technically, no.

                              LARRY
                               No?

                              LT. HARPER
                    Well, this spot looks familiar, though. We
                 shouldn't investigate any further without the
                         permission of next of kin.

                              KELTON
                          Let's go get it!

                              LT. HARPER
                               How?

                              LARRY
               I see what you mean. The gravestone's down there.

                              LT. HARPER
                 Well, let's go down and find out whose grave it
                                   is.

                              KELTON
                               How?

                              LT. HARPER
                      By going down and finding out!

The dialogue intends to say:

1. The policemen don't have permission to "look down" into the grave without the permission of next of kin.
2. The policemen can't find out who the next of kin are without looking at the gravestone to figure out to whom the grave belongs.
3. The gravestone is inside the grave.
4. Thus, in order to find out whether they have permission to go into the grave, they must go into the grave.

Let's break this down.

1. Generally, burial lots are owned by cemeteries and sold for burials under

easement.[54] That means the people buried there and their loved ones don't own the land or the soil—the cemetery does. So next of kin doesn't enter into it, except as a courtesy. The laws about disturbing graves seem to vary widely, and depend on context (whether the disturbance was for some practical reason, or for desecration or robbery). But stepping into a disturbed grave for what I guess are informational purposes does not appear to be a civil or criminal offense.[55] If it was, permission would come from the cemetery, or potentially from the police, whichthese men are.[56]

2. Looking at the gravestone is not the only way to figure out to whom the grave belongs. Cemeteries keep records of such things. Also, these men were *just here*, likely less than a week ago, for Inspector Clay's funeral. How can they not remember that this is where he's buried?

3. The pencil-eraser gravestone fell into the grave, but it's insufficiently clear that the pencil-eraser gravestone belonged to Clay's grave. So this item, too, is disputable.

4. This is a paradox. Lt. Harper is visibly annoyed when he says "By going down and finding out!" as if Kelton should have known exactly what he meant, despite him saying, literal seconds ago, that they cannot go into the grave.

In sum: none of the premises of the scene hold up.

I cannot believe that actors with working brains, moving through this scene, wouldn't ask aloud, *hey, why doesn't this scene make any sense?* I cannot believe that Wood could write and film this scene and not realize how contradictory it is. Everything about these lines of dialogue is inexcusably daft.

Kelton goes into the grave. He asks for a flashlight or a match to read the name on the casket,[57] in a bit of shoe-leather that is a waste of screen time and editing, because he easily could have brought a match or a flashlight into the grave with

---

54 "In nearly all jurisdictions, one who purchases and has conveyed to him/her a lot in a public cemetery does not acquire the fee to the soil." https://www.stimmel-law.com/en/articles/basic-laws-pertaining-cemeteries

55 At least, not according to Dr. Google.

56 The screenplay includes this line from Lt. Harper: "We'll waive regulations this time," after "By going down there and finding out." So it's not as contradictory as the finished film. But that one line does not save the scene. And if it could have, Wood should damn well have shot it.

57 Are names commonly carved into caskets? I truly don't know the answer to this, particularly a 1956 answer, but it seems a bizarre assumption.[a] Also, how could he read the casket when a gravestone has collapsed into it? It seems most likely that the inside of that grave would just be a mess of dirt and a broken casket and a heavy-ass slab of stone, and nothing would be readable.[b]

[a] In the script, Harper asks if Kelton can read the name on the *headstone*. The word "casket" doesn't appear. So it's one of the actors' assumptions, I guess.

[b] These questions are in a footnote because I've spent too much time on this scene in the main text already. It's so much worse a scene than I thought it was.

him and absolutely nothing is gained from him having to ask for one. He then proclaims, looking directly at the wall of soil in the side of the grave, "It's Inspector Clay's grave! But he ain't in it!"

Dissolve to a passenger plane over the Pentagon, which Criswell narrates:

```
                    CRISWELL
         But meanwhile, in the Pentagon,
              in Washington, DC...
```

That's triplicate specificity: the visible landmark, the naming of it, and confirmation of the unobscure fact that the Pentagon is in DC. If only this kind of overdetermined clarity existed in the editing and blocking of the rest of the film.

The scene that follows is about five minutes long. It involves Col. Edwards and his superior, General Roberts, talking at length about the phenomenon of flying saucers from the military point of view. The sequence is loaded with the kind of self-contradiction we previously saw in the scene with Col. Edwards and the captain. Both these scenes have the same problem: Wood had to write a scene about UFOs and military men, yet had to maintain that the military denies knowledge of UFOs. He cannot write well enough to overcome this paradox, so the scenes are circular and nonsensical.[58]

This sequence bears many delights. Apropos of nothing, Gen. Roberts quietly says "I, uh, like you, Colonel," and speaks the phrase "atmospheric conditions in outer space," which makes sense if you do not expend a single neuron considering it.[59] The scene includes an audio recording of Eros, snarking at the human race for our inferiority and referring to our new invention, the "dictial robetary"[60] (the "language computer" or, as it's come to be known generally in sci-fi, the universal translator).

Overall, Eros's message isn't that different from Klaatu's speech at the end of *The Day the Earth Stood Still* (1951): humans are irresponsible, and we build weapons way too dangerous for our own good and the good of the universe.[61] Klaatu's message includes a fascist solution, but Eros's offers no solution at all. Eros claims that "we don't want to conquer your planet, only to save it," which does not jibe with his hostile tone. He threatens with one phrase while offering friendship in the next.

The general says there have been a dozen transmissions like the one we just heard. It's unclear whether they all said the same thing or all bore different messages. That this could be the most substantive message of the dozen is unthinkable, as the recording tells us almost nothing about the aliens' planned actions or priorities. Nor does it articulate ideas that would be sensible for an interplanetary message: a

---

58 This scene is exactly as contradictory in the screenplay as in the film.
59 In the script, it's "Storms in outer space."
60 This is the script's spelling. Rob Craig, in *Ed Wood, Mad Genius*, posits that it's a mix-up of "robot dictionary," which I find cute as heck if true.
61 This idea is at least as old as World War I, but still potent as I type this sentence.

request for a meeting, an explanation of whence it came, a suggestion of what kind of body it represents (an alliance? an army? an HOA?). Also, this last transmission of 12 was received a month ago, which means the military has been remarkably slow to act upon this unprecedented, critically important situation.

Gen. Roberts sends Col. Edwards to Los Angeles—specifically, to San Fernando, where we can now presume the Trents live—to make contact with the UFOs and find out what they want, something their messages might logically have indicated.

We dissolve to the benippled mother ship, and then to Bunny's room. Eros reports on their progress to Bunny,[62] demonstrating the fruits of Plan 9 by presenting Tor, who sort of malfunctions and sort of tries to attack Eros. Breathlessly, Eros spits "That was…too close!" It was not. It was not even close.

The aliens discuss the next step: Eros must sacrifice faux-Lugosi to frighten the Earth people. Bunny finishes off with a series of ungrammatical sentences outlining the ultimate plan: "March [the ghouls] on the capitals of the Earth, let nothing stand in your way. Their own dead will be used to make them accept our existence, and believe in that fact."[63]

Based on this dialogue, the goal seems to be to get Earthlings to acknowledge the aliens, and listen to them, not for the aliens to conquer Earth. Even as I was drafting this essay, I had a hard time understanding that, and kept writing sentences including the phrase "conquer Earth" without thinking about it. It's a major trope of science fiction films, from the 1950s forward, that aliens land on Earth in order to conquer it. These aliens' aggressiveness—in Eros's recorded message, in the details of Plan 9, and in scenes to come—hints at conquering. Why would they march a deadly army of ghouls on the capital cities if they did not intend to kill a whole bunch of the population, leaving us vulnerable? Why would they want us to be vulnerable if they only wanted to speak and be heard?

I theorize that Wood modeled his screenplay after standard science fiction tropes without thinking them all the way through. I think he liked the idea that the aliens wanted to save Earthlings from themselves rather than conquer, but he couldn't make that cohere with the conflict and peril that the genre demanded at the time. He put in scary monsters and super creeps, but neglected to reconsider them in light of the aliens' central motivation; he put in a peaceful central motivation, and neglected to reconsider it in light of the scary monsters and super creeps. Some of the atmospheric inconsistency of the film (that it feels like a conquer-Earth narrative and isn't one), and many of the specific inconsistencies of the film, result from this baseline incongruity.

Dissolve back to the mother ship. Cut back to Earth. A black police car speeds

---

62 Despite his wonderfully florid gestures, Bunny's acting in this scene is unfortunate. His line readings are flat and stilted and his eye movements make it look as if he's not paying attention. When thinking of him, I tend to replace his performance in my mind with Bill Murray's delicious portrayal of him in *Ed Wood*.

63 None of this is in the screenplay. The scene ends with "Report to me when this has been accomplished." I wish I could have looked at the way Wood punctuated these lines.

by on the dirt road, right to left. A saucer floats by in the sky, right to left. A white car zooms by the camera, right to left; a just-readable sign saying SAN FERNANDO is framed center-shot. In a bit of shoe-leather, the police car parks before a black backdrop, and Lt. Harper, Col. Edwards, and Kelton get out. Kelton waits at the car and the other two walk onto the Trents' patio, intercut with a saucer shot for no apparent reason. Finally, three protagonists from separate story threads meet. It is minute 52 of 78.

Col. Edwards begins to ask Jeff and Paula about their "strange experience." Wood does something right here: he elides the conversation. We cut to the same old saucer-landing-in-photo-cemetery shot, and then back to the patio. A pull-back centers Paula, saying "After that, the police brought me home," and revealing three Coke bottles on the table, two mostly empty; Lt. Harper is smoking. These visual details denote that time has passed. The camera move, pulling back, indicates a conclusion,[64] and Paula's words indicate she's finishing up a story. Good job, Ed.

The Trents describe the phenomena a little more, including seeing a "glowing ball" moving toward the cemetery, in contradiction to the "Well, haven't you heard?" conversation between the policemen, as the man who said that line 14 minutes ago sits and listens.[65]

Cut to the exterior of what is meant to be Eros's ship. Faux-Lugosi emerges. Real Lugosi walks through the location cemetery, in his last moment in the film.

Back to the patio. The party hears and smells something. Tension builds (sort of). Faux-Lugosi advances on Kelton, first near the car and then onto the patio. Kelton fires his gun to no effect and gets knocked down. Lt. Harper fires his gun, and the other three characters *stand still* while faux-Lugosi gets closer and closer to them, slowly enough to be outrun easily. Cut to the photo cemetery and a throbbing glow on the horizon. An electric-charge sound occurs and a ray of light spears out from the horizon, and faux-Lugosi drops to the patio floor. Moments later, Col. Edwards lifts his cape away to reveal…a skeleton! EEEK!

Col. Edwards and Lt. Harper revive poor Kelton, who is badly spooked. Duke Moore (Harper) decides to act this scene with an amused, indulgent air, which seems a more and more dissonant choice every time I watch it.

Dissolve to a car parking by the cemetery, from which disembark (in no hurry) all five non-dead characters in the previous scene: Paula, Jeff, Kelton, Lt. Harper, and Col. Edwards. Multiple elements of the film (the danger Paula's in, where she

---

64 Pushing in indicates an opening. A classic example is the "Dignity, always dignity" sequence from *Singin' in the Rain*, when Gene Kelly tells the story of how he got going in Hollywood. The sequence opens by pushing in on Kelly before we dissolve to a series of flashbacks. When these end, we return to the close-up on Kelly, and then we pull back and move on. There are a *lot* of examples exactly like this across classical Hollywood. It's part of the grammar of cinema: push in for opening, pull back for conclusion. Wood either learned this or noticed it, and implemented it here.

65 As a previous explanation of that scene indicated (p. 57), Harper's earlier scene originally meant that sometimes the saucer glows and sometimes it doesn't. But I'm not giving Wood a break here. That scene failed, so it casts doubt on this one.

runs after she's attacked) depend on the cemetery being in walking distance to the Trents' house, so they shouldn't have had to drive there. I can think of no diegetic reasons for this disparity. A non-diegetic reason involves Paula having a place to wait before she's put in danger, which is a bad reason to make this move, but probably the correct one.

Kelton stays behind at the car (again) with Paula in the back seat,[66] while the other three men walk through the studio cemetery looking for...well, even they don't know.

> JEFF
> What do you expect to find out here?

> LT. HARPER
> Well, there's only one answer to that, Mr. Trent.
> We'll know when we find it.

Meanwhile, Eros and Tanna prepare to receive visitors. Tor is sent off for Paula and Kelton, while Vampira is tasked with nothing. The three men gathered at Clay's grave (Jeff, Harper, and Edwards) suddenly notice the throbbing glow on the horizon, after not noticing it at all this whole time, and decide to head that way.

Back at the car, Tor takes out Kelton, and then goes for Paula, whose screams evidently do not reach across the cemetery.

The three men trade inept dialogue—

> LT. HARPER
> Boy, how could anything that big
> hide for so long a time?

—and Eros instructs Tanna to let them in. Throughout all this, Wood expends screen time on Eros and Tanna walking back and forth across the ship set to alternately activate devices and gaze out the window. It's less than ten seconds

---

66 She remains behind because this is a movie and she has to be in peril at least once more, but the argument about her remaining behind contains a minor contradiction with a silly bow of sexism on top:

> LT. HARPER
> **Modern** women.

> COL. EDWARDS
> Yeah, they been that way **all down through the ages.**

The script is less contradictory, if no less sexist. Edwards's reply is "From all I've seen, they've been the same for ages," meaning no, it's not about modern women, all women are argumentative and always have been.

per trip, but it's deeply unnecessary for the set to be blocked so as to waste the audience's time like this. It's the very definition of shoe-leather.

Eros and Tanna explain to each other for the audience's benefit that they plan to kill these three Earthlings, and that they feel sad about the waste of it. In the scene before Tor grabs Paula:

```
                        EROS
    These  are  the  same  men  who  have  been  so  close  so
    often.  They  must  be  halted  before  they  can  inform
                     others  about  us.
```

And now:

```
                        EROS
    Well,  wouldn't  it  be  better  to  kill  a  few  now
    than,  with  their  meddling,  permit  them  to  destroy
                  the  entire  universe?
```

The implication seems to be that because these men have discovered Eros's ship, they must be killed. Previously, Eros and Bunny were both angry that Earth leaders refused to acknowledge them. Why would men who acknowledge the aliens' existence have to die, when acknowledgment is the aliens' goal? How does the meddling of these specific men lead to the destruction of the universe?

This confusion joins with the confusion of whether the aliens are here to conquer, or communicate, or *what*, until the present scene bears an almost pleasant anticipation. We have no idea what will happen when these sets of characters meet, because we can't be at all sure what their motivations are for the meeting. Such uncertainty and unpredictability would be an asset at this point in the movie if it didn't derive from poor storytelling.

In the Earthlings come. They act hostile, trying to take control of the situation with commands and pointing guns, despite being *inside a UFO*, a space of which they have no knowledge, one that is the known territory of another *species*.

The scene that follows is long, tiring, badly written, badly acted, profoundly unscientific, and incredibly funny. Eros gets the lion's share of the dialogue, for better or worse. The scene does communicate an actual idea, if an idiotic one, and Wood gets out of his own way as a director and editor, letting the dialogue pull most of the communicative weight. That means the mechanics of filmmaking in this long scene are not as worthy of analysis as the text. The angles vary between full shots, medium shots, shot/reverse-shots, and closeups of the different characters. The simplicity of this work unfortunately gives Wood's dopey ideas enough rope to hang themselves more effectively than in other, less coherently shot and edited sequences.

Since the dialogue is specifically at issue here, I'm going to annotate it.

JEFF
You fiend!

EROS
I? A fiend? I am a soldier of our planet! I? A fiend?[67] We did not come here as enemies. We came only with friendly intentions.[68]
To talk. To ask your aid.

COL. EDWARDS
Our aid?

EROS
Yes. Your aid for the whole universe. But your governments of Earth refused even to accept our existence. Even though you've seen us, heard our messages, you still refused to accept us.[69]

COL. EDWARDS
Why is it so important that you want to contact the governments of our Earth?[70]

EROS
Because of death. Because all you of Earth are idiots![71]

JEFF
Now you just hold on, buster.

---

67 Dudley Manlove pours it on in performance here, but repetition makes the question seem less profound, not more. Adding another few lines in between might have made the repeated line work better. The incredulousness with which he says it indicates that Eros will explain why the Earthlings are the true fiends. Eventually he almost succeeds at this, but such a rhetorical strategy only works if he repeats the "fiend" theme throughout the speech and follows up on it at the end.

68 As previously explored, this is difficult to believe.

69 Refusal of the aliens' existence isn't the whole truth, based on the conversation in Gen. Roberts's office and Col. Edwards's job "in charge of saucer field activity."

70 GOOD QUESTION, COLONEL. As in the scene between Eros and Tanna on p. 48-49, an answer to this question would make a real scene. Maybe Eros has a good answer...

71 ...or maybe not. The two sentences in this line are equally funny, but Eros delivers the first sentence like a dramatic eleven-year-old.

EROS
No, you hold on.[72] First was your firecracker, a
harmless explosive. Then your hand grenade. They
began to kill your own people a few at a time.
Then the bomb. Then a larger bomb. Many people
are killed at one time.[73] Then your scientists
stumbled upon the atom bomb. Split the atom. Then
the hydrogen bomb, where you actually explode the
air itself.[74] Now you [audio jump][75] brings the
total destruction of the entire universe, served
by our sun.[76] The only explosion left is the
Solaronite.

COL. EDWARDS
Why, there's no such thing.

EROS
Perhaps to you. But we've known it for
centuries. Your scientists will stumble upon it
as they have all the others.[77] But the juvenile
minds you possess will not comprehend its
strength until it's too late.

COL. EDWARDS
You're way above our heads.[78]

---

72 Eros's rhetoric is not improving.

73 Somehow this portion of the speech feels longer than a semester on the history of munitions. We get it; militaries continue to develop bombs, each larger than the last.

74   I am no scientist, but I'm fairly sure this is not how the H-bomb works.

75   In the script, this is the line (which in the film is nipped in the middle by some kind of audio problem): "Now you can destroy whole cities of people in one big explosion. There is only one step left until you and your Earthman's stupidity brings the total destruction of the entire Universe served by our sun." (punctuation Wood's)

76 "Served by our sun." This line implies that Eros's race comes from a planet in the same solar system as Earth, doesn't it? But that's impossible, isn't it? Also, his recorded message said "from a planet of your galaxy," which is extremely unspecific, but at least more likely than him being from a planet "served by our sun," or than the entire universe being "served by our sun."

77 Vague pronoun usage. Subtract ten points.

78 I'm interested in this line. It seems like it's trying to placate Eros, to get him to be helpful instead of insulting, but Edwards delivers it with some contempt. It does little except agree with Eros's prior line. I really do not know what it's for, except to provide a beat between Eros delivering an insult and a piece of information.

                        EROS
    The Solaronite is a way to explode the actual
                particles of sunlight.

                     COL. EDWARDS
              Why, that's impossible.[79]

                        EROS
    Even now, your scientists are working on a way
    to harness the sun's rays. The rays of sunlight
    are minute particles.[80] Is it so far from your
    imagination they cannot do as I have suggested?[81]

                     COL. EDWARDS
    Why, a particle of sunlight can't even be seen or
                    measured.[82]

                        EROS
    Can you see or measure an atom?[83] Yet you can explode
    one. A ray of sunlight is made up of many atoms.[84]

                        JEFF
    So what if we do develop this Solaronite bomb?
    We'd be even a stronger nation than now.[85]

                        EROS
    Stronger. You see? You see? Your stupid minds!
                Stupid! Stupid![86]

---

79 Look at Edwards's last three lines. Two lines beginning with "Why," and ending with contradictions of what's just been said, and one that's needless assent. Bad, bad writing.
80 Technically I think this is true, light being both a particle and a wave, but I can't believe Wood knew the science behind it at the time.
81 This sentence makes no grammatical sense. "They" has an unclear antecedent. Subtract 20 points.
82 "Why," again.
83 Actually, yes, we can measure atoms.
84 No, it's made up of *particles*. Focus, Eros!
85 It's not that important in context of this movie's scads of errors, but this line vocalizes the assumption that Eros is talking just to Americans, not the whole world.
86 I have seen many an audience laugh at this line, this famed, oft-quoted, oft-used-to-sum-up-the-stupidity-of-*Plan-9* line. I don't know how Wood could have written it seriously, nor how Dudley Manlove could have delivered it without knowing how ridiculous it sounded. I see his point, that all Earth men think about is exploding things and having military power, but throwing a tantrum is not going to get his point across.

JEFF
That's all I'm taking from you!
[JEFF LEAPS AT EROS]

LT. HARPER
Get back here, you jerk! Let him finish.[87]

EROS
It's because of men like you that all must be
destroyed. Headstrong, violent! No use of the
mind God gave you.[88]

JEFF
You talk of God?

EROS
You also think it impossible that we, too, might
think of God?[89] [TO COL. EDWARDS] You, who wear
the uniform of your country. You see, I wear the
uniform of my country.[90] Yes, we've had to use
drastic means to get to you, but you left us no
alternative.[91] When you have the Solaronite, you
have nothing. Nor does the universe.[92]

---

87 It's true that Eros has not finished his lecture on Solaronite, but "let him finish" is a weird sentiment for Lt. Harper of all people to offer up. It would have been a better line for Edwards, and different phrasing would have been better still. In the script, I found that Wood agreed with me, in part:

HARPER
Get back here, you fool.

COLONEL
Calm down, Jeff. Let him finish.

88 The sincerity with which this line is delivered cracks me up every time.
89 The awkwardness with which this line was written cracks me up every time. Still, it's a crime against every writer's ear. Subtract 30 points and see me after class.
90 At the beginning of the scene he said he was "a soldier of our *planet*."
91 But Earthlings haven't even developed the weapon yet. Surely there are *many* alternatives to Plan 9.
92 I can't quite parse the antecedent for "nor." The universe has nothing if the human race has nothing and if they do have Solaronite? I think he means to say the universe is screwed if humans develop Solaronite, but the point is badly lost in the sentences.

COL. EDWARDS
You speak of Solaronite, but just what is it?

EROS
Take a can of your gasoline. Say this can of
gasoline is the sun. Now you spread a thin line
of it to a ball, representing the Earth. Now,
the gasoline represents the sunlight, the sun
particles. Here we saturate the ball with the
gasoline, the sunlight. Then we put a flame to
the ball. The flame will speedily travel around
the Earth, back along the line of gasoline to
the can, or the sun itself. It will explode this
source, and spread to every place that gasoline,
or sunlight, touches.[93] Explode the sunlight here,
gentlemen, and you explode the universe. Explode
the sunlight here, and a chain reaction will
occur, direct to the sun itself. And to all the
planets that sunlight touches. To every planet in
the universe.[94] This why you must be stopped. This
is why any means must be used to stop you. In a
friendly manner, or as it seems, you want it.[95]

LT. HARPER
He's mad.[96]

TANNA
Mad? Is it mad that you destroy other people to
save yourselves? You have done this. Is it mad
that one country must destroy another to save

---

93 I should not need to say it, but this is inane. The metaphor doesn't work, but even if it
did, the science is daffy.
94 Whatever Wood's idea is of how light travels through the galaxy, and how close
planets are to each other, it is mistaken.
95 There's no evidence in the movie that the aliens have tried "a friendly manner."
96 I don't really understand why this is anyone's reaction at this moment in the scene.
Maybe the idea is just to discredit Eros? Because what he's saying is too complicated and
negative for Lt. Harper to understand, so he's going to write him off as crazy? He could have
said "Your science is bad," or "We haven't developed a weapon like that," or "Let's go talk to
someone higher up in the government about this to determine if your concerns are valid
about the threat we present," or "What's the deal with the ghouls, then?" or even "Shut up."
But instead, "He's mad." When I think about it, the likeliest reason for this line is to set up
Tanna's little speech, coming next. This is the very laziest kind of writing that exists, when
characters say things purely so you can get other characters to say other things.

themselves? You have also done this.[97] How then is
it mad that one planet must destroy another that
threatens the very existence--[98]

EROS
[interrupting, pushing Tanna] That's enough!
In my land, women are for advancing the race,
not for fighting man's battles.[99] Life is not so
expensive on my planet. We don't cling to it like
you do. Our entire aim is for the development of
our planet.[100]

Phew. That's about seven minutes of scene. The first cut outside the spaceship is to a police car driving along the same dirt road as ever before, and then to Kelton regaining consciousness in the front seat of the police car in the studio. Slow as molasses, a second police car pulls up beside, and Larry questions a distraught Kelton about why he called for backup. It's not a useful scene. Even Vampira walks away from it.

Tor carries Paula…somewhere. Cut to Eros gazing out of the daytime window, doomsaying in a dreary voice. He offers the impression that he's been speaking for many hours. In a comedy, we'd cut from him to the other four sprawled in office chairs, snoring.

At this point, two scenes (really two and a half) are going on simultaneously. The three men and two aliens talk in circles in the spaceship. Outside, in the cemetery, Tor has Paula, while Kelton and Larry search for Paula and the three men. The next few minutes cross-cut these scenes with each other, with fair success. The humans in the ship and the policemen outside it become aware of Tor and Paula at almost the same time. The editing implies that the cops have seen the glow from the ship, too, although the dialogue doesn't. They disarm Tor with a blow to the head, which of course makes no sense, and ADR gives Paula dialogue that also makes no sense, while her mouth does not move.

---

97 Something about the rhythm of these lines feels like Wood's trying to be…grand? Biblical? I'm not really sure. The actress doesn't do a bad job, but the lines feel so strange.
98 Here she says destroying Earth *is* on the table after all. But it's the only line in the film that says so directly.
99 [eye-roll]. Also, how can Tanna be an astronaut at all if this is the case?
100 I truly cannot make sense of these lines. How can you aim to develop a planet without people? What does clinging to life have to do with *anything* that's been said in this scene so far, much less the sexism in the prior line? I grasp for meaning, and can only guess that the connection is about humans having to die so that we don't develop Solaronite. Our deaths would sadden us, but not the aliens, because they place little value on individual human (or alien) life. But I'm fumbling around in the dark. The expensiveness of life on Eros's planet seems irrelevant.[c]

   c Dudley Manlove clearly says "expansive" in the film. The script says "expensive." "Expansive" makes less sense, but "expensive" doesn't make a whole lot more.

Back inside the ship, the humans illogically gain the upper hand, and a physical fight of middling quality breaks out. Eros attempts to hurl sciencey stuff at Jeff, while Tanna frantically tries to make the ship take off. Col. Edwards and Lt. Harper get the door open in their own sweet time.

>   COL. EDWARDS
>   Get out of here, Jeff! The ship's on fire!

How he knows this, I can't say. No fire is visible before he says the line.

The humans flee. Jeff looks back at the destruction he's wrought: a mostly empty room with some toppled equipment and a prone Eros. It is not as disastrous-looking as the music seems to believe it is.

Tanna tries to improve the situation inside the ship, but she is a woman and thus she is panicky and useless. The cast of living humans stands in a line looking up: Col. Edwards, hands comfortably in pockets; Lt. Harper, ever holding his gun; Paula and Jeff, no particular looks on their faces; and Larry, looking approximately like nothing is happening. Kelton stands mostly out of frame. A saucer, afire, lifts out of the photo cemetery. It floats over a spray of city lights. The humans trade some dialogue and reveal the skeleton of Tor.

>   PAULA
>   Have they caught that woman, that thing, yet?

>   LT. HARPER
>   Hey, that's right. There's another ghoul running
>   loose.

>   COL. EDWARDS
>   And it's my guess that she'll look like him.
>   With the ship and the ray gun gone, they have no
>   control.

It's unclear whether Paula ever saw Vampira at all. It seemed to be mostly faux-Lugosi pursuing her in the earlier peril sequence. The editing in that sequence somewhat indicates that Vampira sees Paula, but nothing indicates that Paula sees Vampira. Later, she sees Tor, and the other characters definitely do see both Tor and faux-Lugosi, but there's no direct evidence that any of the surviving human characters see Vampira at all.[101]

---

101 Editing hints that Farmer does, but it's not especially direct. The cops talking about Paula and Farmer's report mention them seeing spirits, plural, but that could be Tor and faux-Lugosi. I'm not trying to be difficult here; I'm trying to say that the character knowledge expressed by these lines has minimal foundation in the film. It's a long-division problem, who knows what and how they know it, and Wood hasn't shown his work.

How do they know there's another ghoul? How does Paula know it's a woman? Further, how do the characters know these are the only three, and that Eros is responsible for all of them?

The film did clarify that Eros was responsible for the ghouls, but it didn't specify the bit about the ray gun. For all Col. Edwards knows, the ghouls could continue to go about their mission indefinitely. Tor could have been skeletonized on purpose, rather than because the ship is leaving and also on fire. *We* know, but that doesn't mean *Edwards* knows. It's a stretch for him to speculate that Vampira will be neutralized too, because the characters have never known (on camera, as part of a scene) what created the ghouls nor what caused them to turn into skeletons.

Col. Edwards's entire line here is written as wrap-up, though. Wood needed to tie off the Vampira situation, so he did it without visuals and with this one hasty line, rather than with a more gradual series of lines and information fed to the audience with care.

> COL. EDWARDS
> We've got to hand it to them, though...they're
> far ahead of us.

This is a Captain Obvious line, and it portrays Col. Edwards as a big man who can admit when he's outclassed. Yet we could read the line as troubling. The aliens mean harm (probably?), and they have the advantage over us. If they choose to come back—perhaps with Plan 10—we're done for.

Tanna screams into a frame almost entirely filled with smoke, and the saucer explodes. Immediately we cut to Criswell, for the last word.

> CRISWELL
> My friend, you have seen this incident
> based on sworn testimony.
> Can you prove that it didn't happen?

No one can prove a negative. But I'm pretty sure this didn't happen.

> CRISWELL
> Perhaps on your way home, you will pass someone
> in the dark, and you will never know it, for they
> will be from outer space.

I won't know I've passed someone *because* they were from outer space?

> CRISWELL
> Many scientists believe that another world is
> watching us this moment. We once laughed at the
> horseless carriage, the aeroplane, the telephone,

> the electric light, vitamins, radio, and even
> television. And now some of us laugh at outer
> space.

Does anyone laugh at the very *concept* of outer space? (Or at vitamins?[102])

> CRISWELL
> God help us...in the future.

The point of this speech remains unclear to me. When I search through the individual sentences for individual or overall meaning, I can't find any. The very idea of meaning slips through my fingers. Now that you've read almost all of this essay, I invite you to break down the speech and try to make sense of it yourself, just as I've broken down as much of the rest of the film as I could. If you find any meaning, please let me know.

I do get hung up repeatedly on the last line, and what it's meant to communicate. It's unexpectedly dire. Plenty of B movies end with semi-concealed messages about the terrors of nuclear war and how dangerous it is to play with space-travel technology, but Criswell's words offer a kind of overarching, unspecific pessimism. Are we doomed? Have we been entertained? Perhaps we are not meant to know.

----

102 One final theft from the RiffTrax for *Plan 9*.

III: In Sum

What you've just read I wrote backwards. I drafted the whole thing, and then, in preparing to write this conclusion, I created an outline of my main ideas and listed the examples I chose to prove them. This outline showed me that I had five things to say about bad movies—listed in the introduction to this volume, p. 8— and I used *Plan 9 from Outer Space* to say them in great detail.

1. Bad movies are unconvincing as movies. Many examples exist of this quality in *Plan 9 from Outer Space*. It's extremely inconsistent, on a scene level. Its special effects are terrible. It includes scenes that try to clear up problems the audience hasn't even thought of—the conversation about why Vampira was buried in the ground and Lugosi was buried in a crypt, for instance, or Lt. Harper's poorly written attempt to explain why the flying saucer that lands in the cemetery sometimes has a glow and sometimes doesn't. The nine non-intersecting aspects of the movie's plot. The time frame of the funerals and the discovery of the gravediggers' bodies. So many elements in this movie push the audience out of the filmgoing experience and make her realize she is watching a simulation, rather than pulling her *into* the simulation, letting her forget the metatextual aspects of her experience.

Of course, we never fully believe we are *part of* a movie, unless we are children or fools. We are bespelled by what we see on the screen in a particular way, and it's a kind of magic to which we consent. But the spell must be strong enough to put us under. Bad movies have no magic of this kind. Because they can't hypnotize the audience, the audience notices the motion of the hypnotizing agent: the pendulum, the 24 frames per second.

2. Bad movies are successful records of attempts at movies. They give the audience a dual, holographic view: of the successful record and of the failed attempt.

Plan 9's holographic qualities are particularly potent. The wobbling tombstones show us that they are props on a set. The existence of props on a set shows the audience that a movie is being made. The movie being made is on the screen, but it is unconvincing as a movie. So we see both: the wobbling prop and the reality of its existence as a prop, *as well as* the whole cinematic context that tries to seal the illusion of this undertaking as a movie.

The police come to the cemetery immediately after Paula and Farmer drive away from it, which casts doubt on the continuity of the story, which makes us recognize it as a story. Some of us might even see the hand of the creator. We might realize that Wood needed the police to come back to the cemetery somehow, so he just had them drive back, and saw no need to build the bridge between the Paula/Farmer incident and the police returning.

When we feel confused and our train of thought is interrupted by the Hollywood montage, we realize the movie isn't making sense to us, thus realizing that it is a movie, and that a writer and director and editor (all the same man in this case) forced it to try and make sense.

A filmmaker must understand with complete acuity what the audience knows and what the characters know, and how these banks of knowledge differ from each other. If we realize Paula is aware of Vampira, when we have no positive proof that she has seen Vampira, the scrim between us and her collapses. We become aware that the same person created everything we're seeing—characters, conflicts, secrets, lies.

Toward the end, when five of the main characters pile into a car and drive to a cemetery that's in walking distance, we realize that either Wood has lost track of his geography, or he needed the car to come to the cemetery for some reason not explained by the plot. The plot is one side of the holograph (the spell, the illusion) and the reason is the other side (the set, the props). We see him trying to make the movie, and we see the movie he's trying to make, both at the same time. The illusion is too thin to disguise the creator; in this case, the Wizard's light and sound show does not distract anyone in Dorothy's party.

3. Knowing more about the context of a bad movie is crucial to understanding and analyzing it, but is hardly a license to excuse it. Back there somewhere I wrote about the stock footage/running time context of *Plan 9*, and how it explains but does not excuse the resulting bad sequences. External factors like the cost of film and equipment, which were astronomical in 1956 compared to the cost of a decent HD camcorder today, also matter. The way *Plan 9* mixes up peaceful aliens with hostile intent, and winds up with a confusing semi-enemy, is part of the film's context, as the film was trying to adhere to two separate and conflicting trends. Some of the stiffness of its acting and the poor quality of its special effects can be explained (not excused) with context, too, though not all.[103]

One element of *Plan 9*'s context I didn't really write about is how its genre impacts its quality. Others have written generously about *Plan 9*'s multifarious genre, its mishmash of science fiction, horror, zombie movie, and military film. I'd like to revise that to say it includes *aspects* of all those genres, but it does not succeed at fully embracing or embodying any of them. At the time it was released, significantly, genre films were almost never of high quality. Pre-*2001: A Space Odyssey* (1968), science fiction, fantasy, and horror were not taken especially seriously by filmmakers, critics, or audiences. A handful of good genre films came out in the late 1950s: *The Incredible Shrinking Man* (1957), *The Fly* (1958). But mostly, a list of sci-fi movies from the era reads like a catalogue of *MST3K* movies.

---

103 As a parallel example, the laughable quality of some computer-generated effects in the mid-1990s can be explained with context—limitations in software and memory, the available skill and experience of effects makers. But Pixar was already doing business by then, so…some, but not all.

Plan 9 is an unusually bad film in a mostly bad genre, and this context matters when assessing it.

Additional contextual elements are the temporary popularity of some of the cast and the lasting popularity of Lugosi's Dracula character. Vampira and Lugosi are (probably) dressed to make the audience remember how much they liked these characters on other screens, and hopefully to endear them to the entertainment on *this* screen. Criswell is totally forgotten today, but he was a fixture on local TV at the time, which made his appearances and voiceover valuable to 1959 audiences. These choices seem strange to a 21st century audience lacking context—who is that lady and why does she look like that? who is that guy and why does he talk like that?—but made sense then.

Ultimately, there's no way to forgive *Plan 9* its flaws just because it was made in a certain way at a certain time. But we can understand and assess it with a more sophisticated eye and mind if we consider that way and time than we can if we look on it as a free-floating page torn away from a book of film history.

4. Bad movies are teaching tools for making and studying good movies. Students of cinema can learn volumes of lessons from this one film:
- Editing cannot carry the full weight of blocking a sequence of scenes.
- The main plot of a movie must be front and center. The scenes and sequences in a movie must have some proportionate relationship to the importance of the plot element communicated in the scene.
- Base-level continuity (not, like, how the glasses are arranged on the café table or how many buttons are on someone's coat) depends on three Ls: lighting, location, and landmarks. Without carrying these elements over between edits, the audience will not assume your characters are in the same time, place, or situation.
- Don't waste the audience's time on shoe-leather. Nor on dialogue that waffles, unless you're carefully building character over a long period of time.
- If you're filming a sequence mainly of dialogue, make damn sure that dialogue is interesting and not stupid.
- Montages should call back to what has already occurred in the film and hint at what comes next. They should not introduce important characters.
- Show stakes, don't just tell them. Remember, this is a *motion picture*.[104] The best way to explain danger is to *show* the outcome of that danger when not avoided.

5. As teaching tools, bad movies are best studied in aggregate. There is so much more to learn from bad movies. *Plan 9 from Outer Space* doesn't make all possible film mistakes, although it surely makes a lot of them. The only way to understand the thousands of small and large ways a movie can go sideways is to watch a ton of them and take notes.

---

104   Stolen from *MST3K: The Dead Talk Back* (1957 / 1994).

For example, Criswell's voiceover, though unhelpful, rarely duplicates the action on the screen in a way that renders the voiceover superfluous.[105] The scene on pp. 59-60 does this, as the visuals already did the work that Criswell does a second time, but it's just about the only occasion. Even if a film uses voiceover to make sense of what's on screen rather than overexplaining it, screenwriting teachers discourage the technique, as it can lead to lazy writing. (Why would you take the trouble to show something when you can narrate it instead?) Wood uses voiceover to bridge gaps in his incompetence, not in his laziness, but many filmmakers do the opposite. Further, there's always the negative example of a film like *Monster a Go-Go* (1965), in which filming produced very little usable sound, so the movie relies on voiceover instead of dialogue. That's incompetence, too, but of a different kind than Wood's.

Figuring out what's going wrong in a movie becomes a worthy puzzle. Some movies take themselves much too seriously. Others cast actors who have no chemistry with each other or the camera. Still others depend on titillation or gimmicks, either of which can fall flat or offend. Pacing problems can sink a movie; too much money can make a movie tedious; a script that changes too often or remains too rigid can overturn everything good about a movie. Combining a lack of budget with an egomaniac at the helm often results in terrible cinema (Wood, Wiseau), but sometimes that combination can create something incredible (Kenneth Anger, Darren Aronofsky).

Patterns, not individual elements, characterize and predict bad movies. A few of the problems in *Plan 9* are part of these patterns: the poor usage of day for night, cutaways disguising mistakes or bad takes, filler and shoe-leather scenes, the triangulation of genre with time period. These characteristics exist across a huge swath of bad movies. Yet for the most part, *Plan 9* is lit well (if sometimes a bit strongly), and its music is not overtly terrible. Wood knows how to use an establishing shot to show the audience where we're going, and knows not to linger too long on it. His scenes, despite how badly their dialogue is written, all have beginnings, middles, and ends. Because *Plan 9* is certainly terrible, it's hard to remember to give credit to stuff like this.

But plenty of movies have problems *Plan 9* doesn't. Bad lighting and bad music are endemic to sub-par movies. Inexperienced filmmakers often allow establishing shots to hang out onscreen for the better part of a minute, whether to hammer home the point to the audience or to let a music cue finish or because they don't have a good grasp of pacing.[106] And poor writers will chop

---

105 The cut of *Blade Runner* (1982) with voiceover is a terrific example of this error. The voiceover doesn't explore the inside of Deckard's head or any of the film's abundant subtext, it just reexplains what's already on screen.
106 A movie that will drive you to the nuthouse, *A Talking Cat!?!* (2013), favors establishing shots over substantive shots. They often have no relationship to the plot, nor do they even establish where the next scene will take place, sometimes (which is the whole point of an *establishing* shot), and they last for ages.

off scenes in the middle rather than truly concluding them, or will fail to give the scene a middle at all, often robbing it of a purpose.

The best way to understand what a bad filmmaker like Wood is doing wrong, and what he's doing right, is to watch so many movies of all qualities that the patterns jump out. You begin to notice what all the bad movies have in common just as easily as you notice what all the good ones do. The more you watch, the starker these contrasts become, and the more the established grammar of cinema makes sense. In the right hands, violating that grammar has remarkable results (early Brian De Palma), but in the wrong hands, it just makes a mess (James Nguyen).

A secondary point, better made about other films than *Plan 9*, is that **bad movies are wonderfully surprising, because they upend audience expectations.** If you can't use bad film as a teaching tool, consider it a change of pace from the irritating rigor of mainstream American film. Most of what goes on the big screen in the current moment in the US is proscribed, and prescribed, down to the minute. There are three carefully proportioned acts with predictable plot moves and character choices, dependent in their particulars on genre. There's bloat in the third act, usually, although sometimes toward the end of the second. The color palette is showy and artificial. Shakycam abounds, especially in difficult emotional scenes or action scenes for which the actors are inadequately prepared. Most of the film is staged to be watchable on a small screen, which means a preference for medium shots and close-ups rather than wide and landscape shots. Plots revolve around miscommunications or grudges or central personality flaws. The women are thin and the men are ideally tousled.

I am so weary of these characteristics that I barely follow contemporary cinema anymore. Friends tell me this or that movie is super good and really different, so I watch, and no, it isn't. Around one film I watch per year genuinely is different, but it's never the one I think it will be, and it's *definitely* never one the Oscars have lauded.

This supreme boredom—and I know it's not attractive—leads me to weird rabbit-holes. It leads me almost anywhere that can offer me a surprise. Most reliably, it leads me to bad movies. I find absolute delight in a movie that breaks all the rules, even if that movie does not hold together and I could never sanely recommend it. I don't watch these movies out of masochism or misanthropy. I watch them because they do what their higher-quality cousins cannot: they show me something I have never seen before.

All the ways in which *Plan 9 from Outer Space* should make sense and doesn't, should be decent and isn't—those missing qualities, if fulfilled, would make it just like every other movie. As a passable movie, it would sit among dozens of similar B pictures from the late 1950s, in reasonably good company on a forgotten library shelf. As a bad movie, it is unique, shining all alone in the darkest cavern of bad art.

I hope you have found this useful. I hope you watch some bad movies with a spirit of exploration, with a notepad, with a ready laugh. I hope you can read *Plan*

9 from Outer Space as a failure that has a great deal to teach, or as a success in chronicling sheer will and ambition. I hope you write or make something better, but I hope you see writing and making as acts of building on the bad as well as the good. No discourse, no art form, is complete without both.

SOMETHING TO
SING ABOUT:

WHY *COP ROCK* FAILS

COP ROCK (ABC, 1990) was a real television show that existed. It was a police procedural with musical numbers.

The plot of the show chugged progressively from episode to episode like any police procedural. The songs in the show occurred with clockwork regularity, as in any musical. The characters—police officers, suspects, lawyers, bureaucrats— resembled characters in fraternally related shows like *Law & Order*, except that they sometimes burst into song. I promise this is true.

I first learned of *Cop Rock* from a video posted almost as an afterthought by a friend on Facebook. When I watched the video—it was "Let's Be Careful Out There" from episode seven—I went through a series of reactions. *Is this a fan parody of* Hill Street Blues? *Is this an elaborate SNL sketch?* I denied and disbelieved, and only gradually, with the help of Wikipedia, came to accept that the show existed.

I am explaining this because you may be feeling something similar. Before you read any analysis of *Cop Rock*, you must believe that it aired, which is a process, not a light switch. Even when watching the show, its ridiculousness does not wane, but simply rolls over itself, like waves on the shore. By the end of the final episode, a viewer may have succumbed to a new reality in which *Cop Rock* is normal, but it's a little like accepting cult conditions: it only occurs with immersion and a fatally open mind.

Here are some other things to know about *Cop Rock* before we truly begin:

- The show ran for eleven episodes before cancellation.
- Its creator, Steven Bochco, had previously created *Hill Street Blues*, *L.A. Law*, and *Doogie Howser, M.D.*

"The height of
    the Bush era was
 a *weird,*
    giddy time."

—STEPHEN THOMAS ERLEWINE ON MILLI VANILLI'S
        GIRL YOU KNOW IT'S TRUE (1989)

- All of these shows were memorable and successful, although very differently so. *Blues* is easily one of the most influential television shows ever made.
- Another hour-long musical TV show, *Hull High*, also debuted in 1990. It ran for nine episodes.
- Across the eleven episodes, the cast sings 54 songs.
- All of the songs were recorded live, not dubbed and lip-synced.
- *Twin Peaks* also debuted in 1990. So did *Beverly Hills, 90210*. So, in fact, did *Law & Order*, which certainly would not exist, in any of its permutations, without *Hill Street Blues*.

1. GENRE

Although *Cop Rock* is bad for apparent reasons—its musical numbers are exceptionally undistinguished, its dramatic tension is consistently undermined, its plotlines are slow and generic, its characters are either paper-flat or totally bizarre, and its tone never coheres for longer than half a scene—it's also bad for fundamental, genre-based reasons. Any lesson from *Cop Rock* is a lesson about genre, and how genres work, together and apart.

Police procedurals are a specific genre of television, one largely codified by Bochco's own *Hill Street Blues*.[1] The police procedural (cop show) has a teeny-tiny wheelhouse with infinite items inside. Although networks can make a ton of different shows from the formula, the formula itself is quite restricted, limited to what can fit inside its doorway. Bochco's success and expertise with this genre must have convinced him that he could combine it with another fairly regimented genre: the musical.

He was wrong. I am certain that he did not know enough about how musicals work, and for all I know, he may have been mistaken about cop shows, too. The 1,100 hours of television comprising *Law & Order* had not yet passed through CRT tubes at the time *Cop Rock* ran, and that means all of us knew a lot less about how modern cop shows work.

Musicals, in their mechanisms, haven't changed much in a long time. For several years I went to as many operas as I could, attending live broadcasts from the Metropolitan Opera of New York in movie theaters, and it dawned on me somewhere in the middle of this obsession that Broadway musicals descend directly from opera. The latter used to be popular entertainment, after all; that it's become an esoteric art form mainly enjoyed by rich people is a quirk of time and evolution, not an inevitable outcome. (Broadway musicals may be headed for the same outcome if ticket prices don't even out.)

The point is, songs in musicals accomplish many of the same purposes arias in operas do. They expand upon character, capture a ceremony, gather a crowd under a particular purpose, or explain a circumstance. Most importantly, songs and arias illustrate transitional emotional moments. Something is changing inside

---

1 *Dragnet* (1951-8, 1967-70) started the engine, and structurally, cop shows still do more or less what *Dragnet* did. But the shakycam, the production design, the typical characters, the blending of private and public life, the "realism" are all modeled on *Blues*.

a character's heart, or a character is revealing something inside her heart to others. It can be love, or joy, or heartbreak, or determination, or fury, or jealousy. It can be any number of emotions. But there is always a change in emotion that the song encapsulates, a move from one mood to another, both for the characters and within the show. The audience is prodded by the song to feel something, and likely it's something different than we felt a little while earlier. The show transitions from mood to mood until the final bow, and then the experience is over.

I'm sure there are exceptions to this general rule, but nearly every song I can think of from a musical follows it. Songs from Disney movies fall into limited categories, as Justin McElroy memorably pointed out on Twitter, but even those categories are largely about transitional emotional moments, too. Songs from *The Sound of Music, Repo! The Genetic Opera, Hamilton, Bye Bye Birdie, The Phantom of the Opera, Frozen, Cannibal! The Musical, Singin' in the Rain*, and many more conform. Not *all* songs featured in *all* musicals follow this rule, but I'd wager that most do, even if the emotion they express is satisfaction or stable *joie de vivre*.

COP ROCK PROMOTIONAL CAST PHOTO

After all, what is music without emotion? Why say it with a song if not to infuse it with extra feeling?

In *Cop Rock*, this rule does not apply. Some of the songs do indeed express an emotion that the audience would not access as deeply without the song, such as "She Chose Me" and "If That Isn't Love." But in other cases, a minor character (or even a character we never see again) sings an emotional song—"Beautiful Eyes," and "Nobody's Fault"—rendering a dead end of emotional exposure. In most cases, the song isn't about an emotion of any kind— "Black Is Black," "He's Guilty," "Let's Be Careful Out There," "For the Record," "Clean It Up," etc., etc. The majority of the songs on *Cop Rock* are situational, reiterating or embellishing a moment that could just as easily exist in dialogue.

This is an essential, insurmountable problem with the show. The songs, although often performed well, are needless, which makes them awkward to sit through. A moment that would take a few lines of dialogue on another police procedural is stretched into a three-minute song ("Baby Merchant," "LaRusso's Back," and perhaps most regrettably, "Bumpty Bumpty"). There are also flashy fantasy numbers that don't fit at all, like "Perfection," and pointless songs that remind us upsettingly what 1990 was like in music, such as "Lineup," and "In These Streets." None of this arises from emotional urgency or genuine feeling, but instead functions as gimmick. Or as requirement: sing five songs per episode, no matter how crappy or shoehorned they may be. Since they don't happen naturally, the songs fail, on the whole.

There are exceptions. "Good Life" is sung by partners who have been coping with unwelcome sexual tension. Although the fantasy elements of the song (the partners magically change outfits and a phantom wind blows at their clothes) are out of place, the song showcases and heightens the tension, it's sung well, and considering the rest of the show's catalog, it's not badly written. "Garbage In Garbage Out," a song about bureaucracy and recidivism, has strong energy and a palpable emotion: frustration. Some of the songs, if stupidly written, are extremely well-performed, like "Reasonable Doubt" and "You Lied."

Still. The reason for the song is rarely organic, which leads to an audience wondering why we're sitting here listening, when the point of the song has already been made. Steven Bochco, in an interview, proudly noted that all the songs advanced the plot. This is not true, but even if it was, it's not generally what songs are for.

This basic misunderstanding of why musicals work the way they do is a columnar problem with *Cop Rock*, but it's not the only genre-based problem.

COP ROCK PROMOTIONAL CAST PHOTO

Plenty of genres can blend into musicals surprisingly well, but police procedurals are uniquely poorly suited for this task.

2. MEMBRANE

In any fiction, a membrane exists between the audience's real world and the fiction's false one. The thickness of this barrier depends upon a slew of factors, genre not least among them. Rupture the membrane, and the audience remembers or realizes they are absorbing a fiction, and their relationship to the art changes. Sometimes this is a deliberate action (*Deadpool*, *Funny Games*), and sometimes the art is so unconvincing that the audience is thrown, disappointed, out of hypnosis.

Musicals have a funky relationship with the membrane.[2] The very idea that one would break into choreographed song due to unfettered emotion might be enough to shatter the spell, but if not, only in certain stories is it unsuspicious that all the characters within the fiction can sing and/or dance professionally enough to entertain outside the fiction. Lots of musicals write in professional singers and dancers as characters (*Swing Time*, *Chicago*), or are backstage musicals, written to capitalize on this dynamic instead of succumbing to it.

---

2 To me, *all* genres have at least an interesting relationship with this barrier, but if I enumerated them all, I'd be writing a totally different essay.

You have to think about it, when you're writing a musical. You have to make the musical so captivating, cast such a spell, that an audience will fall in love with what you're doing enough to forgive you for the farce of your premise. And the audience has to walk into the musical willing to forgive. Any cynicism (theirs) or shoddiness (yours), and the whole framework of the thing will collapse.

Police procedurals, on the whole, intend to display realism. To a fault, perhaps. Writers of cop shows try to tackle current issues, consult with real police officers, be gritty. Nothing about a police procedural communicates that you're watching a fantasy.[3] It asks of its audience only minimal suspension of disbelief: the ordinary kind of "get metaphysically absorbed in these small moving pictures that are plainly simulacra." What we're asked to believe once we're in there is not different from what could conceivably happen if we were living in the circumstances depicted by the show.

Compare this to the audience investment required in a musical, with its proliferation of fantasy. Everything about a musical is fake—not *simulated*, as with many fictions, but falsely conceived. In the course of their ordinary lives, people do not ever behave as they commonly do in musicals.

In short, a cop show asks its audience to believe we're watching something real, while a musical contracts with its audience to watch something artificial. Blending these two genres was just never going to work. Or, at least, it wasn't going to work under these circumstances—in 1990, on television, with the demands of a major network in play.

This isn't to say that *drama* has no place in musicals. Terrific dramatic musicals exist, like *Les Misérables* (in its time, a novel that realistically showcased wretched poverty). But dramatic material has to be poured carefully to move from one genre jar to another without spilling the whole lot. A dramatic musical has to offer extremely compelling context for the characters to sing. *Les Mis* is an all-sing for a reason; it's less jarring that these starving revolutionaries sing everything they say to each other than it is to imagine them having dialogue-driven scenes together and occasionally deciding to sing.

3. MOOD

Mood and tone also require careful management in a musical, and these elements are often simple or even monolithic in a cop show. Occasional flares of dry comedy barely disturb the undulating dramatic mood of the average cop show. Meanwhile, in a musical, the mood of a song will dominate the scenes around it, and ordering the songs manages the audience's emotions across the course of the piece. The creators of *Cop Rock* did not understand this at all. The songs that do have emotional resonance (few and far between) are placed without regard for the episode's story-based momentum, and the songs that have some other purpose disrupt the episode's emotional momentum.

A song like "Baby Merchant" is profoundly jarring not just by its own lights

---

3 Although of course it bears saying that these shows always offer a fantasy version of police officers and departments, whether they intend to or not.

(its lyrics are impossible to take seriously, its melody poor), but because the smug, surreal tone of the song contrasts with the dramatic situation. Two undercover cops are pretending to be a couple desperate for a child in order to arrest a…well, a baby merchant, and the cops' preexisting sexual tension plus the dual performance aspect are plenty to manage. The song overloads the scene until it collapses into comedy, which puts the surrounding dramatic scenes in jeopardy. Besides, it's a particularly pointless song. The singer is a bit player at best in a wider dramatic arc. The song's purpose is theoretically to convince the play-acting couple that the singer can get them a baby, which they already believed before the scene even began.

It's not the only song that completely halts an episode for a baffling tone change. In "Choose Me," a passel of female officers are disguised as prostitutes for undercover work, and they sing and dance suggestively to convince the male officers they're realistically prostitute-y. This song is a waste of time in every possible way. Before it starts up, the tone is a bunch of cops at a briefing, and then suddenly we're watching a PG-13 stripper number (amazingly, the second one in the episode). It's sexist and gratuitous, and the situation isn't even an important part of the overall plot.

The number, meanwhile, is almost a leap into fantasy. The audience should be able to understand a fantasy song as a jump away from the ordinary, but should also be prepared to accept it as part of the fabric of the work. Neither of these requirements exists in "Choose Me." In *Grease*, "Beauty School Dropout" works because nearly everything about it is visually distinct from the rest of the film— the sets, the costumes, the lighting, Frankie Avalon—thus marking it as a fantasy, but also, the tone of the film is generally light, and a goofy number like it is not conceptually off the table. In *Cop Rock*, occasional fantasy numbers ("Perfection," "Your Number's Up") don't work at all, because they only *exaggerate* the regular surroundings, and because the tone of the show is mostly dramatic—and, again, realistic, as a police procedural, not fantastic, as a musical.

Indeed, the songs vary much more widely in mood than the rest of the show does. Generously, the songs attempt to vary the overall mood of the show. But they are so poorly integrated into the plot and character development that they just amplify the shoehorned feeling most of the songs already convey.

4. 1990

The sheer mediocrity of *Cop Rock*'s music represents one of the larger problems of the show. It doesn't grab an audience well or immediately. And even if the audience believes the characters are genuinely motivated to sing their feelings (which we almost never do), it's even harder to imagine that the characters' feelings could or should be expressed as feebly as *this*. Again, the crunch of a weekly 45-minute show, answering to network producers nervous about the rise of cable channels, is probably the worst imaginable context to write and deliver 54 musical numbers. Given that, and the contemporaneous music (Vanilla Ice, MC Hammer, Michael Bolton), it's no wonder that *Cop Rock*'s songs are mostly crap. But it remains astonishing that such crap was aired.

The songs are largely synth junk, strings of idiom and cliché, and shallow, repetitive melodies, along with a surprising amount of vamping from certain singers (Carl Anderson, of *Jesus Christ Superstar* fame, plays a judge twice; Loretta Devine, of the original Broadway cast of *Dreamgirls*, kills it as a singing juror). However, the show's musical talent includes Randy Newman, who composed the theme song as well as songs for the pilot. My opinion of Newman is not high, and I realize this opinion is not commonly shared, so I'll say only that his work on this show is fairly typical for, and recognizable as, his.

That opening credits sequence, though. It depicts Newman performing "Under the Gun" in a soundstage rigged as a studio. There are other musicians in the semidarkness, including a second pianist and three woo-woo girls, and Newman is in headphones. Cuts show the main cast of *Cop Rock* sitting around in directors' chairs or standing nearby, watching and enjoying the song. Some are bopping along. Some are smiling in a manner that does not seem voluntary. All are dressed in clothes that don't resemble the characters' costumes on the show, and they are eye-catching, even for 1990—ugly sweaters, huge jackets, hideous patterns.

COP ROCK DANCE NUMBER / 20TH CENTURY FOX

I watched these credits many times, and they only got weirder on each repeat. No realism in sight: the lighting is such that musicians can't see to read their music, and the acoustics in the space seem unacceptable for recording. So it's clearly a setup for the sake of filming the credits sequence, yet it continually tries to convince us that it's a spontaneous thing. Ronny Cox, shouldering a tote bag, walks up to stand next to Barbara Bosson's chair, as if he's just arriving on the set for a day's work. The actors continually look at each other and grin: "Hey, wow, this is really cool, huh?" They move to the music as if it's *awesome*, as if they're *feeling it*, but that is simply impossible, given what we are hearing. Anne Bobby has an openmouthed smile that suggests she can't believe what she's seeing and has chosen amusement as her reaction.

This sequence oozes artificiality, but it purports to be showing something real. That's really a key assessment for all of *Cop Rock*. It crashes the fakery of choreographed musical numbers into the (purported) realism of a police procedural. With better music, more time, and more complex plots and characterization, this collision might have resulted in a pleasurable, paradoxical tension. But 1990 was the wrong moment in pop culture to try it, cop shows being early in their evolution and music being what it was at the time.

Sometime around the year 2000, Stephen Thomas Erlewine retrospectively reviewed Milli Vanilli's 1989 hit record, *Girl You Know It's True,* for Allmusic.com. I have remembered this review for twenty years, as its assessment of the pop gestalt in the early 1990s is so sharp and so intriguing.

Ironically, at the end of the '80s, MTV changed the rules for mainstream pop, putting the emphasis on image and overall package, to the extent that major artists lip-synched in concert so they could deliver better dance routines. So, it really wasn't that extreme to have a group with two faces—one to make the music, one to market it. And, face it, the fluffy dance-pop and slick ballads on *Girl You Know It's True* were of their time…The fact is, with dance-pop (especially Euro-dance!), just like *Playboy*, artificiality is the name of the game, and that's what is good about it. It's the distinguishing characteristic, its identity, the core of its being. On that level, it's hard not to listen to *Girl You Know It's True* and marvel at the level of [producer Frank] Farian's studiocraft, since it doesn't even sound like he programmed a computer to make this music; it sounds like something the machine wrote on its own accord. There are no natural sounds or human emotions on this record, just a bunch of shiny hooks and big beats, all processed and precisely assembled to be totally irresistible to a mass audience. […]

The height of the Bush era was a weird, giddy time, when the mainstream was filled with effervescent, transient pop, and nothing sums up that era as well as *Girl You Know It's True*. This isn't just music that's all surface, this is music that gives the impression of having a surface, then not delivering on that.[4]

He's talking about the *texture* of the record, and I've been talking all this time about the way fakery manifests more broadly, in genre. But the way these ideas conjoin in *Cop Rock* continues to fascinate me. At a time when pop music was especially dumb and powerless, *Cop Rock* tried to alchemize two naturally opposed genres *with pop music*. The experiment could only fail.

The credits sequence epitomizes a lot about the show: how enthusiastically everyone involved threw their lot in with Bochco's terrible idea; how very much a product of 1990 the show is, a quality which becomes more noticeable with every passing year; how thoroughly the genuine is papered over with badly made fakery, and how that seems like it'd be cool and fun and instead is obvious and awkward. Showing the actors out of costume and character (although, no doubt, they are acting) also hints at metatextual concerns, which pop up again unexpectedly, and perhaps transcendently, in the finale.

5. FINALE

In all these words, I haven't offered a summary of the story arc across the eleven episodes of *Cop Rock*, nor have I said much about the characters. When I considered what I wanted to say about this show, these elements kept slipping to the back of my mind. I found them irrelevant to an assessment of *Cop Rock*, because

---

4 He also calls the record "intentionally disposable." (See my essay on the Teen-Agers for more about that.) Should we even be listening to and assessing Milli Vanilli, thirty years on?

they are inconspicuous compared to everything that makes it fail so spectacularly, everything that makes it a rare artifact. Still, they do require a mention before we tackle the finale.

The major plot threads have to do with a wrongful police shooting and its consequences, a drug addict who sells her baby daughter, uneasy partnerships between different genders and races of cops, the mayor considering a Senate run despite her unfortunate looks, the batshit insane chief of police, and various marriages. There are shorter plotlines about a movie star and her stalker, a rookie losing his innocence, and the mayor's gay assistant. These are all pretty undistinguished. Only one of the show's threads interested me enough to feel faint regret that there was no more to the story, and that largely because the characters and their actors were likeable, not because the story was especially original.

For the most part, the characters only pop out of cliché in order to be really odd (the police chief is obsessed with cowboys, a female cop goes full Pepé Le Pew on her partner after breaking up a fight). Elaborating on them would be to point out how indistinguishable they are from characters on other cop shows. The actors in this experiment are generally game, and they acquit themselves well enough, although some of them haven't learned the trick of singing and/or listening to singing with stillness that belies the song's length. The songs mostly seem long and out of place, and although the most meaningful reasons for that are laid out in detail above, the actors are also inexperienced at staging them properly. Aside from this, they're appealing, particularly Anne Bobby and David Gianopoulos. Even some of the weirder scenes have undeniable chemistry, with Ronny Cox and Vondie Curtis-Hall presaging the greatness of Aidan Gillen and Reg E. Cathey in *The Wire*.

The show does not indicate that it might be ending until the final scene of the final episode. Prior to that, the plot churns on, slowly, dully. But then, after a song that concludes in meaningful looks from two decent cops about the reinstatement of a corrupt cop, Curtis-Hall walks into an office set and sits across from Cox, who says, "I can't believe they cancelled us." The two actors have a conversation about the songs they sang in the show, and how much they enjoyed the experience of working on it. Cox presses a button, a door off the set opens, the cast (not in costume) spills in, and the music begins.

The cast starts singing, all together, and the handheld camera captures them as well as the musicians playing just off the set. The number grows more elaborate, showing a zaftig woman on a swing that rises up into the air ("it ain't over till the fat lady sings") as the cast vamps shamelessly. The song's lyrics refer to the show and its folly—name-checking famed disaster *Heaven's Gate* and *Cop Rock*'s network, ABC—but has a generic positive message of overcoming obstacles and fond farewell. The final shot is a crane angle of the set, cast, crew, lighting, etc. on the soundstage.

This blindsides the audience completely. We had no indication at all that the episode, much less the series, was properly over, and all at once we are deep in metatext, watching actors rally in song about the cancellation of their dreadful show. Although there's plenty of precedent for metatext in musicals, there's very little in police procedurals, which adds incongruity. I must credit this move for being clever, but this was not a particularly clever show, which makes the number yet stranger.

Perhaps it's fitting that the opening credits and the finale song both traffic, to different degrees, in metatext. *Cop Rock* is so weird, top to tail, that it's almost impossible to become absorbed in it as art, even if the art had been original and exceptional enough to warrant that absorption. We might be able to set aside our shock and surprise about the existence of the show for the length of a scene, but back it rushes once a song begins. The holographic way we consume bad art, at once perceiving the finished art and the record of the makers' attempt at art, is, if not constant, at least frequent, rematerializing five times per episode.

Both the opening and finale sequences ultimately leave me at a loss, gaping at them, all my intellectualizing about their function and context fading to a murmur. I can use everything I've read and seen to interpret what they're doing and how and why, to illustrate similarities and conclusions, but I cannot tamp down my amazement that they really went on film and then on the air. Even in 1990.

6. FEELING

If you'd like a look at how a genre-restricted television show can do musical numbers successfully, watch *Buffy the Vampire Slayer*'s sixth season episode "Once More with Feeling." Even the title acknowledges what the writers of *Cop Rock* did not understand about musical numbers: their basic purpose is to convey a transitional emotional moment. Every major song in the episode reveals a character's emotional struggle or situation, and even the miniature filler songs about parking tickets and removed mustard stains have actual moods behind them (pleading and joy, respectively). These songs reveal character in ways that have been building all season long, and in ways that will drive the plot in following episodes. "Once More with Feeling" accomplished something great: it blended two kinds of art that shouldn't go together—or, at least, that usually don't—and it made of them a unique harmony.

In my kinder moments, I wonder if Bochco was trying to do something similarly great. "Once More with Feeling" was a tremendous risk, and so was *Cop Rock*. But Bochco didn't do the work to understand the trickier of his two ingredients. In the spirit of the early 90s, I believe, he wanted it all to happen quickly and synthetically. To dazzle with a light show instead of creating authentic illumination.

COMPLEXPLOITATION:

SWITCHBLADE SISTERS AND POWER DYNAMICS

SET ASIDE, IF YOU will, everything that makes *Switchblade Sisters* (1975) a less-than-serious film. Just for a couple thousand words. Give no thought to the performances, the costumes, certain plot contrivances, nor even the color of the fake blood used in the film's many violent scenes. For a moment, think of it as an homage to *Othello*: a schemer massages the insecurities of a flawed leader, throwing suspicion onto a blameless but convenient scapegoat. *Othello* is about jealousy and power, and these intangibles drive *Switchblade Sisters*, too. If it seems like a movie about chicks with knives, that is only because writer/director Jack Hill understood profitability and exploitation.

Unquestionably, we are in exploitation-land. The plot has dubious continuity and realism; the camera lingers on violent scenes and sleazy situations; early on, there's a needless women-in-prison scene with an abusive lesbian warden. These elements make the film valuable to an exploitation audience, which was, if nothing else, a source of profit in the 1970s. "Exploitation" as an adjective for cinema usually implies "bad," and for someone accustomed to sleek Hollywood productions, *Sisters* might be rough going. However, the film is unexpectedly rich when it focuses on power dynamics.

The plot is about gangs: the Silver Daggers, a gang of high school boys, and the Dagger Debs, a gang of high school girls. The film centers on the Debs, and more specifically on two women—Lace (Robbie Lee), the longtime leader, and Maggie (Joanne Nail), a newcomer. The leader of the Silver Daggers, Dominic (Asher Brauner), is Lace's boyfriend, although his affections transfer to Maggie. The Daggers and the Debs stir up trouble with a rival gang, led by the flamboyant Crabs (Chase Newhart), and retaliation from one side and the other gets increasingly violent, up to and including a machine-gun attack at a roller rink and an *Animal House*-esque tank-car driven by Black militants. The Debs drive the Daggers out of command and rename themselves the Jezebels. Infighting leads to a group arrest at the close of the film and a dramatic monologue by Maggie about, subtextually, the power of women to rise from the ashes of disgrace and death.

The real story is between Maggie and Lace. Lace's second in command, Patch (Monica Gayle), riles and manipulates Lace into seeing Maggie as an enemy. Patch (so-called because she lost an eye in service to the Debs and wears a silver, butterfly-embellished eyepatch) insists that Maggie wants control of the gang and Dominic, too. Maggie has no real designs on either and has genuine, uncomplicated affection for Lace. This might sound familiar; change the names to Othello, Iago, and Cassio, and you've got Shakespeare.

When Maggie gets released from juvie, Lace gives her a letter for Dominic. She insists that Dominic receive it alone, but when Maggie delivers the letter, Dominic reads it aloud to the gathered Daggers. Hill cuts between Maggie, angry and embarrassed for Lace; Dominic, shamed by Maggie's awareness of his cruelty; and the Daggers, hooting over Lace's bad, heartfelt poetry. Maggie finally snatches the letter out of Dominic's hand and slaps him, and he nearly hits her back. They exchange looks, and Joanne Nail expresses an awful lot in that moment: fear of his fists, loathing for his cruelty, and attraction to his swagger.

Although it seems like Dominic has the power in this scene, since he's cock of the walk, Maggie's opinion of his behavior subtracts from that power, as does his need to remain tough in front of the guys rather than enjoying Lace's affectionate words. Hill carefully communicates all these shifting forces, rather than merely offering information about Lace and Dominic's relationship or about Dominic's callousness.

In the next scene, Dominic forces his way into Maggie's apartment and rapes her, overpowering her with force but relatively little violence (he slaps her once but does not punch or choke her). Nail's performance demonstrates that Maggie has some attraction to Dominic but does not consent to sex with him, a fine line to walk when "date rape" was not yet in the lexicon and marital rape was legal in 49 states. After, the dialogue indicates Dominic does not understand what happened as rape, a typically misogynistic position ("You asked for it, didn't you?"), and Maggie falters at calling him out, insulting rather than contradicting him. She begins to cry and drops her head on his chest, and he comforts her. It shows how alone Maggie is in the world: she must seek comfort about her own rape from her rapist.

In case it's not clear, rape is about power, not sex. Hill knows that. The dynamic in this sequence is complicated by the presence in the apartment of Maggie's mother, an alcoholic, who turns out to be cavorting with the building manager behind a closed door. Maggie resists Dominic as quietly as possible, plainly wanting to keep his presence a secret from her mother. If her mother was sympathetic to her, Maggie could have made more noise and perhaps resisted Dominic successfully, but instead, the rape is a secret Maggie keeps through the end of the film. Dominic sees in an instant that he has power over Maggie not just physically, but psychologically, because of whatever keeps Maggie quiet when she could yell for her mother's help. He takes advantage of that power.

The following scene, too, contains a complex power dynamic. At the outset, it's a sort of dutiful scene indicating that the Debs and the Daggers are high school students, which, outside of exploitation-land, is ridiculous, given the actors' apparent ages and the characters' abundant free time. As the teacher (Paul Lichtman) begins his lecture—not coincidentally, the topic is laissez-faire government—a non-Dagger student, Harold (John Voldstad), makes rippling, fruity fart sounds with his hands. The teacher loses his temper at this interruption, and Harold taunts him: "You'll what? Hit me? Come on, you chicken-ass! You can't, can you? Or you'll lose your job." Meanwhile, Lace and Maggie have sauntered up beside Harold. They punch him in the gut and uppercut him with a thick book. Lace sits in the teacher's chair, puts her feet up on his desk, and encourages him to go on teaching the class; the teacher thanks Lace and Maggie for putting Harold in his place.

Here, the teacher is not able to hit back at a student who's being a jerk, and he's grateful to hoodlums for acting as his proxy, even though he shouldn't be endorsing their bad behavior. This outcome reinforces his powerlessness and Lace's and the Debs' power. In real life, this set of actions would make things much worse for the teacher in the long run—certainly he can only teach for as long as they want him to, as long as it serves their interests. Lace is no Robin Hood. A surface read says that Lace doesn't want the teacher to be bullied by a kid like Harold, but the text supports a more complex reading of Lace's motives. She doesn't want to let Harold's insolence stand because he is not affiliated with the Daggers, but she *also* wants to assert power over the teacher. It has nothing to do with the teacher's feelings or the purpose of high school.

To further complicate things, the scene finishes up by delivering the punchline of a relatively harmless prank. A Deb has replaced the teacher's handkerchief with a pair of girls' cotton undies, and after the women knock Harold out, the teacher wipes his brow with them. The whole class laughs, and Lace sketches a small bow. She has embarrassed the teacher immediately after helping him, asserting her dominance for the only audience that matters: the students.

As *Switchblade Sisters* moves forward, Patch continues to poison Lace against Maggie, either with lies or on very thin evidence. Lace and Maggie, in their scenes together, seem to truly like each other. During the roller rink massacre, when Lace is hurt, Maggie screams her name with such anguish that it's clear they have a special bond. Yet by the end of the film, Lace forces Maggie into a brutal knife fight. Patch's treachery is the cause, and the reason for her treachery is as obvious and as obscure as the reason for Iago's. Patch seems to like stirring the pot, as a personality trait, but she's also jealous. Whether she wants Lace's power in the gang or her sole devotion as a friend (or more?) is up for speculation, but she definitely does not want Maggie to have either of these prizes. Eventually, her scheming gets the better of her. In the final scene, the gang, arrested, proudly asserts their membership in the Jezebels, but they claim Patch "ain't with us," despite Patch's protests. She is shut out of the gang; shut out of punishment, but also of belonging.

SWITCHBLADE SISTERS PROMOTIONAL PHOTO

However, Patch's conniving weaves in with other factors at work in the dynamics of the group: Dominic's preference for Maggie, Maggie's keeping the secret of his assault on her, the macho hierarchy of the Daggers and the Debs' growing frustration with it, Maggie's natural leadership talent coming to the fore while Lace is in the hospital, Lace's betrayal of the roller rink plan to Crabs. In the same way Maggie's bad relationship with her mother worsened the outcome of Dominic's attack, these factors agitate what goes on within and among the gangs.

Even Lace's leadership style assists in her downfall. Early in the film, she bullies Donut (Kitty Bruce), but by the concluding scenes, Donut has gained confidence from Lace's absence. When Lace yells at her and slaps her, Donut reacts calmly, placating Lace without showing submission. This makes Lace seem insecure and hysterical in the eyes of the other Debs, which lowers her standing. Following Dominic's masculine example, aggression is her only tool. Conversely, Maggie, leading the renamed Jezebels no longer reduced to being "anybody's Debs"—makes the women feel valued.

And, honestly, so does this film, on the whole.

Most exploitation films wouldn't bother, but *Switchblade Sisters* isn't most exploitation films. This film quotes Mao that "political power grows out of the barrel of a gun," illustrating its interest in power dynamics quite clearly. This film's male characters are exclusively stupid or brutal or weak, and its female characters are tough and smart and ambitious. *This film passes the Bechdel test.* Maggie, in defending the new name of Jezebels, defines the word as "an immoral, shameless, impudent woman." In marking these adjectives as positive, she is doing a thing later called reappropriation,[1] or reclaiming, before our very eyes. Critics have reexamined Jack Hill's work with a feminist lens long before now, but this essay's point is a little narrower: in *Sisters*, Hill constructs a story about women that investigates power dynamics—usually the terrain of male-centered stories.

By some criteria, *Switchblade Sisters* is a melodrama: it exaggerates and sensationalizes a recognizable world, its characters often speak with high bombast, and it depicts female hardships, female desires, and family issues (of a sort). Yet in most classical Hollywood melodramas, the power dynamics appear in, for example, a heroine constrained by an overbearing father or a loveless marriage, or an ambitious woman reduced to manipulating men to earn power of her own. These stories feel circumscribed by traditionally feminine worlds in a way *Sisters* never does. The Debs are constrained by the misogyny of the Daggers, but they are not trapped in corsets or kitchens, and they demonstrate real, palpable power as few melodramatic heroines ever do.

Perhaps melodrama only potentially applies here because this is a story about women, and melodramatic stories about men (*Wall Street*, for example, or *Midnight Cowboy*) tend to be categorized as regular dramas rather than consigned to a "lesser" genre. But all of these stories concern power to some degree, whether melodrama or morality play, misogynist or feminist. Hill's work in *Switchblade Sisters* elevates exploitation cinema to Shakespearean tragedy via a carefully choreographed exploration of power dynamics. The film offers an opportunity, beyond the obligatory sex and bloodshed, to see something unique and valuable at the purported bottom of the barrel of American cinema.

---

1 Per Wikipedia, reappropriation is "the cultural process by which a group reclaims words or artifacts that were previously used in a way disparaging of that group. It is a specific form of a semantic change (i.e. change in a word's meaning). Linguistic reclamation can have wider implications in the fields of discourse and has been described in terms of personal or sociopolitical empowerment."

AT THE END OF A
THOUSAND YEARS:

THE BAD NOVELS OF PENN AND ROS

THE DIFFICULTY OF WRITING a good novel means there are a lot of rotten novels out there, published or not. But sometimes writing is bad in a grand, towering way; sometimes the badness of a novel is so overwhelming that it warrants recording and remembering. Such is the case with Sean Penn and Amanda McKittrick Ros, whose bad novels have a great deal in common.

At a glance, the two authors have little to do with each other. Ros was an Irish teacher born in 1860 who lived a mostly quiet life and died in 1939; Penn is an American actor born in 1960 who has lived a flamboyant, well-recorded life since the early 1980s. Ros self-published her first book, *Irene Iddesleigh*, a slight novel of Victorian-style romantic fiction, while Penn's first novel, *Bob Honey Who Just Do Stuff*, which strains to be political satire, was published by an imprint of Simon & Schuster with wide availability. Although these writers are a century apart and completely different on the surface, their work bears astonishing similarities, from the way each author assembles sentences to the bombastic, preposterous ego hovering without sufficient disguise behind the work.

Both books are bad, but "bad" does not suffice. A little word of three letters does not plumb the depth of these books' failures. The critic Barry Pain wrote that *Iddesleigh* "is a thing that happens once in a million years. There is no one above it and no one beside it, and it sits alone as the nightingale sings." The critic Claire Fallon called *Bob Honey* "akin to the product of a postmodern literature bot. It doesn't seem quite possible that a human person wrote this mess." Ros's prose is so bad that little societies formed around her in the early 20th century, reading her work aloud as a contest to see how long one could keep from laughing.

Penn's prose is so bad that social media shared around pictures of his sentences for ridicule at the time of his book's release.

Similarities abound.

1. Sentences, generally. Both Penn and Ros write *terrible* sentences. Both fall victim to the agony of overwriting, using phrases of unnecessary complexity; Penn writes that music "attenuates in amplitude" (i.e. gets quieter) and that Bob desires to "recommit to the seeking of social connectivity" (i.e. make friends). In Ros, Lord Gifford "sat burying in the silver receptacle that lay by his side the deadened ashes of feathery manufacture produced by the action of his thin lips" (i.e. put out his cigar). Their sentences wind around the reader like boa constrictors, misusing vocabulary and syntax freely.

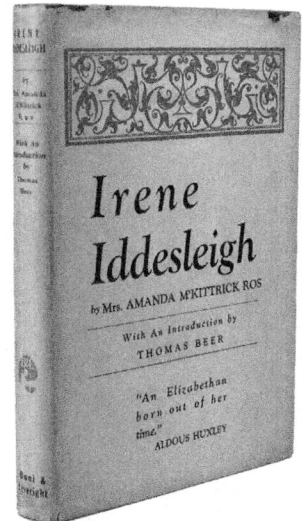

Ros: Now he stood supported by the strong giant he so often before had hugged because of its silence, its secrecy, its shade, trembling in every nerve lest the virtue his loved-one claimed would pass for ever from his crafty capture to that of some equally depraved digit of distrust and distinction.

Penn: Normalization of commercial compromise had left this medium as one of dominantly irrelevant fantasies adding nothing to the world, and instead providing a perfect storm of merchanteering thespians and image builders now less identifiable as creators of valued product than of products built for significant sales.

2. Absurd alliteration. What is it about continuous alliteration that makes bad writers revel, and that makes experienced readers cringe and cry out in pain? Penn and Ros both use handfuls of two-dollar words in long runs of purposeless alliteration.

Penn: He realizes that not only in road-roaming reality has romance been relinquished to ruins, but the cinemas themselves have been caged and quartered into quixotic concrete calamities or corporatized cultural capitulation.

Ros: The living sometimes learn the touchy tricks of the traitor, the tardy, and the tempted; the dead have evaded the flighty earthly future, and form to swell the retinue of retired rights, the righteous school of the invisible, and the rebellious roar of raging nothing.

3. Poetic rhythms. Ros wrote two volumes of poetry, *Poems of Puncture* and *Fumes of Formation* (alliteration was her lifestyle choice). Penn incorporates poetry into his novel, to no real advantage. They favor similar rhythms.

Penn: He observed a familiar sensation
in sensing himself alone,
Might next he go to prison,
or die there on his own?
Would his body be poked and prodded
or simply left to rot?
Then his recall brought back the words
of Egypt's own Sadat…

Ros: I stood while the ground was hollowed
To admit this pile of stink;
They placed the coffin upside down
(The men upon the brink).
How the stony mould did thunder
Upon the coffin's rump,
The louder grew the rattle,
The deeper Jamie sunk.

Penn also writes passages full of sentences with rhyme, but little meter:

> But inside the room, the television is on. A *Duck Dynasty* star speaks conventionally for the artist of con. Pundits report their version, already inured to the preposterous perversion. A singularly immoral inversion.

4. Vituperative rants. Approximately once per chapter, Penn offers a few paragraphs of pointless ranting in the voice of an old coot with a well-thumbed thesaurus, thinly disguised as Bob Honey's interior monologue. Here is something about the Pentagon, or possibly the Department of Defense in general:

> Dollars dispersed with impunity to contracting companies operating without elected oversight. Their employees, often good eggs doing the dangerous and difficult work, and just as often, assholes in need of attitude adjustments. A grab bag of seasoned former soldiers, security specialists, and small-town truck drivers toiling for tax-free tender, with government gifting grandly to these corporate gunslingers, be they of guts or greed.

Ros, for her part, lashed critics, lawyers, and other enemies repeatedly with the same switch: her words. The preface to her second book is an 8,000-word, sentence-by-sentence response to Barry Pain's review of *Irene Iddesleigh*, and a number of her poems are little more than exercises in gloating over deceased foes.

Beneath me here in stinking clumps
Lies Lawyer Largebones, all in lumps;

A rotten mass of clockholed clay
Which grows more honeycombed each day.
See how the rats have scratched his face?
Now so unlike the human race;
I very much regret *I* can't
Assist them in their eager 'bent'.

5. Outlandish ego. Here things get interesting. Of course Penn has a big ego; he's a rich, famous, Oscar-winning celebrity who's had rapturous praise thrown at him from all quarters for decades. And that ego bursts out of *Bob Honey*, both in the content of the novel (Bob Honey never doubts the rightness of his own behavior, even when that behavior entails murdering senior citizens with a mallet) and in the novel's very existence. Penn evidently did not doubt that he could write a novel and it would be good. He, totally untrained as a writer, elected to write in potentially the most difficult genre to get right (satire), to imitate writers whose work stands alone in quality among many inferior attempts at its characteristics (Pynchon, mainly, but also Bukowski), to write prose that individually offends an astounding array of people (women, people of color, Jewish people, military, anti-military, elderly people, non-Californians, non-Americans, dog lovers, Katrina survivors, just…anyone you can think of who isn't a middle-aged white man).

With such hubris, it is no wonder his book is an artistic failure. But at no point did he appear to examine any of the presumptions behind this effort, to think that perhaps writing a novel isn't as easy as putting words on paper for 150 pages. At no point did he think to himself, hey, maybe a person literally rowing through the immediate aftermath of Hurricane Katrina, observing floating bodies and houses on fire, should not be feeling "a cathartic sense of momentarily connected bliss; the kind he might, in a pinch, one day pick from his back pocket, were he ever in the greater Gulf Coast area again, and in need of sensory soothing." Maybe writing that is not such a hot idea? No. Never. Penn can do anything; everything Penn does is worthwhile. That is the assumption underlying the awful reality of *Bob Honey*.

It's the same assumption that brought Ros's work into the world. Everything divides the two writers; Penn has many years of fame and privilege on which to base his opinion of himself, but Ros would likely have lived a totally forgotten life had she not decided to put her work in print. Yet her voluminous correspondence records an ego that matches Penn's. She once asked a friend if she ought to "make a dart" for the Nobel Prize in Literature, having just heard of it. "I am prouder of my Works than ever," she wrote to a correspondent—

> Surely there must be something strangely great about my Works when they create such a furore amongst the World's noblest and best down to the 'Hogwashing Hooligans' whose sole foundation is based upon spleen. I pity such poor apes.

This superiority complex bleeds through her novels. She looks down her nose at drinkers, Catholics, women, lawyers, anyone who is not a member of the peerage, and "that class who subsist on the prostitute penny" (i.e. prostitutes). Most chapters of *Irene Iddesleigh* begin with a paragraph of condescending purple prose meant to teach some kind of life lesson: be grateful for blessings, beware of ambition, "Torture trifleth not." The prose in these paragraphs operates in the mood of a hard-won, Melvillian revelation, even if the point is contradictory or incredibly obvious. What a boon to the sad, sorry human race that we have this countrywoman from Ireland to teach us such things. "I expect I will be talked about at the end of 1000 years," she wrote. A thousand years! Even the major romantic novels of Ros's time are hardly read after only a hundred and fifty.

A similarity less obvious, but perhaps most instructive, is the sheer boredom in the subtext of both writers' works. Ros could not have been satisfied with her life; she exaggerated its circumstances at every opportunity. Her books are (intended to be) breathless romances, where stakes are high and life is short. The opposite was true in her life, as she lived to nearly eighty, and her grand fantasies

remained in her head and on the page. Penn's book touches on some of the major political disasters of the recent past: Baghdad in 2003, New Orleans in 2005, Benghazi in 2012. It is jammed with pointless military jargon, often footnoted patronizingly, as well as large, unlikely accidents (a helicopter falls into a house for no reason). Through all this, Bob Honey's life is practically static, and his motivations never emerge. Penn, too, must have a great deal of time to sit in his home and do nothing, now that he has purportedly retired from acting. Unlike his character, Penn has not been a propulsive force in any world events; he has played roles around them, often very well, but that is all one can say of his life.

It's as if Penn is writing the boy version of Ros's fantasies. His take place in the political realm, while Ros's take place in the domestic. But both write of inflated lives from a perspective of no real consequence.

Both possess the time and the ego to try at writing, fail at it, and move forward as if they have succeeded. It's appropriate, then, that aside from the century that divides them, the major disparity between Penn and Ros is power. Penn's power as a male celebrity propelled his book into print, granted him reviews from major publications, and landed him a blurb from no less than Salman Rushdie. So, of course, he writes about power, about the political landscape. Ros, who had virtually no power at all in her lifetime, writes about marriage and manor-house intrigue, and her book's initial publication was her husband's gift to her—she could not even propel herself into print.

Perhaps this is why Penn's book is so unpleasant to read, while Ros's book delights. The two writers' sentences are equally risible, and their pugnaciousness is equivalent, but Penn rages at a world that has given him so much, while Ros sniffs at that world primly after being denied its pleasures. Penn's book would be repellent if it were not so stupid, while Ros's books would be stupid if they were not so funny.

The uncanny similarity between the sentences and tendencies of each writer cannot be explained by simple incompetence, because incompetent writing does not always sound and feel like this. Although their similarity is amusing, it's the distinctions between the writers that may reveal something significant about what happens when bad writing transcends obscurity. The difference may be the century that separates Sean Penn and Amanda McKittrick Ros, but it may also be gender, or power—or some significant mixture of the two.

INTENTIONALLY DISPOSABLE ART:

THE TEEN AGERS FILMS

I AM NOT THE only person unduly fascinated by a series of eight cheap, forgettable films released by Monogram Pictures between 1946 and 1948, all starring a malleable cast of diminutive, fully adult actors dubbed the Teen Agers. Podcasts and conversations have convinced me that the Teen Agers films hold a rare fascination for certain people. These people, like me, have been around the block a few more times than necessary on bad movies, and know more than a little bit about twentieth century film. We see something remarkable in the sheer mediocrity of the Teen Agers movies: their transparent disposability, their utter superficiality, somehow becomes intriguing, even unique.

The fact that these movies are still around is itself a puzzle, as they were not created to survive. Yet they did, and we can watch them, long after everyone involved in them is dead and gone. Art that should have expired but didn't has a strange aroma, like vinegar and deserted libraries, difficult to hold in your nostrils and interpret, but sharp and unsettling. I've smelled it on art from all over the twentieth century, from Virginia Woolf to Flash Gordon. It squeaks like Styrofoam under pressure and it cracks like Bakelite when dropped from a decent height.

These are not good movies. They are not memorable or worthy, and they don't even offer much useful information as cultural artifacts. Yet something about them stuck with me—and not just me, but others. I want to figure out what it is.

1. CONTEXT

Let's break up the first sentence, for context.

Monogram Pictures

Monogram was a prominent Poverty Row studio in midcentury Hollywood. Poverty Row is/was a term of art referring to small, independently operated studios that produced mostly B pictures from the silent period until the breakup of the major studios some forty years later. Sometimes these companies came and went in a matter of months, and sometimes they operated for many years; occasionally they evolved into major studios (Columbia Pictures) or were absorbed by other companies (Liberty Pictures). Should I fail to offer enough information about this ecosystem, there are whole books about Poverty Row.

eight films between 1946 and 1948

This is not an error. Monogram turned out films like Detroit turned out cars. In twelve years, the studio made 48 films about the Bowery Boys. *Forty-eight!* The Teen Agers films seem positively sparse in comparison.

diminutive, fully adult actors

None of the main cast of "teens" was taller than 5'7", and main heartthrob Freddie Stewart was only 5'5". The shortest of them, Frankie Darro, who would later inhabit the carapace of Robby the Robot for *Forbidden Planet*, was nearly 30 when he was cast as a Teen Ager. June Preisser, aged 26, had already married and given birth when she signed on for the films.

There is nothing wrong with short actors, and it's something of a grand tradition to cast actors in their twenties for teen roles. They're easier to work with—more stable, better skin, not subject to pesky labor laws—and if they're short, you can cast taller actors to make them look younger, which seems really weird as I type it out, but is absolutely a strategy the Teen Agers films employed. The particular angle these films took on adolescence makes the illusion of youth more interesting than usual.

dubbed the Teen Agers

I'm not the first or best person to tell this sociological story, but the idea of teenagers, as a discrete phase of life between childhood and adulthood, has not been around for long. Prior to the 1940s, teenagers were, culturally, like little adults with more innocence and worse judgment. By the 1950s, movies like *Blackboard Jungle* and *Rebel Without a Cause* (both 1955) hypothesized that this phase of life had meaning and boundaries. Again, there are a ton of sociological reasons for this—national changes in labor practices, education infrastructure, etc.—but those aspects aren't as relevant to this essay as the simulacra of those years: how teens appeared in media. Portrayals of "the American teenager" were coming into existence, a new phenomenon, as the Teen Agers films were in production. This matters to how they operate.

A good deal of popular midcentury film and radio, almost all of which has faded into obscurity, provided precedents for Monogram's work. Two teen characters popular in the late 30s and early 40s, Andy Hardy and Henry Aldrich, were touchstones, as were the Bowery Boys, who evolved across 20 years from gangsters to rascals. Surely there was a lot more art like this, and I just don't know about it; I'll tell you what I do know so I can get on to the Teen Agers films and why they're so weird.

Andy Hardy was portrayed by Mickey Rooney in a series of 16 films from MGM, which generally revolved around Andy getting himself into social or financial trouble and then finding his way out. Originally the films were written around Andy's family, but Rooney proved such a draw that Andy became the whole point. Henry Aldrich began life on the stage, moved to radio, appeared in eleven films from Paramount, and spent four years on television before finally being assumed into family sitcom heaven. He can't easily be distinguished from Andy Hardy. Each character is a high-schooler of unspecific age whose behavior is sometimes that of a mini-adult and sometimes that of a boy, depending on the convenience of the plot. Henry Aldrich is often cited as a predecessor for *Leave it to Beaver* (1957-63) and other foundational sitcoms.

(Those 1950s sitcoms, whence decades of TV sprang, didn't come out of nowhere. They came out of radio and plays, ur-texts that we can barely enjoy anymore, so many iterations have come and gone since then. It all seems basic and childish, sketches on the cave wall.)

CAMPUS SLEUTH/MONOGRAM PICTURES

And then there's the Bowery Boys. In 1935, a play called *Dead End* cast a bunch of young actors to play New York street kids. It was a huge hit, and United Artists hired the original stage cast for the film of the same name (1937). The actors became known as the "*Dead End* Kids," and they made a handful of films for Warner Bros. before rebranding as the Little Tough Guys, and then the East Side Kids, and finally the Bowery Boys, all while moving studios, changing membership, and causing trouble. In 1946, they wound up at Monogram, where they continued making films until the franchise ended in 1958. *Dead End* was a serious drama, but the Bowery Boys films evolved gradually into slapstick. As the films got cheaper and quicker, they got less and less serious. I think this evolution pertains to what the market demanded during the twenty years the Bowery Boys films were being made, as well as what could be written and delivered quickly as they moved down the studio ladder toward Monogram. All that has bearing on the Teen Agers films.

But the main reason I'm writing about the Bowery Boys is to introduce the notion of a Poverty Row repertory company—a group of actors Monogram gathered and pumped for obscene amounts of work until they were no longer useful or profitable.

Of course every studio had a menagerie of actors they liked to parade across their movies like puppets on a series of stages; that was the point of having contracts, and contract players. Teaming the same actors in multiple films, one after the other, has persisted from the silents to the Coens. James Cagney and Humphrey Bogart played essentially the same two guys opposite each other in a handful of indistinguishable gangster films in the early 30s. Christopher Guest rotated the same little company of brilliant improvvers among his films in the 90s and 00s.

This happens a lot.

But Monogram, in the 1930s and 1940s, did something slightly different. The studio created little gangs of actors with varying talent and made them play the exact same characters in one uninspired scenario after another. There is no name for this, as it's not a saga of films with meaningful time and character progression (i.e. Star Wars, *The Godfather*), nor is it a rotation of contracted actors in different screenplays that strongly resemble each other (i.e. the Cagney/Bogart situation).

FREDDIE STEPS OUT/MONOGRAM PICTURES

Nor is it a franchise centered on a single character who gets recast from time to time (James Bond, Doctor Who). It's just a monotonous run of content without beginning or end.

That's a perfect transition into puzzling over what the Teen Agers movies are *for*, but first I have to address the movies themselves.

2. SUMMARIES

There are eight Monogram films that use the Teen Agers: *Junior Prom*, *Freddie Steps Out*, *High School Hero*, *Vacation Days*, *Sarge Goes to College*, *Smart Politics*, *Campus Sleuth*, and *Music Man*. The first few films revolve around seven Teen Agers: Freddie (Freddie Stewart), Dodie (June Preisser), Betty (Noel Neill), Lee (Warren Mills), Roy (Frankie Darro), Jimmy (Jackie Moran), and Addie (Judy Clark/Ann Rooney). Subsequent films dropped one character after another; only Stewart, Preisser, and Neill appeared in *Music Man*. The plots of these movies involve hijinks, misunderstandings, and music (Stewart was blessed with a honeyed, near-countertenor croon, and Monogram was clearly positioning him for bobby-soxer stardom that never arrived).

Junior Prom (May 1946): Freddie and Jimmy compete to be class president, and to win Dodie's heart. Jimmy has hardly a chance on either of these quests.

Freddie Steps Out (June 1946): Freddie's doppelganger, a famous singer, goes missing. This one's unusually plotless; seemingly half the runtime is actors yelling "Whose baby is that?"

High School Hero (September 1946): The high school football team's secret weapon is Dodie. A horny female singer named Chi Chi is involved.

Vacation Days (January 1947): The gang goes out west after their teacher inherits a ranch. The plot relies on backstory—old grudges, hidden crimes, another doppelganger.

Sarge Goes to College (May 1947): A daft but friendly WWII veteran tries to settle into life at junior college, with the kids' help. Unfortunately, the veteran is Alan Hale, Jr., aka the Skipper of *Gilligan's Island*.

Smart Politics (January 1948): The corrupt town mayor tries to, at once, help the gang build a youth center and stop them from building a youth center. Novelty acts abound.

Campus Sleuth (April 1948): A murder occurs, and Lee tries to solve it, despite the body disappearing twice. Under an hour of movie here.

Music Man (September 1948): A songwriting team of two brothers breaks up and gets back together over girls, money, and misunderstandings. This one isn't set in the Teen Agers Cinematic Universe, but includes some of the cast of the prior films, so it's lumped in with the other seven.

None of these movies is good. The plots are thin and predictable, the characterization is meaningless, the camerawork is totally unremarkable, and the acting is middling at best. The early scripts are loaded with slang (terrif, drool-man, date bait) and the films depend on musical numbers—often set pieces recorded elsewhere and inset with transitions—and novelty acts— June Preisser's self-taught acrobatics, a harmonica quartet, elastic-limbed dancers, and Candy Candido, famous in an Urkelesque way at the time for the catchphrase "I'm feelin' mighty low"—to appeal. The comedy is of the take-my-wife-please variety, adjusted for a teen audience.

Freddie is a pretty standard juvenile hero: good kid, great singer, equal parts natural leader and sensitive artist. Dodie is written as a desirable girl next door, but Preisser isn't quite pretty enough to pull that off; plus, Dodie's temper and jealousy often make her obnoxious. Betty, Dodie's sister, is a nerdy newspaper editor, and her priorities pull her away from romance and toward schoolbooks, which is obviously backwards for a girl in the 1940s. Lee, Freddie's best friend, is comic relief—a dork with a store of one-liners and exaggerated facial expressions (except in *Campus Sleuth*, where he drives the plot, which is odd and kind of refreshing). Roy more or less provides hoodlum energy throughout the series; he's scrappy and sometimes underhanded, interested in Betty but not in her brain. Jimmy is Freddie's competition and foil—tall, athletic, as interesting and well-characterized as boil-in-the-bag rice. Addie is the third sister, and she's essentially a convenience; she adds dialogue and plot contrivance as needed, with no character consistency. After the first film, she was recast, and after the third film she disappeared altogether.

A handful of other characters offer one thing or another to the series. A teacher, Miss Hinklefink, and a principal, Professor Townley, provide adult contrast or comic relief. Tiny, a soda jerk played by two different actors (like Addie), provides additional comic relief, if it can be called that, in the first three films. Monogram took full advantage of its actors, casting them as needed, continuity be damned. Donald MacBride appears as Lee's father in *Campus Sleuth* and as the mayor *and* the mayor's father in *Smart Politics*. Douglas Fowley (recognizable as the short-tempered director from *Singin' in the Rain*) is a talent manager in *Freddie Steps Out* and the football coach in *High School Hero*.

All the Teen Agers movies contain musical numbers, and some of them roped in significant talent: Gene Krupa, Les Paul, Jimmy Dorsey. Multiple bandleaders and instrumentalists appear whose names are long forgotten, but who were likely recognizable in their day: Abe Lyman, Charlie Barnet, Eddie Heywood, Jan Savitt. This talent, juxtaposed with the novelties, give the movies a grab-bag flavor, as if Monogram was throwing whatever tiny water balloons of notoriety they could contract at the studio wall to see what made the biggest splash. Some of the songs are good, most of them are banal, and a few are can't-look-away bizarre ("Mi Caballo" in *High School Hero* involves the singer, Isabelita, imitating a horse in both Spanish and English). All of them attempt to prop up the movies, since the usual load-bearing elements (plot, character, visual style) cannot. It's possible that Monogram hoped one or more of these songs would catch on as a single, but I don't believe any of them did.

3. DISPOSABLE

On the whole, I'd describe the Teen Agers movies as desperately mediocre. Clearly Monogram had ambitions to *sell* the pictures, to distributors and audiences, or it would not have combined affordable talent with flash-in-the-pan novelty and splashed these dubious assets all over posters and lobby cards. That desperation to *create a product* oozes from the films, every minute of them. The flash, the surface appeal, is the point. Weak inner scaffolding makes this obvious. The scripts are meaningless; I cannot detect a single ounce of innovation in the writing. Characterization has minimal relevance to how the plot unfolds, when there is a plot. Even the slang feels like pressed and chopped language rather than something organic, something real.

The movies are, thus, disposable. They were *created* to be disposable, to increase Monogram's bottom line and be forgotten in a few months. There is no reason to remember the dialogue, the performances, the camerawork, or even the songs beyond the length of time required to sit through the film. The films are exactly that mediocre, and, crucially, Monogram did not create them with an ambition greater than earning a few bucks.

I have long wondered how to interpret disposable art that lasts beyond its intended expiration date. What do we do with the Teen Agers movies, which were no more intended to be seen 75 years later than a dinner cooked in 1947 was intended to be eaten in 2021? Surely we should not judge them by the standards of art made in the same moment that was built to last—*Black Narcissus, The Lady from Shanghai* (both 1947). Monogram's output cannot enter the ring with Orson Welles and remain standing; it's not a fair fight. Any critical assessment should take these films' disposability into account, but should it be done at all? What do these movies have to tell us?

Advertising, also intentionally disposable art, offers us anthropological information about the era whence it came. Do the Teen Agers movies do that? It's hard to say, if only because it's difficult to determine the level of artifice in the film and toward what it aimed. Monogram's low budgets mean that the films' costumes were probably more accurate to the way real people dressed than the clothes in more expensive films of the time. But the way the Teen Agers behave—was that meant to be accurate, or aspirational? Did kids dance politely and well at teen canteens (which did exist), or did they brawl and bully each other? Would a fine singer be more popular in high school then than he would be today? Or was it all so artificial as to be *entirely* divorced from the way young people lived, and thus an entertaining fantasy? Maybe the adults writing these scripts hoped they could actually shape teen behavior. Remember, the whole notion of the teenager was just coming into existence. But then, the obvious age of the "teens" makes the fantasy angle even stranger: they're fresh-faced, but they don't exactly seem innocent.

Compared to its precedent media, the Teen Agers were squeaky-clean—friendly, naïve, free of smirks and irony. I suspect this is part of why the films weren't as popular or long-lasting as their siblings, since the roughneck aspects of the Bowery Boys are part of their appeal. But this posture may offer some clues about the purpose of the series. The films were made and released immediately following the war, at a time when America was trying to put its psyche back together after a long, severe hardship. A little Up With People energy does not go amiss at a cultural moment like that.

HIGH SCHOOL HERO/MONOGRAM PICTURES

Did Monogram make these films as entertaining fantasy deliberately, to distract? Did the war contribute to the meaninglessness of the Teen Agers films? Any content produced at a fraught cultural moment requires study for potential resonance. Maybe there is none in this case; maybe Monogram was just churning out junk by whatever means possible, and didn't think too deeply about the psychic purpose it served for the audience.

I can't answer any of these questions. I don't know who these movies are for. Surely few adults could enjoy such thin films explicitly about young life; surely no actual teenage audience could enjoy them, either, as inane and unrealistic as they are. It would have been like asking me to watch weekly youth ministry pageants instead of *My So-Called Life*.

4. HUMANS

Whenever I'm faced with this question—*who is this art for?*—and can't come up with an answer, the art tends to be filler. Like the bag of plain Lay's chips at the party. It's just there to make the snack table look full. People will eat the Cheetos and the salt & vinegar chips, because people like flavor, and will only turn to the Lay's when everything else is gone. The Lay's are marginally better than nothing.

The Teen Agers movies read like filler: like something, only just better than nothing, to put on the movie screen when required. The way Monogram changed and recycled the cast, the speed with which the films were shot and released, and the general mediocrity of the whole endeavor are clues to its nature. No one was meant to see these films more than once. No one was meant to see them after about 1950.

In the decade after Monogram stopped producing Bowery Boys films, television stations came calling. The stations needed content they couldn't afford to produce anew, for time slots that didn't draw a lot of viewers. The Bowery Boys films were perfect for slots like this: natural filler, parked in times and places that needed content which was marginally better than nothing. I don't know that the wider culture gained much from these films being on television for a couple of decades in spots that would otherwise just be dead air. They served a purpose as filler, but I think that's about all.

This equation becomes painful when I consider the actors. The Teen Agers films were not for an audience, exactly, and they weren't for art, nor posterity. They were for a bottom line. Where does that leave the living, breathing human beings who performed in them? If these people understand the nature of the contract they've made—if they understand that Monogram is almost never a first stop for talent, but instead a tar pit; if they recognize that their place in media history is a footnote at best, and are fine with that; if they contentedly accept their paychecks instead of dreaming and aching for stardom—then filler like the Teen Agers movies hardly harms anyone.

Alas.

Noel Neill, who played Betty in seven Teen Agers films and Kitty in *Music Man*, is best known as Lois Lane in the original *Adventures of Superman* TV show (1952-8). Of all the Teen Agers, Neill seems to have had the healthiest perspective on her job as an actor. She took a shrugging, at-least-it's-good-fun attitude toward work and fame.

Perhaps that's why she's the only one to transcend the tar pit. Neither Freddie Stewart nor June Preisser ever made another film after *Music Man*. Warren Mills died by suicide. Frankie Darro drank himself to death. Their stories are sad and ugly, tales of disappointments huge to their sufferers but miniature and predictable to the world at large. Of course Freddie Stewart wasn't going to be the next Bing Crosby; he was 5'5" and radio crooners were passing out of fashion. Of course Warren Mills couldn't be a major comedy star; he had virtually no magnetism and undistinguished schtick. But these people did not see such bald, unkind logic when they looked at their own lives and careers. They saw talent and drive, and a willingness to work that Monogram tapped until it was dry. Their (minimal) talent was used to make filler, but they did not see it that way, which hurt them.

And it hurts me to think that these actors truly believed they could be somebodies if they gave their energy to material as poor and meaningless as the Teen Agers films. I hope that is not true. I hope there is mitigation in there somewhere, a lack of fooling oneself, when one sees there are no retakes for flubbed lines and the films are released two or three per year and the narrative logic doesn't cohere and the songs and jokes are so bad. I hope the cast no more pretended that a week's shoot for a Monogram film bore a relationship to decent filmmaking than they pretended these films depicted realistic teenagers. But striking this bargain in the first place, agreeing to sing and dance for Monogram for whatever they got paid, makes me doubt.

5. FAILURES

After watching these films dozens of times, after writing about them for thousands of words, I'm still awash with fascination for them—these dinky, drab little movies made a lifetime ago. I think they intrigue me so because they're disposable art in a form I once considered permanent. At one time I couldn't reconcile *any* movies as disposable, and seeing something that purported to be a movie, but was so artistically valueless, shocked me. Understanding the media distribution norms of the 1940s well enough to understand these movies as disposable art was, itself, a process. (That's why this essay expends so many words on context. If we're to understand how they operate, these films require loads of context: where they came from, what they're capitalizing on, what was meant to be done with them.)

I comprehend that these are failed films. They are workmanlike and unambitious, which naturally slots them into a different category than the output of Welles and Wilder, but even in their proper category, they are not good art. The acting is sloppy; the comedy does not please; the sets are dingy; the directing and photography traffic in mediocrity. The musical numbers are the excuse for the film, or the film is the excuse for the musical numbers, but neither of them is solid enough to genuinely buttress the other. Everything about the films seems half-assed, especially their initial choices: casting, writing, music.

However, each film fails a little differently.

Junior Prom has an air of enthusiasm that does not match its hackneyed script, and some of its musical numbers ("Keep the Beat" and Eddie Heywood's appearance) are clearly shoehorned for novelty. The songs that do fit the plot ("Trimball for President" and "Teen Canteen") aren't good. Nothing in this film relates to real life; its glaring artifice makes it impossible to take seriously, and yet hypnotic. Like an MGM musical with a tiny sliver of the required budget and talent. These first couple of movies, though, do expend some time and money on numbers with choreography and choruses, while later movies drop the group numbers altogether. Less rehearsal time, fewer actors to pay.

Freddie Steps Out has just a whisper of plot, and even that revolves on misunderstanding. The characterization is off (Lee plays a harmful joke on Freddie which sets things in motion; Freddie loses his temper), the group number is awful, and none of the other songs relate to the plot at all. Although the ballads make more sense in this film, given a character who is a professional singer, his resemblance to our Freddie is a silly contrivance. This film plods through its paces in a tiresome way, with a rigid grin.

High School Hero demonstrates actual momentum, but its ideas are fatuous and inconsistent. Dodie is the football team's secret weapon at practice, but then she shows up at the big game in a majorette outfit, so it's as if the ruse was never actually going to play out when the stakes got high enough to matter. Chi Chi tries to seduce Freddie, but is rude and bratty to him at the same time. It's not clear why he's repeatedly visiting her, when it's her boss he really needs to speak to (and only once, to ask a favor that never materializes!). The songs are thin, strange, and overcaffeinated. Generally, the movie throws a lot at the wall but none of it sticks.

Vacation Days is less a Western than it is Western-adjacent, involving clothes and clichés from the imagined West[1] but little of its consequence. This makes it more fetishistic than fixed in a genre. The film seems to reach in its bag of Western Stuff to pull out another idea just when it runs short on plot or character: the boys go to a saloon, Freddie sings "Home on the Range," Freddie rides a horse, the gang is involved in a holdup. This doesn't really ascend to being a story, and it certainly doesn't cohere into meaning. The movie has such shallow investment in its genre and its script that it reads almost as pastiche, but it doesn't know that's what it's doing.

Sarge Goes to College is so packed with songs that it has little room for anything else. Yet its 63 minutes drag like hell. It's not the only Teen Agers entry that refers directly to the war, but it's the only one in which the war is a significant aspect of the plot or characterization, and this makes matters worse instead of better. Sarge's intellect is unrealistically low, even for an Alan Hale, Jr. character, and both his comic scenes and his sentimental scenes are ineffective. Also, the whole film is about the show Freddie's planning (he plans a show in nearly every film—sometimes this planning process is central to the film, sometimes not), but the movie ends before we see the show. *No musical comedy does this.* The show is always the third-act set piece. That's the rule. If you're going to break it, you better be doing something damned subversive, but in this case it seems like the production just forgot to put it in.

Campus Sleuth fails in a mundane way. It's a comedy-mystery movie (we have now attempted a Western, a postwar film, a sports film, and a family comedy in this series, so why not?), but the mystery tangles in the middle so the audience can't follow it, and the comedy doesn't have enough backbone to succeed. Lee's father is an abusive lunatic, rather than a character whose rage is funny; giving Lee the central part betrays how shallowly he's been written. In all, *Campus Sleuth* feels like a pretty normal B picture that's lesser than the sum of its parts. Nothing about it works, but all its failures are recognizable. Compared to the other Teen Agers movies, which feel so deeply weird, it's almost a relief to watch.

Smart Politics tries a couple of framing gimmicks that it doesn't have the sophistication to pull off. It opens with a Black maid singing a bluesy song about fixing the boss's breakfast, which could be a decent way to set out the parameters of the story. But we almost never see the character again. The boss she's fixing breakfast for is not the mayor, who is the main antagonist of the film, but the mayor's *father*, who narrates the film to the audience, looking right at the camera

---

1 "The imagined West" is a term of art for the largely ahistorical Western environment that appears in films, books, and the popular imagination. It focuses on white settler perspectives rather than indigenous ones, and it features various typic characters: the gunslinger, the innocent, the bandit, the hooker with a heart of gold, et cetera. This set of fictions has a multifarious reach and is more three-dimensional than either myth or folklore, which is why "the imagined West" is such a useful term. Richard White has written at great length on this issue in *"It's Your Misfortune and None of My Own": A New History of the American West.*

and addressing us. Such a device wasn't uncommon at the time, but the Teen Agers movies have never done it before, and there is no explanation as to why this character, whom we've never met, knows so much about the story he unwinds. We, veteran Teen Ager viewers, surely know more about Freddie and Dodie and Lee and Betty than he does, and yet *he* introduces them to *us*. The film also has a repetitive script, more novelty acts than previous entries, and musical numbers less organically integrated than ever before.

And finally, *Music Man*. It's closer to an actual film than the others, since the characters are all adults rather than the same teens we've been following for seven movies. This means they're not infantilized, and there's less of a sense that these characters are trapped in a cage and prodded into performance. But it also means the film has to come up to par with other movies about adults, and it cannot. The scenes are too short, the comedy does not provide relief, the love triangle is unconvincing, and the plot is very specifically about the struggle between brothers and collaborators to write music together. Such a narrow purpose means it's difficult to connect to the story. It's a paper-thin B musical, with the added anomaly of recontextualizing Freddie, Dodie, and Betty into adult life under other names.

None of these films is so bad as to be laughable. In the following decade, Edward D. Wood, Jr. would astonish the world with his incompetence; Bert I. Gordon would poorly convey his wondrous imagination to the screen; and Roger Corman would begin drafting the most checkered filmmaking resume imaginable. Their bad movies became filler that behaved the same way as the Teen Agers series, as they finished out a double bill or made a middling profit at the drive-in. But Wood and Gordon and Corman all had more ambition than skill, which causes their movies to fail spectacularly, making a huge *splat*, rather than falling noiselessly into the gray desert of mediocrity. The operating principle in the Teen Agers movies—bad, but not painfully so; competently but indifferently created—was once a distinction too fine for me to draw.

6. REMNANTS

The more I have watched these movies, the more I have marveled at them, and the more I consider them a breed apart from other films of the time. They don't quite do the same things as their Aldrich/Hardy/Bowery peers (they are not as comfortable to watch, and the teens' behavior is proscribed in a different way), and they cannot compete with their noir and war and Western contemporaries. They don't portray teenagers accurately, but they also don't portray them quite like the art that preceded or followed did. They appear minimally influenced by the war that had just ended, but perhaps their disposability is, in fact, all about that war. At times, they seem desperate to succeed, but they were never intended to be good; they were only intended to *be*, to exist, to serve a small and temporary purpose and then to vanish.

It's quite difficult for me to reconcile this intention. Perhaps that's why the films have such a grip on me.

Only by spending a good chunk of my adult life on the internet have I begun to grasp that very little art will last. The more content comes and goes, the more trends rise and fall, the more I tweet, the more I understand this with my gut instead of resisting it, fearing it, pleading for preservation and sanctifying archivists. (My obsession with this has something to do with mortality, I think, but that's a subject for a much more personal essay.) I have written articles that I do not intend to save until the end of my life; I have written blog posts better dissolved into their component bits. But applying this understanding of impermanence to film is an extremely difficult mental project for me. Nitrate film deteriorates into flame, but modern film has a base of polyester—that unnatural polymer which, in its molecular composition, will outlast stone and wood and iron. How can anyone put film in a camera and assume this act will be forgotten?

Part of me wishes the Teen Agers films had been lost after all, so I wouldn't have to think about them. I wouldn't have to acknowledge their flaws while searching and scrabbling for whatever it is that makes them intrigue me so. I wouldn't have to consider the heartbreak of those stars, what they hoped and what did not come to pass, perhaps *because* they sold their time to a studio that didn't value film as a lasting medium. I would be able to grieve, without complexity, for all the film and TV from the twentieth century that's been lost forever due to decay and obscurity, instead of realizing a more complicated truth: plenty of that stuff is not worth grieving.

We can't always make sense of what gets saved from the fire, or why. No one watches *Scarlet Street* (1945), a sexy, violent, funny, devastating noir by Fritz Lang, but *The Maltese Falcon* (1941), which drags in places and has a painfully moralistic ending, remains a classic. Nearly all of Johnny Carson's earliest *Tonight Shows* are lost forever, but the Teen Agers films are still available. I don't think any of this is unfair, or inexplicable, or karmically sound. It just is. But it's hard for me to bear. Isn't what we gain from keeping everything, despite the unwieldiness and the intellectual near-impossibility of keeping everything, more than what we gain from discarding any of it? How else are we going to keep in touch with the culture that shapes us, the culture that we shape?

The problem, specific to the Teen Agers, is reconciling what was *meant* to be lost with the fact that it's still here. All those Styrofoam Big Mac containers sitting in landfills, intact, 40 years on. What does it say about us that such things remain, while books and films decay?

The paradox of the Teen Agers films is that we *can* still see them. Parsing out their context helps us understand them, understand their intended meaninglessness (and how they likely have meaning nonetheless). But nothing can unravel the riddle of their remaining available at all. Now, and maybe, unintentionally, forever.

PARATEXT, BITCHES:

HOW *BEST F(R)IENDS* SUBVERTS CONTEMPORARY FILM

THIS ESSAY IS NOT about Tommy Wiseau. And it's not about *The Room*.

What this essay is about: *Best F(r)iends*, the two-part film by Justin MacGregor, which received a fragmented theatrical release in 2018 and finally dropped on Blu-Ray in January of 2019. It's about the way the film makes weird weird again, how it uses audience foreknowledge to its advantage, how it surprises and delights a totally jaded viewer. It's about questioning how we move forward in American film, how we find a way out of the deadening bigness and loudness that Hollywood insists we want. And it's about paratext.

A wide release was not possible for *Best F(r)iends* and its teeny-tiny production, but the film got national attention because of its stars: Greg Sestero and Tommy Wiseau, formerly of the infamous *The Room*, working together again after 15 years. This time, Sestero, rather than Wiseau, is at the creative helm. He wrote and produced the film, and toured indie theaters to screen and promote it for well over a year.

Two different marketing platforms for this film exist. Publicity has been based entirely on the first, more attention-getting one: Wiseau and Sestero together again! In another wacky indie project! Come see a second *Room* for the first time! It's a sensible way to promote *Best F(r)iends*, because fans of *The Room* are legion, they are devoted, and they are accustomed to midnight screenings and weird shit. But the fact is, *Best F(r)iends* has almost nothing to do with *The Room*. Although comparisons between the two are likely to sell the former to fans of the latter, it does *Best F(r)iends* a disservice to consider the film only as a follow-up to *The Room* (and to *The Disaster Artist*, Sestero's 2013 book about Wiseau, later adapted into a film of its own in 2017).

The other platform is *Best F(r)iends* as an indie movie with its own merits. This is a far harder angle to sell, for any production, and it's pointless for a production with a preexisting platform to build a challenging one from scratch. So I understand why the production team sold the film the easier way. But it means that the film may not reach much beyond *Room* fans.

Which is a shame, because I liked *Best F(r)iends* more than any other 2018 film. Mainly because, unlike any other 2018 film, it surprised me. I wasn't expecting it to be especially bad or good, but I was expecting it to be ordinary—to copy the form and style of contemporary cinema on a smaller budget. It is not. It does not.

For example, its montages don't communicate the way montages normally do. A montage of a trip to Las Vegas shows Harvey (Wiseau) and Jon (Sestero) having substantive conversations with each other and unexplained, but clearly significant, encounters with people and landmarks. It's as if the montage depicts real, specific scenes that have been chopped up and muted, rather than joining clips that gesture to clichéd scenes. As if the montage is cutting together, let's say, character-building encounters between the coach and the boxer, rather than cutting together the boxer's training and progressive victories, which are predictable enough that they don't require full scenes. Montaging scenes that evidently matter is a novel choice.

BEST F(R)IENDS PUBLICITY PHOTO/SESTERO PICTURES

The film alternates between long periods of silence and rapid, often improvisational dialogue. The characters talk in circles in an irritating way, but they also say things I've never heard in contemporary film: a nervous CPA type who runs a hotel says "Don't forget to sign the guestbook...*bitches*," and Jon, when his girlfriend snoops in his carry-bag, says "I know it's weird to see a mask, and teeth and shit, but it all adds up." The use of music feels a little bit uncontrolled, but this film is a study in the distinction between inexpert filmmaking and fresh filmmaking. I tend toward believing MacGregor capable of the latter.

Overall, *Best F(r)iends* and its characters carry a pervasive weirdness. And not the acceptable, Hollywood kind of weird (Steve Buscemi's characters, for instance), but *really fucking weird*. Harvey runs a private morgue where he makes silicone death masks and extracts teeth, which he saves, for no apparent reason. There's a whole scene involving a dead clown on the mortician's table, fully decked out in rainbow wig and floppy shoes, and a cheerful discussion about how the clown ended his life with two candles in separate orifices. An old hippie locksmith (picture Dr. Jacoby in *Twin Peaks*) turns out to be a greedy, sadistic killer. The only genuine cliché in the film is Rick, a dude obsessed with football and pussy who owns a .44 Magnum and a vintage Ford Bronco. Somehow it's the intensity of the cliché that causes him to fascinate, that makes his every line of dialogue hilarious.

The varietal of weirdness on display in *Best F(r)iends* is compelling because it's so abnormal, but so harmless. Like Wiseau himself.

Sestero has said in interviews that he wanted to assemble a project that would showcase Wiseau properly, and this film certainly is that. More than once, the film depicts the way people commonly react to the real Wiseau, as described in *The Disaster Artist*. The encountering characters have a similar unsettled, slightly angry look on their faces, and they each struggle to maintain control over their side of the conversation as Harvey says one strange thing after another. In particular, a scrap salesman, Andrei, acts as a mirror for audience reactions to Wiseau. He asks where he's from, what drugs he's on, what even is his whole deal. No answers satisfy.

Again, though, *Best F(r)iends* isn't really about Wiseau. It blows the Wiseau wad pretty early, in fact, and the rest of the film is sort of a grim crime caper, involving road trips, a dental underworld, and an impenetrable safe made out of an ATM.

There are missteps. The famed Black Dahlia case is integrated really unsuccessfully as an element of Harvey's backstory, and the way Jon's girlfriend Traci transforms from a real person into a stereotype, pitted against Jon's best male f(r)iend, is disappointing. Plus, I mean, the title. There's something bold about going ahead with a title that cheesy, but the one doesn't redeem the other.[1]

The total run time for the two volumes is about three hours, and watching them back to back demonstrates that there's an awful lot of padding—establishing shots, repetitive conversation, long and loving shots of Sestero in fading light. It's not lyrical slowness like Tarkovsky; it's dead time. The actors are reasonably charismatic, and the level of novelty in the film's structure, editing, and story maintain audience involvement. But it's still pretty soft in places.

In truth, I don't really understand why the film wasn't cut together into a sharper single volume once it went to home video. It was a unique choice to put together two film releases several months apart, doubling the press (and the publicity burden on the cast and crew). But now that *Best F(r)iends* is on Blu-ray for all time, the hoopla that accompanied the film in theaters—and the excess runtime that made its dual nature possible—could have been stripped away, leaving behind one hell of an interesting film rather than two pretty interesting ones.

Then again, cutting or changing the films for home video would remove some of their paratext. In literary studies, paratext is stuff like a book's back cover summary, epigraphs, and any introductions or acknowledgements. The unavoidable accompaniments. I'm borrowing it here to mean the affiliated but not integrated elements of *Best F(r)iends*, like the trailer, *The Disaster Artist*, audience knowledge of *The Room*, and the film's unusual release strategy.

Best F(r)iends blends its paratext with its text in a way I haven't really seen

---

1 In 1999, Werner Herzog released a documentary charting the bizarre, abusive, and fruitful partnership between Herzog and his frequent leading man, Klaus Kinski. The title is *My Best Fiend*. A parallel between the friendships of Wiseau/Sestero and Kinski/Herzog does exist, but I don't find it compelling enough to believe anyone had Herzog's film in mind when titling this film. I would like it on the record that I'm not calling Herzog cheesy.

before—in a way that transcends easter eggs. In the theaters I went to, screenings of both volumes were accompanied with a video for the Neighbourhood's "Scary Love," which stars Wiseau, even though the video and the film are otherwise unconnected. A teaser for the second volume immediately follows the first volume, both in theaters and on the Blu-ray. The teaser clashes with the integrity of the joined volumes—as if the filmmakers had inserted a teaser for the second half of *Amadeus* or *The Sound of Music* immediately before its intermission—but it also points back to the existence of trailers and film promotion generally. A close-up on a basketball that Jon and Harvey use shows that it's official Wiseau merchandise; the shot makes visible the URL for *The Room*'s official website. The film stock varies between somewhat grainy DV and a cleaner medium, with no obvious logic, in a way that makes it plain we're watching an indie production. Which reminds us all over again of what we're watching and why.

These choices aren't exactly metatextual. They don't refer to the practice of filmmaking as a whole, but to *Best F(r)iends* alone, to the personalities involved in making it, and to the whole mechanism of how films are promoted and released. A teaser for the second volume of the film is a necessary addition to the end of the first volume. It doesn't serve as a coda to the first volume, but it does remind the audience of the film's unusual two-part release method. To forget that would be to forget the film's context, which includes Wiseau and Sestero as people and artists, *The Room*, *The Disaster Artist*, and everything else associated with their little solar system of creative work. Even though *Best F(r)iends* isn't *about* that context, it cannot *avoid* that context. Rather than making external context the elephant in the room, the film makes it into the room's wallpaper.

In other words, *Best F(r)iends* embraces the paradox at the heart of star studies—the fact that the actors we see in films are neither their characters nor themselves but an amalgam of the two. Harvey isn't Wiseau, but he also sort of is; someone says offhand "What are you, D.B. Cooper[2] or something?" and the scene with the branded basketball refers (and kind of panders) to the football stuff in *The Room*. Sestero in the film is partially Sestero, not merely Jon. Wiseau and Sestero working together again is no different than Astaire and Rogers working together again in *The Barkleys of Broadway* (1949), but that film does not make references to how Astaire and Rogers impacted Depression-era audiences, nor how Astaire's collaboration with Hermes Pan led to wide shots and long takes that showcased his and Rogers's exceptional dance chemistry. *Best F(r)iends* does the equivalent of these things. It holds up a mirror not to the practice of filmmaking, as Deadpool and Ingmar Bergman alike have done, but to the audience's role, and the audience's mental calculations, in watching films.

I've written about *Best F(r)iends* at such length mostly because it reminded me that contemporary cinema too rarely includes surprises. Three-act save-the-cat structure has become mandatory. You know who's going to live and who's going to

---

2 An internet joke/conspiracy theory says that Wiseau's real identity is that of D.B. Cooper, an unknown man who committed a 1971 plane hijacking and vanished without a trace.

die from minute six. Screenwriters have prioritized the formula above the content that goes in it, while producers have prioritized the actors above the characters. I've seen so many mainstream movies that I no longer enjoy them; as Debbie Reynolds pronounced in *Singin' in the Rain*, if you've seen one, you've seen 'em all.

It's beyond frustrating to watch mainstream film move back into safety and common denominators—elements that occupied the art form throughout the 1980s and, before that, dominated the classical period (late 1930s – late 1960s). American film in the 21st century is continually getting bigger and dumber and louder. I keep thinking these elements have reached their nadir, but then there's another bigger, dumber, louder sequel to something and I find I was wrong. The stakes keep escalating until trucks are crashing into helicopters and Dwayne Johnson can vault into a skyscraper. Any decent writer knows that artificially high

stakes are the cheapest, most shortsighted way to entice an audience, whereas if a character's developed properly, a dropped teacup is a nuclear bomb.

BEST F(R)IENDS PUBLICITY PHOTO/SESTERO PICTURES

In this context, *Best F(r)iends* is a storyboard for the next stage of American indie film. The plot picks up gradually instead of immediately, trusting the audience instead of trying to hook it. The film makes the most of editing as a resource: cross-cutting during conversations and monologues leads to novel juxtapositions, and the second volume reverses a framing device by cutting back to the frame in the same rhythm that an ordinary film would cut to the flashback. It's about such strange topics and characters, but that's part of why it's a mesmerizing story. Why not make films about benign morticians in back alleys of Los Angeles, instead of white-collar professionals from New York City?

For that matter, why not mix up what montages do? Or when the plot points land in the screenplay? The grammar of film has been the same for a century, and some of its syntax has been frozen for decades. Audiences in 2019 have been watching films at a high volume from early childhood, and they are well-versed enough in the formula that they can handle (or, you know, *desperately need*) a little variety. *Best F(r)iends* is proof that varying the formula can make an inexpensive little film into a one-of-a-kind artistic success. Or, as Harvey tells Jon at the end of the second volume, "Different is what pushes life forward."

NEVER EXPLAIN HOW:

DEATH BED IS GOOD, ACTUALLY

TO BEGIN WITH, *DEATH Bed: The Bed that Eats* is exactly what it says on the tin. It's a horror movie where the villain is a bed, a gigantic bed in a stark black basement that laughs and snores and, as promised, eats. It was written and directed by George Barry with an attempted release in 1977, lost for decades, and officially released at last in 2003.

Unexpectedly, though, for an indie horror flick with its wacky premise written into its title, *Death Bed* is good. Not great—it's limited by its minuscule budget and inexperienced creative team—but good enough that I recommend it whenever possible. It has a well-balanced tone, strong camerawork, and a surrealist sensibility all its own.

1. PREMISE

Death Bed divides into four sections: Breakfast, Lunch, Dinner, and The Just Dessert. Lunch and Dinner include multiple flashbacks to decades or even centuries past, but the main, present-day thread of the film socially connects the victims of Lunch, Dinner, and Dessert.

The manner in which the bed eats its victims varies across the film, but in essence, the bed envelops objects, limbs, and whole bodies in narrow crevices between two sections of its sheeted mattress. These crevices are supernatural, and are only physical as a film effect—not apparent to the victims before they climb upon the bed. Sometimes the bed emits toxic-looking yellow foam around the object of its hunger; sometimes it seems to drug or hypnotize the unlucky people who climb into it, so they don't notice they're being consumed until it's too late. Often, the people bleed, inexplicably. The process is most often one of sinking

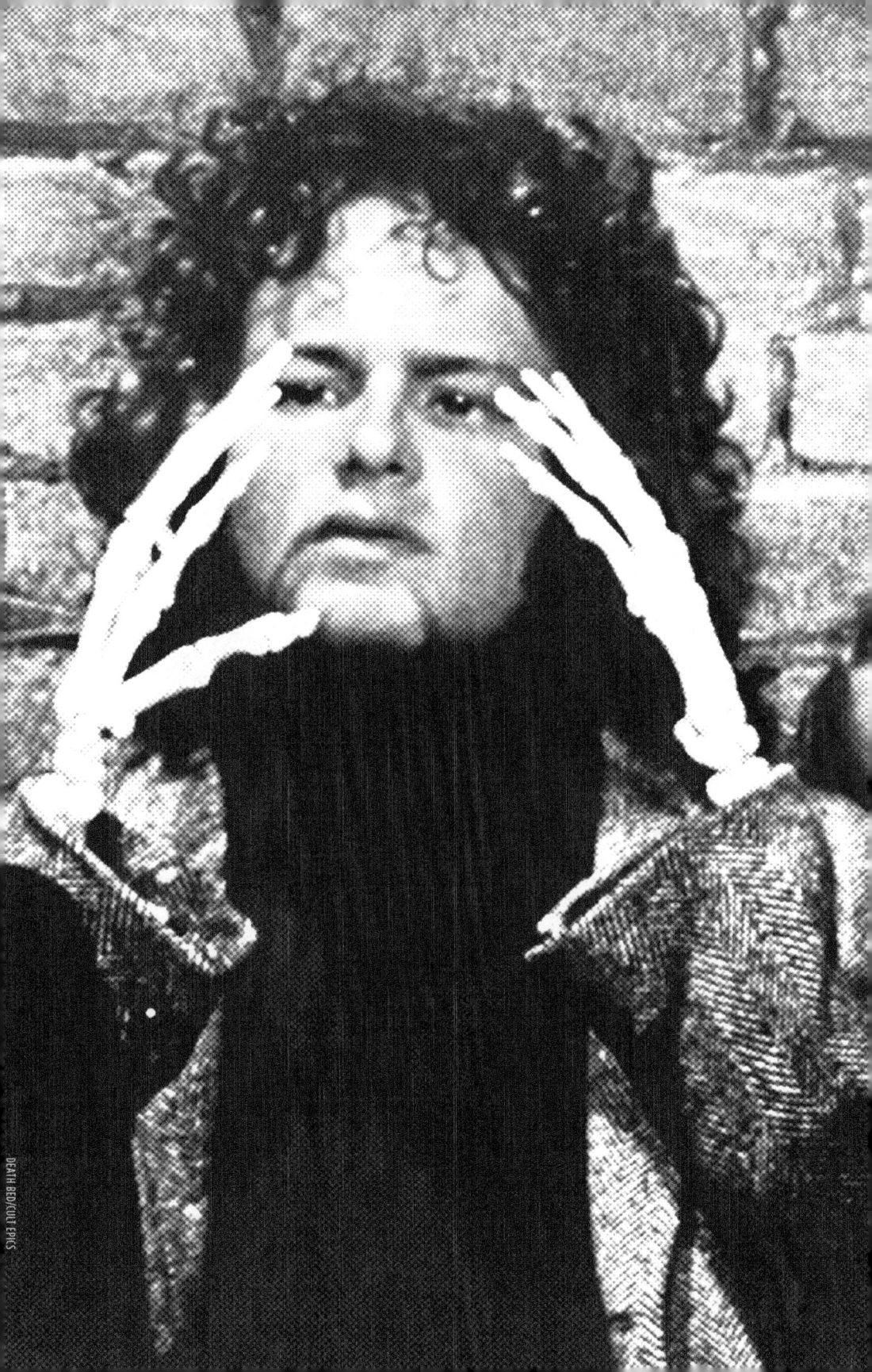

down into the bed, and although this process is not quick, it reads as inevitable, irreversible.

The Breakfast victims, a young couple who neck on the bed next to a meal of takeout fried chicken, apples, and wine, have nothing to do with that main thread. (Their clothing is just anachronistic enough that this section could be set in the 1950s, not the 1970s, although there's little other indication of that.) Their death sequence, which takes place before the credits, functions as a teaser. It indicates who the villain is and how its victims will die—setting up the rules of the universe before telling the story the filmmaker wants to tell about it. This is a reasonable, and reasonably sophisticated, way to structure a horror film. The premise of *Death Bed* is strange enough, and the justifications for that premise are convoluted enough, that easing the audience into its peculiar logic seems wise.

In the main thread of the film, three women—Diane, Sharon, and Suzan—come to "the country" to get out of "the city," following a tip from a friend. Barry leaves their backstories a bit murky, but the vibes are off the chart: Diane and Sharon are on a secret lovers' weekend, and Suzan, oblivious, has invited herself along for fun. Diane reads like a leader, canny and resourceful; Sharon flip-flops between capable and inert; and Suzan is oversensitive and marked virginally (cross necklace, timid, associated with flowers).

Meanwhile, the story of how a bed came to be a supernatural monster is related to the audience by a would-be victim, the Artist. His situation is unusual enough to captivate; he narrates while crouched in a cubic space in the wall behind his own illustration of the bed. (This character is, thus, eternally trapped in his own deathbed.) The Artist died of tuberculosis ("consumption") in the bed at the turn of the 20th century, and the bed spared him its own consumption and gave him a liminal form of existence in the wall. He speculates that it did this because he fed the bed's vanity by painting it.

The Artist explains that, centuries ago, in the course of seducing a maiden (the Resurrected), a demon wept tears of blood into the bed he created to make love with her. These tears "took root into the bed," and "from this root a life sprang." Thus, the bed is not *possessed* by a demon, but is a bed-shaped supernatural creature with "hunger."

Suzan is Lunch, alas. After she, her suitcase, and her bottle of Pepto-Bismol vanish without a trace, Sharon elects to drive back to town for help finding her. Diane stays behind, falls asleep, and becomes Dinner, in a lengthy sequence in which she almost gets away.

In the meantime, Sharon's brother has been trying to find out where she's gone for the weekend, and eventually, he traces her to the bed's home. Sharon returns from an incomplete trip to town (the car breaks down) just in time to witness Diane's final struggle, an experience which renders Sharon nearly catatonic. In this state, Sharon's brother (unnamed in the film, despite having more lines than she does; I will call him Rusty, after the actor) finds her. The bed eats Rusty's hands, and then itself falls asleep, which occurs only once every ten years. The Artist "can talk beyond my painting" when the bed is asleep, and so he instructs Sharon in a ritual to destroy the bed, which she and Rusty fulfill. The bed burns, gloriously, and the movie ends.

That's a summary, but there's a lot of movie that this summary doesn't explain: Suzan's and Diane's extraordinary dream sequences, the Artist's colorful recounting of the bed's many prior victims, the connection of the Resurrected to the bed's demise. Like so many good horror movies, *Death Bed*'s whole is greater than the sum of its story.

Although slow, the film has structure, and it does a good job moving between flashback and present-day action in order to unfold the bed's history as well as the story of the three women. It doesn't linger so long in one timeline that we forget where we were in another (not that any of the timelines is too complicated), and it uses sharp editing and generous sprinkles of humor to keep things moving. The only part of all this that is poor in craft is the bed's convoluted origin story. Everything else entails good storytelling and good filmmaking.

It's easy to mistake *Death Bed* for a bad movie because of its premise. An inanimate object is a hard sell as a villain, especially if that object isn't something like a doll or a car, which make more sense causing fatalities than furniture without limbs or moving tonnage. Yet as long as the audience can refrain from spluttering at the premise across the running time, *Death Bed*'s positive qualities, its cinematic integrity, transcend its inherent silliness. It wins you over.

While baffling to an audience accustomed to more mobile monsters, the rules of what the villain of this movie can do are internally consistent. The bed can psychically lock and unlock doors from great distances, use its sheets as prehensile limbs, cause fires, induce dreams, and etch messages into playing cards. How it does these things is not explained. In fact, "how" is the main unanswered question of *Death Bed*. Barry demonstrates skill at cueing the audience to *what* the bed is doing, and often *why*, but *how* is rarely on the table. (I editorialize that *how* is not really necessary to make this film work, because, as several critics have noted,[1] it has a dreamlike quality. Dreams do not deal in hows as often as they deal in whats.)

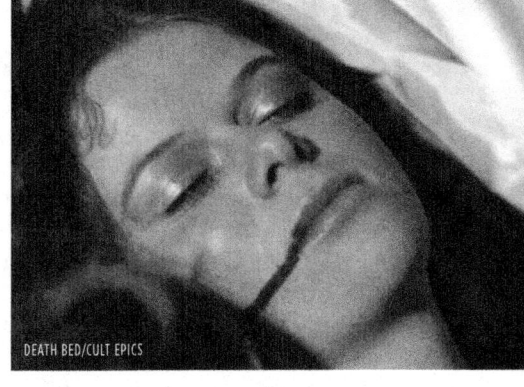

DEATH BED/CULT EPICS

When the bed consumes people and objects, the film cuts to a tank of yellow liquid, shot with various effects (physical, visual, and sound) to indicate it's the bed's innards. This tank is not under the bed, or inside the mattress; it's metaphysical, a supernatural place where the bed's victims go. Physical effects do occur here—flesh dissolves, apples are bitten down to the core—but this does not make the

---

1 Michael Adams in *Showgirls, Teen Wolves, and Astro Zombies* (2010); Harry Knowles of Ain't It Cool News upon release of the *Death Bed* Blu-ray (2014); Barry Meyer in *Film Monthly* (2004).

tank implausible, exactly. Instead, the film encourages the audience to think of this space, and this monster, as following different rules than those of the real world, or of other horror films.

So, how it's possible that the sheets stay dry and clean, despite the gross yellow foam, remains unanswered. How the bed "spits out" things like chicken bones and eyeballs, and gifts the Artist with jewelry and even a lit cigarette belonging to its victims, Barry doesn't reveal. How the bed's telekinetic powers work, we will never know. But at no point in the film do these actions contradict each other— at no point does the film contradict itself. *Death Bed* may be outlandish, but it is not sloppy.

This was the weirdest conclusion that came to light when I studied the film: all signs point to *Death Bed* being a good movie.

2. QUALITY

The normal markers of bad movies are, in general, (a) incompetence in the mechanics of filmmaking (bad camerawork, lighting, focus, sets, costumes, editing) and (b) low-quality raw materials (bad script, acting, effects, music). Almost always on the list, too, is unintentional comedy.

(a) Incompetence in the Mechanics of Filmmaking

George Barry demonstrates some incompetence—his lighting is uniformly bright, he overuses zoom-ins—but not much. Certain pips of incompetence actually add to the film. For example, a few day-for-night shots are apparent (as day-for-night usually is in color), but it has an interesting effect; the colors in those shots pop uniquely, like twilight at sea, and bright, surreal dots of yellow and white wildflowers add mood. The film's foley is bold throughout, almost intrusive, but it gives the viewer lots of clues as to what the bed is doing. It even contributes deliberate humor, as when the sound of a marble rolling on a hard surface accompanies a shot of an eyeball rolling on the bedspread.

Unmistakably, Barry knows where to put the camera. His framing is always good, even excellent. Sometimes he shoots people standing by the bed from the bed's surface's point of view, a perspective that shows them as victims, or as existing only in relation to the bed.[2] The square framing of shots in the dream sequences makes them more surreal, and the sequences themselves are inspired, despite dream sequences from debut directors being something of a cliché. The shots of Suzan and Diane dreaming while lying in the bed, at separate points in the movie, are identically framed, adding consistency. The hideous spectacle of the Breakfast couple making out helps us not to feel too sorry for them; at the same time, the angles on them look entirely new to me, despite the hundreds of make-out scenes I've witnessed. The images of Suzan's reflected eye shattering as her compact breaks in her hand, and the mirrored book full of flame, and the Resurrected in

---

2 In an interview (in Stephen Thrower's *Nightmare USA*), Barry called the bed the "star" of the film.

her cozy satin-lined coffin, remain indelible. It may not be noticeable that Barry has a terrific eye, as the stuff going on in the frame is so unusual and viewers only tend to notice framing when it's bad, but repeat viewings have convinced me that he does.

Other filmmaking mechanics are similarly in place. The basement (set) where the bed lives seems strange—many steps down from the door, black-painted brick, a fireplace not connected to a chimney—but it suits as a habitat for the bed. It might seem claustrophobic, but we go elsewhere occasionally: to pleasant natural surroundings, to the small cemetery where the Resurrected is buried, to a gas station where Rusty makes a phone call, etc. Props are minimal, but the bed itself is enormous, much larger than any ordinary bed, and built to be sturdy and imposing: a terrific prop. The editing is very good, making use of fadeouts, abrupt cuts, and overlay effects, the latter to particularly artistic effect during Diane's dream sequence. The costumes aren't distinguished, but they give us clues about the characters. Rusty, who wears a corduroy blazer, has his life together. Diane, in denim, a kicky scarf, and skull earrings, is somehow both rebellious and tidy. Sharon, in jeans and a shapeless t-shirt, has nothing in her life to dress up for. Suzan, in a matching skirt and vest, is conservative and naïve.

And although Barry couldn't afford sync sound for most of the scenes, jumping from one character's voice-over to another works well. It makes the film a subjective narrative for each of the characters, without lapsing into chaos, as it moves forward. The primary voice in the film is the Artist's, but his scorn and eventual treachery force us to conclude that we can't trust him as an objective narrator, either. These are subtle moves, easily lost under the audience's own (probable) scorn for a movie about a killer bed. Despite what we expect from that premise, Barry proves himself competent to the task of filmmaking through multiple mechanics.

(b) Low Quality Raw Materials

Low-quality raw materials can result either from bad judgment or from limitations that are not the filmmaker's fault. Someone with a budget as small as Barry's cannot hire Meryl Streep, for instance, or Janusz Kamiński. Money doesn't guarantee a good movie, but it usually improves the quality of the raw materials. However, if the filmmaker has bad judgment, he will accept poor-quality raw materials without recognizing that he could do better (cf Ed Wood).

In the case of *Death Bed*, Barry mostly worked within his limitations and used good judgment. He doesn't have elaborate music or effects, but he doesn't need them to tell the story. Simple film reversal will do to slurp up blood and draw the bed's curtains. The shots with the stereotypical spinning newspapers read a bit cheaply, but they are clearly supposed to be funny, and the cheapness skates by on humor. The bed's tank of a digestive system and the way it eats people can look pretty weird, but the whole concept is weird, and making it look "better" would remove enigma and charm. (What on earth would a "realistic" version of a bed eating people look like?) The script rarely drops to the level of *bad*, and aside from some of the Artist's exposition, it offers just about the right blend of information and mystery to keep the audience engaged. The film stock is not great, and the blowup from 16mm to 35mm is pretty apparent, but this middling visual quality doesn't interfere with enjoyment. None of Barry's actors is especially charismatic, but their flat delivery is deliberate, according to Barry himself:

> I also remember feeling…the delivery of their lines should still range from low-to-middle soap-opera recitation—earnest and banal. This was more of an instinctual notion, that if the story is a bit over-the-top, the acting should run counter. If the bed is outrageous, the people should be "downed out" a bit. [3]

He's right. As a counterexample, see Faye Dunaway in *Mommie Dearest*.

The only material element that truly worsens the film is the original music that went with the credits,[4] but thankfully it was replaced with music by Cyclobe for the film's legitimate release in the early 2000s.[5] Everything Barry did on *Death Bed* conforms to what he had to work with at the time, and within those limitations, the film excels.

The final criterion for a bad movie is **unintentional humor**. All the great bad movies exhibit it, from *Reefer Madness* to *The Room*. I have never laughed at *Death Bed*, except in moments when the audience is encouraged to laugh with it— which is often. Even before the credits roll, the bed eats fried chicken and regurgitates bones. Newspaper headlines announce the bed's reign of terror with tongue planted in cheek ("Strange Munching Sounds Heard at Night!"). A sequence involving a quack sex therapist, Dr. Graham, and an orgy described as the bed's "one great  feast," is altogether bawdy and irreverent. A priest dies haplessly, perplexed at the blood dribbling from his mouth. George Barry's own grandmother reads a dirty newspaper advertising "Oral lesbians! Big butts! B'zooms! Crax!" before, inevitably, being devoured.

The segment when the bed eats Rusty's hands is funniest of all. The bed audibly slurps the flesh off his bones, and then he yanks his arms out of the bed to find skeleton hands protruding from his cuffs. The film dissolves to Sharon looking at them, and then through them, toward the camera. My notes ask "Is this funny or horrible?" The pair sits by the fire, a bit melancholy, with Rusty's

---

3 *Nightmare USA* interview.
4 The old music is a feature on the Blu-ray of *Death Bed*, and it is genuinely awful, generic and dated and poorly performed. The new score, dominated by organ, is simple, but it suits the film beautifully.
5 The story of *Death Bed*'s path to legitimate release is long, magical, and well-covered elsewhere.

skeleton hands held up before them. When a finger bone falls to the floor, he says "Great. Cartilage is decaying," with slightly less pathos than Charlie Brown saying "good grief." It's absurd, and it might tip over into bad. Yet the film offers a sense that we're *supposed* to be laughing—that this is not unintentional comedy.

That's the element that most convinces me *Death Bed* is not a bad movie: it has no unintentional comedy at all. If you are laughing at it, Barry almost certainly meant for you to laugh. I've been taking the film seriously across this essay, and I believe it's best read that way. But if you laugh at it, I suspect you're actually laughing *with* it.

3. SURPRISE

Perhaps the film's innate sense of itself is what draws me to it. *Death Bed* knows it's a low-budget movie about a killer bed, and unlike other films that exploit deliberately bizarre or silly ideas (*Sharknado* and its cohort), it has no cynicism mixed into its disposition. The film moves toward fun and joviality about as often as it moves toward art and surrealism, which makes it an unusual blend but, for seasoned viewers, an enjoyable one. Inexperienced viewers are likely to see *Death Bed* as a jumble, because it doesn't conform to expectations for the genres it purportedly belongs to. A low-budget genre film usually isn't this thoughtful, and a funny film doesn't usually have such striking images, and a horror film doesn't usually eschew so many tropes, and a film with a gimmick doesn't usually require this kind of investment.

But it's possible to read so much into *Death Bed*. Consumption and greed, as themes. The man of the Breakfast couple is pushy, consuming his girl before the bed does. Nationally, America had to start rethinking its use and waste strategies in the 1970s, given the gas crisis, a sudden turn toward environmentalism, and campaigns addressing litter. The film creates slushy, poetic boundaries between life and death: the Artist's existence behind his painting, the Resurrected lying in her coffin half-alive for a few hundred years, and the red flower that grows almost immediately out of Suzan's skull after the bed devours her. It leans to the Gothic, which attaches it to a separate tradition than low-budget horror of this era most often invokes,[6] and opens up a new avenue for interpretation and comparison.

Even if these artistic ideas fail to captivate, the film has one ace up its sleeve: it is relentlessly surprising. Outsider art offers the jaded critic something new to appraise, something that she cannot fit under the same umbrellas she commonly uses to evaluate art. George Barry is not an outsider artist, as he was clearly aware of certain film tropes—the sexually active couple who must die messily; demon possession, which saturated cinema in the 1970s; the spinning newspaper as exposition device. But he assembled this film without regard to audience expectations, to the narrative and cinematic patterns (ruts) into which any film should fit (*thunk*, like a bowling ball in the gutter) in order to be classified and

---

6　For pedants: yes, Hammer horror is quite Gothic indeed. By the 1970s, American low-budget horror was moving away from the Gothic and toward gore.

understood. Thus, for instance, the villain with its own rules and reality, rather than those resembling other horror villains. *Death Bed* meanders, slots in backstory where and for as long as it wants to, trims interstitial scenes to nothing.[7] It uses humor almost in self-deprecation, and adds splendid, unique imagery to goofy sequences. It's a film without interest in conforming, which could make it a tiresome and self-indulgent project. But the result is, instead, wholly surprising and even refreshing.

I've glossed over some flaws to the film. Whatever's going on with Sharon before she comes on this weekend trip is a little too obscured. No one seems to bother about the sheets being clean, even though the bed has been abandoned for years at a time. After the bed begins to eat Diane, she crawls across the floor for three straight minutes of screen time, making uncomfortable moans and groans, before the bed lassoes her back with its sheets. (I could spend a while analyzing the effect this sequence has on the viewer, as a mini-dose of slow cinema, but it's still pretty hard to watch.)

All this pales for me in comparison to the surprise of *Death Bed*, the sense that it's made by a mind and eye undiluted by others' expectations or precedents. Every time I watch, I fall a little more in love with it. Few bad movies act on anyone in such a way.

---

7 Note this particularly when Sharon, inside, says she will go find Suzan, and the film cuts immediately to Sharon taking Suzan's hand, outside, and dragging her up a hill. Ordinarily these scenes would have an interstitial of Sharon walking outside, *on the way* to Suzan.

WHEN BAD
IS BAFFLING:

AFTER LAST SEASON

LET'S TALK ABOUT OUTSIDER art for a minute. This term refers to works created by people who are not traditionally trained or skilled in the artistic fields in which they create. Sometimes these people are mentally ill or otherwise marginalized—whether on the margins of the regular world or the art world can vary. A word that often comes up with regard to outsider art is "naïve"—the notion that this art has a capacity to charm and appeal that professional artists no longer possess, having honed their talent into skill and their naïveté into experience. A famous outsider artist is Henry Darger, a janitor whose thousands of pages of writing and visual art was discovered, a treasure, shortly before his death. His work is in museums now.

Whether any films, of any length or style, can truly be considered outsider art is a question I can't answer. How could a regular American live her life without absorbing, and thus being influenced by, moving pictures? The moving image infiltrates our neurology from babyhood, most of us. With it comes an acceptable syntax of cinema, a set of structures that the subconscious mind registers even if the conscious mind doesn't. Like language. A native speaker understands all kinds of weird particulars in English that they can't explain with linguistic terms. We are all native speakers of cinema.

It's possible to argue for certain filmmakers as outsider artists, but I generally consider this a fun intellectual puzzle rather than a legitimate theoretical avenue. I believe that any filmmaker born after 1940 who has access to a camera, a script, lighting, and actors has some knowledge of what he's doing, what body of work he's supplementing. Tommy Wiseau did not understand why it made no sense to use a film camera and a DV camera taped together to record scenes, but he did understand, on a basic level, where to put the camera(s) and what kind of dialogue to put in a scene. He understood this because he had seen movies, and he thought of them as he was making his own. He was not detached from cinema the way Henry Darger was detached from fine art. Wiseau had seen romantic comedies, he had seen melodramas, and he made a film that imitated aspects of both genres. His script doesn't understand narrative set up/knock down very well (the way it brings up Lisa's mom's cancer just to drop it off the map, for instance), and his sets are unconvincing as genuine environments. But Wiseau had a comprehensible motive for adding cancer into the script: he believed it would add drama. He had a reasonable idea of what sets were supposed to look like. His film misses the mark, but he is aware that a mark exists. Not knowing that a mark exists is what defines an outsider artist.

And the closest film I've ever seen to genuine outsider art is *After Last Season*. It's also the only film I've seen, out of thousands, that utterly stumped me. I did not know what to make of it, in a fundamental way: what it sought to do as a piece of art. Upon studying it, I have a few ideas about this, but first a little background.

After Last Season came out in 2009 in four theaters. Some of the theaters were told by distributors to destroy the prints rather than returning them, as returning them cost more than the distributors made from the film's release. Shortly thereafter, DVDs became available from online retailers, but they sold out within a few years, and that was that. The film's production company, Index Square, does not appear to exist anymore; the film's website is defunct; the actors are available to contact, but the filmmaker(s) are not. The director, Mark Region (evidently an alias), sat for a single interview with *Filmmaker Magazine*, which offered only a modicum of useful information. The film was not a hoax, Region clarified, and he stated that the plot is "very logical" and "all in there." It was shot in less than a week, and the crew was minimal. Region claims that the budget was $5 million, with under $50,000 of that going to practical production and the rest going to digital effects. Few people who have seen the film find this plausible.

A plot summary of *After Last Season*, even if it were not speculative—which it necessarily will be, as the film doesn't make sense—cannot convey the experience of watching it. The plot has to do with neurology and/or psychology students doing an experiment, unless that experiment is all a dream, and a serial murderer, unless the murderer has only killed one person. But many of the conversations in the film are meaningless small talk, concerning family history, car travel, a shrimp allergy, or mundane scheduling matters, so "plot" is a loose indicator at best of what *Season* does to occupy 90 minutes. The two characters who have the most screen time are Matt (Jason Kulas) and Sarah (Peggy McClellan), the neuro/psych students. Also appearing are Sarah's roommate, Sarah's roommate's friend, a doctor, the doctor's wife, a patient of the doctor who is also an FBI agent, another patient who is also a friend of the wife, and the doctor's two sons, who may both be dead by the end of the film. And a ghost. Who is probably one of the sons. Unless that part is a dream.

The experience of watching *Season* mostly consists of boredom, with significant frustration and a teensy bit of humor thrown in. This film is *slow*. It's not slow in a good way, because it's a supremely unbeautiful movie, and the long periods when little happens don't help to clarify the parts of the movie that don't make sense—as in a thriller, when the film occasionally slows to let you catch your breath and put some pieces together. No, every minute is as baffling as the minute before. Because the human mind gets so bored and yet so confused by *Season*, it's a film almost impossible to grasp, aesthetically or practically. As Tim Brayton wrote for Alternate Ending, "One's body simply refuses to absorb it, like accidentally eating a small piece of plastic." The mind tends to let go of whatever it can't comprehend, which makes *Season* a difficult 90 minutes to remember, let alone interpret. It's cinema through a sieve.

When a film makes this little logical sense, a critic must rely on elements other than logic to make it cohere. *After Last Season* does have visual patterns: it contains a lot of lines, doors, and chairs. Lines in particular are everywhere. The set design contains a great deal of paper taped together to cover walls and tables, rendering lines everywhere the edges of the paper meet. Characters don their lab jackets right out of the bag, plainly, without ironing the factory creases out. Plus, one of the doors is marked by two short, perpendicular lines, like so:

—
|

This image echoes the initial, pre-title shot, as well as the lines and polygons in the "virtual reality" space that Sarah and Matt occupy for the majority of the film's runtime.

Many doors and many chairs get their own shots in this film. Some of these bridge two other scenes, attempting to establish location or otherwise convey information, but some of them seem altogether random. The chairs vary in style:

wood-and-upholstery waiting room chairs, banquet dining chairs, padded computer chairs, steel folding chairs. They are all generic and easily available to a set decorator, but their repeated inclusion made me notice the focus on them. Doors vary less, but there sure are a lot of shots of them. Doors are threshold spaces, but this film seems to use them as limiting factors, closing off something inside or outside, making a distinct world behind a door or outside it.

I'm observing, not drawing conclusions; I don't necessarily think Region did any of this on purpose, to communicate a particular idea. But it's useful to pick out elements of *After Last Season* that occupy the film visually, that take up a lot of room in what passes for an aesthetic in this film. That's how I'd work on a surrealist film, or a film by someone without a lot of clocked hours watching movies. I'd focus on whatever the camera focuses on most.

But is that a stupid thing to do in this case? It assumes Region has an aesthetic, a sensibility as an artist, that his film does not prove he has.

After Last Season does not hold together as an artistic project of any kind. The framing is bizarre: sometimes it traditionally centers objects or people, and sometimes it holds objects off-center or people in the bottom third of a shot otherwise filled with empty walls. The dialogue can't be trusted: most of it is mundane, but occasionally a character will slip something into conversation that relates to the mysterious plot or the even more mysterious title, which makes it hard to dismiss the chitchat altogether. The editing is maddeningly inconsistent: sometimes it cross-cuts between two locations or situations effectively, while frequently it juxtaposes shots and scenarios that make no sense together. Attempted (and failed) connection between unrelated scenes through editing is a common choice among unskilled directors, but *Season* tries this maneuver with unmatched peculiarity. In the opening "MRI" sequence, the film cuts to a shot of a domestic ceiling fan for no apparent reason. The fan does not indicate a location, it's not a subjective shot from a character's perspective, it doesn't have symbolic meaning, and it's not unusual or attractive. It's just a ceiling fan, and thus, it's unjustifiable as a cutaway shot.

More puzzlingly, the film doesn't seem to communicate anything artistically (much less narratively). Outsider artists create because they feel a creative urge so strong that it overcomes lack of training, community, and historical awareness. Underground filmmakers especially must be artistically motivated, as making a film is much more expensive and difficult than drawing a picture, and it requires corralling people and resources in a way other art forms don't. Wiseau's passion for his material shines through his incompetence; he wanted to tell a story that he felt was novel and emotionally fraught. No kind of passion ever surfaces in *After Last Season*. Its imperative to exist remains obscure.

The film's other flaws are numerous. Timing: shots begin before the actor has taken action and last long after they should end, and the order of shots in a scene is sometimes backwards (the doctor explains to Matt and Sarah what an MRI machine does *after* he shows them a patient's scans with the implication that Matt and Sarah can read them). Sound: a lot of dialogue is inaudible, and most of it echoes against the surfaces of the sets or rooms, while the sound effects in the virtual reality sequences are inconsistent or meaningless. Lighting: horrific, with strong key lights and no fill lights, causing sharp shadows behind the actors in most scenes. Music: mediocre at best, varying between minimal piano melodies and unpleasant synthesized woodwinds. It comes and goes entirely at random, dropping in and out of scenes not to cover up poor ambient sound or a lack of foley (as in other bad films) nor to emphasize the emotions in a scene (as in good films), but with no logic at all. Acting: I have no quarrel with the actors, as they seem to be doing what they can in truly strange conditions, but their performances are uninspired and multiple flubbed lines make it into the finished movie. Sets: off-kilter in every way, from the cardboard MRI machine in a pink-painted bedroom to the derelict but blindingly white-walled warehouse space which stands in for college classrooms and apartments. Domestic items show up in professional spaces and vice versa; in one scene, a refrigerator blocks the base of a staircase, and in another, beige metal filing cabinets fill a wall in someone's bedroom. Costumes: mostly the wardrobe looks like the actors', which means it adds little to the proceedings. Matt and Sarah seem to mirror each other in the long warehouse section that consumes most of the screen time (almost 50 minutes), each wearing a blue button-down and jeans in one part of the sequence and a white button-down and jeans in the other. I don't know how this signifies.

But elements like that, the two actors noticeably being costumed the same in a very long sequence, makes me think there must be more to *After Last Season* than incompetence so extreme it becomes inscrutable. Maybe it's the naïveté of outsider art that's at work here. Yet how can this be? How can a director who has lived in the moviegoing world not know when to start a scene, what handful of seconds to cut off the top of the take so the action looks natural to an audience? Is it possible he's never seen a movie before, or somehow didn't correctly interpret how scenes begin in other movies?

Here is where my sanity begins to dissolve; here is where *After Last Season* defeats me.

Shots like the one of the ceiling fan don't just make me question the capacity of Mark Region or the nature of this film. They make me question the underlying purposes of cinema, and possibly life, as I know it. Is the shot of the ceiling fan intended to convey information? Are any of these shots intended to convey information?

Should any shots in a film intend to convey information?

Does information exist in art?

Does art exist?

Do I exist?

I'm not saying every person who watches *After Last Season* is bound for an existential crisis. But it really is that strange a film. During the VR sequence, Sarah sees a crude rendering of a woman in her mind, and we see her too. Sarah says, "Her left arm is bleeding!"—but, as we can see, it is not. So what Sarah says is incorrect, unless she is trying to offer information to us that we cannot see, rather than describing something we can see. The most likely explanation for this is that the digital effects people who worked on *Season*, those wretched souls, could not render a bleeding left arm, but the dialogue still needed to exist to indicate what Sarah was seeing, and the filmmaker did not perceive any inconsistency there because he is an idiot. However, the other possibility is a desire to destabilize voiceover's usual purpose, to force the audience to question what it's seeing and why. This seems unlikely, but it still floated through my mind as possible, because the likely explanation is so depressing, and it closes the film instead of opening it to interpretation.

Similarly, I realized through my boredom that Matt and Sarah, sitting with VR chips stuck to their temples, were having a shared vision. That is the very nature of watching film. They describe the vision to each other even as they're having it to gain insight. They help each other to interpret what they're both seeing. It's Sarah's vision, but she understands it no more than Matt does. That could be Mark Region and me, sitting in those cheap chairs in an overlit warehouse, watching *After Last Season*. Couldn't it?

(No, probably not.)

A series of shots in the warehouse show black and orange arrows taped to the wall. Sometimes these arrows point left or right, and sometimes they have other signs, like FLOOR 4, next to them. In the world of the film, presumably these signs guide people in one direction or another, depending on where they want or need to go. But the internal geography of *Season* doesn't make sense to the audience in any way. We know that in the world of this film there are apartments, a house, an MRI screening room, a few rooms on a college campus, and the Prorolis Corporation, but shots of these locations don't establish, distinguish, or consolidate them. They're too similar to be different places, or too different to be a single place. It's a labyrinth, these places and their supposed locations, as characters wander between and within them. The arrows point inward and outward but ultimately nowhere. The film acts this way, too; the plot is a labyrinth that leads nowhere, no conclusion, indicating connections but no relationships between characters.

That there is a symbolic link between the geography of the film and the structure of the plot, one I can point to and interpret, makes me think, yet again, that *After Last Season* is up to something. However, the confusion of both plot and geography

AFTER LAST SEASON/INDEX SQUARE

could be due to incompetence. *All* of this possible meaning could be due to incompetence. An incompetence that could answer everything I've questioned and failed to understand about this film would be so titanic, so absolute and singular, that I cannot truly conceive of it. I try to think of other things *Season* could be and mean in order to save myself such terror.

In his film, Region sometimes indicates that he is not an outsider artist. Matt looks at a paper in his hand and the next shot is a close-up of the text on that paper—typical clarify/consequence shot. But there are so many shots like the one of the ceiling fan. Sometimes the shared vision of Sarah and Matt is a virtual space that looks dumb and terrible, like *Virtuosity* made on somebody's 1984 Macintosh, and sometimes it's an ordinary kitchen, which Sarah and Matt describe inaccurately. This is not cross-cutting, it's just mess. But then some proper cross-cutting *does* occur, between the shared vision and a man knocking on a murdered woman's door, and it shows that Region knows how to do that. He doesn't do it correctly for most of the movie, but he does it easily once or twice. If he *can* do it, why does he not do it every time?

Are we misinterpreting this film? Could it be a play in the Theatre of the Absurd, *intended* to make us fall to our knees and plead with the universe for a scrap of sense among the chaos? I don't believe this, not really, but I also thrash and plead at the (many) doors of this baffling film, *make sense to me*, because it simply doesn't. It doesn't fit into any pattern I know for bad film, let alone good. It doesn't instruct me about what it is or what it's doing, in a fundamental way, which leads me to question its nature and my own. It doesn't follow any coherent plan or rule for how to make a film that I'm aware of, yet it shows tiny threads of coherence from time to time, just frequently enough that it doesn't read as coincidence.

So I keep returning to outsider art. Part of the reason this film stumped me when I first watched it was something I wrote in my notes the second time: "judging this film by what other films generally look like doesn't work." Judging Henry Darger's work by the standards of the Impressionists or the Cubists doesn't make sense, because he didn't create art in those traditions and possibly wasn't aware of those traditions at all. Pretending that *After Last Season* is a film in the Griffith/DeMille lineage, that it's poorly replicating the syntax of regular cinema, only obscures it. Understanding it as a completely different kind of artifact—as a film potentially made by someone who did not know what "making a film" involved, and never learned—helps. Even if, ultimately, nothing can fully explain that artifact.

A DISAPPOINTING
LACK OF MAYHEM:
ATTACK OF THE 50 FT. WOMAN

DESPITE THE FAME OF its premise, the delight of its poster, and the juiciness of its scenario, *Attack of the 50 Ft. Woman* (1958) disappoints. Ordinarily this conclusion would be enough; a critic who writes such a sentence should perhaps move on to consider some other, less disappointing film, but I cannot. Nathan Juran's giantess story sticks, a burr on my cuff, nagging me either to excuse its flaws or to like it better. I refuse to do either. The closer I look at *50 Ft. Woman*, the more flaws I find, and the less excusable I find them.

Why does *this* movie have to be so awful? A lot of bad monster fare was turned out in the 1950s, and a nonzero amount of it made the human into the monster (*The Amazing Colossal Man* or *I Was a Teenage Werewolf*, both 1957), but this one makes a *woman* into a monster without making her appearance monstrous. It hands her the power to destroy, reversing the pattern in which male-gendered monsters repeatedly destroy women's bodies. It offers a premise in which a woman is a walking fetish, but she's also remarkably empowered. And then it takes her offscreen for half the film and gives her a measly nine minutes of rampage. This should be a feminist fantasy, and instead it's a misogynist dud.

Attack of the 50 Ft. Woman is mishandled in almost every detail. The plot is so thin it can hardly buoy 65 minutes: a woman sees a UFO in the desert while her husband and his girlfriend plot to seize her riches; later, she grows unnaturally tall and kills both of them. Aside from certain miniatures that pass muster, the special effects are noticeably inferior. The sets are few and minimal, which makes the movie feel claustrophobic, like a TV play. The characters are unlikable and underdeveloped: Nancy Fowler Archer, at normal size, is an unstable, alcoholic harridan. Her husband, Harry, is a dishonest, cowardly womanizer. The object of

Harry's extramarital affection, Honey Parker, is an oversexed, murderous gold-digger. The acting is either hysterical (Allison Hayes as Nancy), flat (William Hudson as Harry), or one-note (Yvette Vickers as Honey). Even the focus puller comes off looking bad. It's incompetent material made worse by incompetent execution.

So what? Why not toss *50 Ft. Woman* on the same junk heap as dozens of other forgotten drive-in flicks? Why kick it around for analysis at all if it's so impossible to redeem?

Because missed opportunities are always more interesting than simple successes or failures. *Attack of the 50 Ft. Woman* manages to oppose the feminism that's baked into its very premise—a missed opportunity rather rare among 1950s monster movies. Particularly in light of a 1993 remake that, despite being a minor film, uses this premise more effectively than the source material, the forces that drag *50 Ft. Woman* down into ignominy prove worthy of study.

1. PSYCHOLOGY

Nancy and Harry suffer from insufficient dimensions, but the psychology of their failed marriage matters to the movie's problems. Nancy is bitter because Harry cheats, and because it's starting to sink in that he married her not because he loves her, but for her fortune ($50 million,[1] a staggering amount of money in 1958. "A man can ignore one million dollars," snipes an unkind voice in Nancy's mind, "but fifty! That's too much to ask"). Harry is greedy and lazy, among his other imperfections. He schemes vaguely to get Nancy's money away from her, but when Honey suggests that Nancy's death is the simplest way to make that happen, he balks at taking any action.

The dynamic in the marriage includes, in the subtext, Harry feeling emasculated because of Nancy's money. The glimpse we get of Harry indicates that he wouldn't exactly be out there a-toiling if that money didn't exist, but it's still a source of shame for a 1950s man to be kept, instead of to provide. He acts out under this shame: drinking too much, lying to Nancy's caretakers, latching on to a floozy who makes him feel like a man. With these actions, he's rebelling, childishly, against the control he perceives Nancy as having because she has the money.

Nancy doesn't seem to care much about why Harry acts this way, or who has the power in the relationship. She just wants to be loved. The movie sets her up as pathetically desperate for Harry's affection and attention, and to dull the pain of his rejection, she drinks a worrying amount of alcohol. She has minimal control over her emotions—she cries, she yells, she throws things, she swings wildly from one mood to another.

This husband and wife make each other miserable. I can invent a history between them where Nancy was a sheltered rich girl, Harry showed her how to have fun, and years later, the fun has dried up but the liquor keeps flowing. (Nancy's butler, Jess, has abiding affection for her, which indicates she wasn't always such a

---

1 Is it coincidence that 50 is the number of her millions and of her eventual height? Probably, given the minds at play here, but perhaps not.

mess.) Harry is clearly the worse human being, as he's venal and mendacious, but Nancy comes off as an immature shrew, lashing out at everyone around her when she can't get her needs met. I want to invest emotionally in the dynamic between them, but there's no richness to their on-screen interaction (aside from what I'm inventing in this paragraph), just unpleasantness. Neither of them makes a good protagonist, although Nancy comes closer to having our sympathy. That's why it's so curious that the film fails to make her a genuine protagonist, since no one else deserves the slot, either.

2. SUBJECT

It's unfortunately common in the classical period for films to make women protagonists without granting them subjectivity. They are maintained as objects in the audience's gaze instead, objects of ridicule or revulsion or desire. (This happens to Joan Crawford in the 1950s a lot, but the lovely noir *Laura* [1944] is perhaps the most extraordinary example.) Nancy Archer is no exception, whether normal-sized or fifty feet tall. She is ridiculous in her hysteria, repulsive in her drunkenness, and desirable in her clingy black dress—and all three when she's tall enough to squash any man in town. But the subject of her own life? Not really.

Women in genre movies of the era are often subjected to egregiously sexist writing. In *Cat-Women of the Moon* (1953), the first thing a woman astronaut does when she comes out of space-sleep is not attend to her duties, eat, or speak to the others, but pull out her compact and apply lipstick. In *Dinosaurus!* (1960), Kristina Hanson's Betty is subject to numerous scripted indignities, including being made to faint from surprise while underwater and a "funny" scene about a caveman wanting to rape her. In countless drive-in flicks, women scream and cower helplessly when monsters approach or men fight with each other, taking no active role in any conflict. There are exceptions—Peggie Castle's sassy reporter in *The Beginning of the End* (1957), for example—but they prove the rule.

ATTACK OF THE 50 FT. WOMAN/ALLIED ARTISTS PICTURES

So a woman protagonist in a 1950s genre film is bound to be written with confusion, dually hamstrung by objectification and sexism. The premise of *50 Ft. Woman* offers agency to Nancy that the screenwriters can't deliver, and instead of resolving this issue in a feminist way, the film repeatedly shuts down her sentience. That is, they can't figure out what she should do, so she doesn't do anything. She is offscreen for a large part of the picture, sedated and then chained up in her bedroom after her alien encounter. The film restricts her destructive motivations to her husband, despite the wealth of interesting things she could either do or wreck once she's fifty feet tall.

Every time the film starts to favor her point of view, her mood shifts so radically that we lose touch with her perspective. Even her introduction does not appeal: she opens the film proper by losing control of her car and screaming wildly, her face grotesque with terror. When policemen disbelieve her account of the UFO, we should sympathize with her indignation, because we saw it too, but she defends herself with paranoia and hysteria, and we recoil. Later, when a broadcast criticizes her life too specifically to be anything but a hallucination, she throws a bottle and destroys the television, an expensive tantrum in 1958. Who could relate to such a rich, loud, erratic woman?

In keeping Nancy from true subjectivity, the film maintains a distance between her and the viewer, and this is part of what drains Nancy's rampage of its pleasure for the audience. Maybe we could enjoy her destruction more if we believed she was seizing the control she had been denied or revenging herself upon Honey and Harry. But the film hasn't seriously invested in her point of view. That means, when she grows big enough to tear her own roof off, we don't know whether to be alarmed about a monster or excited about a superhero.

3. POWER

Perhaps the filmmakers themselves could not decide which tack to take. A fifty-foot-tall woman, a woman who dwarfs even the tallest and strongest of men, implies enormous power. During a decade of nationwide, pathological sexual repression, such a woman triggers fears and desires that likely inspired as well as confused the men who dreamed her up.

As demonstrated above, the film does everything possible to make Nancy a difficult personality, to keep us from liking her too much. It also gives her power twice over—in her wealth, and then in her size. These choices can only be connected. No woman with power is a nice woman, a likable or relatable woman. And so, the film thwarts, minimizes, and shunts Nancy's power at every opportunity. It makes her unstable and dependent, drugs her heavily, physically restrains her, and ultimately kills her off. She's the richest woman in town, but she dresses cheaply (for the era), in striped capri pants, big gold earrings, and highlighted hair, which repels the "respectable" viewer. Instead of demonstrating her wealth with understated elegance (in cashmere and pearls, for instance), she wears a diamond pendant so large it's vulgar. Her reputation is bad; the policemen she approaches about the UFO she sees in the desert take her only as seriously as her money forces them to. "Poor mixed-up Mrs. Archer," the sheriff says.

None of this works to keep Nancy in check: her emotions and her body won't be contained. The audience can only wait in anxiety (and, for some, fetishistic excitement) to see what she does with her power.

Not much, is the truth. The failure of *50 Ft. Woman*, most notably in its conclusion, is a failure of imagination. On her nine-minute rampage, Nancy meanders into town, wrecks a hotel room, destroys the only bar (killing Honey with a roof beam), and collects Harry. Then the sheriff shoots out what appears to be a telephone switching station at her eye level, and, as she dies, she accidentally (?) squeezes Harry to death. Hardly the mayhem promised by the poster, which shows Nancy crouched over a busy freeway overpass, a car in her hand, tiny men fleeing her grasping red fingernails. Surely the budget did not allow for big-city mayhem, moving cars and complex overlays and so on, but why not build additional static models? Why didn't they let Nancy smash through a scale version of town, throwing scale cars and kicking scale neon signs? Was that a budget limitation, or was that discomfort with what she could really do with the size and strength she's given?

Allison Hayes does her best to invest Nancy with appropriate fury and confidence during these scenes. Gone is her earlier hysteria and melodrama; as she lifts a kicking Harry out of the wrecked bar, her nostrils flare and her eyes narrow, showing all the emotion we need. But she calls out for Harry again and again, seeming, as she has all along, to *want* him, not to want him dead. Even at a monstrous size, even with enormous power and driving anger, all of her motivation is tied up in the mean slob she's married, the one who grabs a gun and shoots at her enormous hand reaching through the bar's doors for him.

This is not relatable and it's not especially satisfying. We don't sympathize with Nancy's desire for Harry, nor with Harry's violence and cowardice, so the scene gives us a showy physical conflict in which we root for no one. There's no levity here, either, as Nancy's desire is equal parts dangerous and pathetic.

These scenes also aren't particularly well-shot. Nancy's face is often in shadow or she's walking away from the camera at an angle that doesn't give us much. Either Nathan Juran did not know enough technical tricks to make the scale look good, or these scenes were shot with unusual carelessness for the big finish of a monster movie. Where the monster happens to be a woman.

4. MONSTER

In other monster movies, the big destructive rampage that closes the film is often more fun than worrisome, thrilling but not scary. Think of Godzilla in his first film: it's not that we *want* him to destroy mini-Tokyo, but most of the characters to whom we have any meaningful attachment are far away from the monster himself, working on the problem he presents in distant, safe laboratories. However, Godzilla is not a human monster, and his destruction derives from animal instincts, not the wish to be loved by his spouse. Nancy is a more complicated monster than the filmmakers seem to want her to be for their finale to fit the pattern of similar movies.

That's why her rampage isn't a lot of fun. Not only because the filmmakers don't do a lot with her in the sequence, but also because her characterization is so muddy. Maybe we want to see Nancy crash through two dozen buildings and squash the lusty deputy between her finger and thumb, but the filmmakers don't; maybe the filmmakers want to see her as powerless as possible, but they acknowledge the need for *some* kind of rampage. The result, which should be terrific, never quite lifts off. A turn of events so off-kilter is the price of failing to give women characters subjectivity.

Nancy not only lacks subjectivity, she also can't rightly be called the hero of the piece. No male character steps in for the role, either. Harry is clearly a negative force, not only by our modern standards (additionally offended, for the record, by Nancy's paternalistic doctors and how Nancy herself is written), but by 1950s standards as well. He fools around with Honey in plain view of anyone who enters the town's only watering hole, and he spends his wife's money on booze. But the real death knell for his likability comes when he drives Nancy to the desert and they locate the UFO. When a giant (alien) man appears, he gets in the car and drives away, leaving Nancy screaming for help. Such cowardice is totally unacceptable in a man of the era. Harry can never be the hero of this film.

Without Harry as a hero, and without Nancy as a heroine, the film has an empty spot for its protagonist. Thus, its stance is equivocal. Often, low-budget genre movies contain weak moral summations, closing out the mayhem with a lesson about the dangers of radiation or medical experimentation delivered by a positive character. *Attack of the 50 Ft. Woman*'s last line is "She finally got Harry all to herself," delivered by the doctor who has made so many bad decisions on Nancy's behalf. Not much of a lesson, and an oddly inaccurate statement, as both

she and Harry are dead. Perhaps the moral is for men not to cheat on their wives, but that has nothing to do with the UFO that caused Nancy's growth. The line betrays how little this film resembles other monster movies, and how illogical its stance is.

An *un*equivocal stance would be to treat the woman as a destroyer, a devourer—an utter antagonist. But for that line of flight to have any lift to it, the man opposite the destroyer would have to be a slightly worthy human being. Nope. Another stance could be a sneakily feminist one, in which Nancy takes back the power she's been denied and then some. But then her behavior wouldn't be so erratic when she's still normal-sized, and she wouldn't be so fixated on Harry once she's tall. The film does not nail down its attitude toward its characters or events, which makes it less a story than a disorganized batch of events. Again, the filmmakers' inability to write Nancy as a subject or a protagonist is the biggest reason for this disorder, and for our disappointment in the final product.

5. SPACE

"Women and girls are so often told, in ways both obvious and insidious, that we are not supposed to take up too much space," Hannah Walhout writes, in a terrific essay for Catapult that folds *50 Ft. Woman* into her contemplation of female tallness. Nancy is large even before she's physically so—her body is too well-displayed, her voice too loud, especially to all the doubting, suppressing men around her. It's a shame the script of *Attack of the 50 Ft. Woman* couldn't give her even more space than it did.

The 1993 remake of the same name corrects this error to some degree, more capably building a metaphor about how difficult yet empowering it is to take up space as a woman. Nancy (Daryl Hannah) is still overly attached to her sleazy husband (Daniel Baldwin), and she's still got more money than self-determination. Other weaknesses involve too-topical references, the limited resources of a made-for-TV movie, and the stylistic absurdity that saturated early 1990s genre filmmaking (thanks, Tim Burton). But the movie, directed by Christopher Guest and released by HBO long before it became a prestige content hub, does a lot more with its premise than the original. Nancy is enormous for much more of the running time and the special effects around her are better. The script has a keen if dated sense of humor, and it showcases silly gimmicks without relying on them. Some pastiche of 1950s monster movies occurs, along with many callbacks to the source film. The sense that this is someone's fetish made into film is stronger, and yet the inherent feminism of the premise gets a full airing. When men treat Nancy badly, the film calls it out as harmful. Her size increases as her anger does—appropriate, since angry women are as socially acceptable as tall women. In general, the remake fashions this story into the feminist fantasy it should rightly be.

Further, once Nancy gets used to being big, she gains a confidence she never had as a normal-sized woman. Her interest in making her life what she wants it to be is appealing, and far more meaningful than the previous Nancy's vague, husband-related motivation. "I'm not saying the old Nancy still isn't in me," she explains to her doctor. "I can hear her inside, rattling around in the dark, bumping into things, always apologizing. But less and less." She turns her attention back to the spool of cable in her hand. "Less and less."

ON THE FILMS OF NEIL BREEN

IN THIS SPACE SHOULD be a detailed essay unpacking the fascinating films of the self-taught, financially independent director Neil Breen. However, Breen threatens litigation on anyone who so much as talks about his films on YouTube without contacting him first, so I have chosen not to write or publish this essay to save myself from legal entanglements. Ask me about him in person and we can talk for hours. My favorite is *Fateful Findings* (2012).

DUAL PLOTS, DEMON POSSESION, DE PALMA:

RUBY AS INTERESTING FAILURE

RUBY (1977) DRIPS ANACHRONISM, emits confusion, and refuses to resolve so stubbornly that it ends up with appeal. At first, it seems to be an embarrassing failure, but looking closer, it's an interesting one. On the surface, standard bad-film problems abound: the sets look motel-cheap, the special effects are poor, and the majority of the lighting is dead flat, all to the detriment of the film's atmosphere. Although the film is set in 1951, the actors wear long pointed collars and floppy hair, courtesy of 1977. The screenplay makes acrobatic leaps in logic, some casting choices are bad, and multiple characters slot easily into cliché.

Down a layer or two, *Ruby* makes for an unusual case study in bad film. Unraveling its special badness is harder than it looks. Piper Laurie acts with as much extremity here as in the prior year's *Carrie*, but just as in that film, her exaggeration works extremely well for the character. Centrally, the plot is really two plots, smashed together like colliding trains. In the wreckage is a mess of a movie, but one that has ineffable pleasure embedded in the viewing experience.

1. DUAL

At the macro level, I know exactly why *Ruby* doesn't work. It's clearer every time I watch it: those two plots. One of them is a gangster movie about Ruby Claire, and the other is a demon movie about her daughter Leslie. I don't really know if, with some movie, someday, you could mix these two genres successfully. The demon movie trend of the mid-1970s required the spirituality crisis the nation was undergoing at the time to cohere, while the fast-'n'-sleazy type of gangster movie *Ruby* imitated had been out of fashion for decades. Plus, the gritty realism of one genre clashes with the supernaturality of the other, so you'd have to tap-

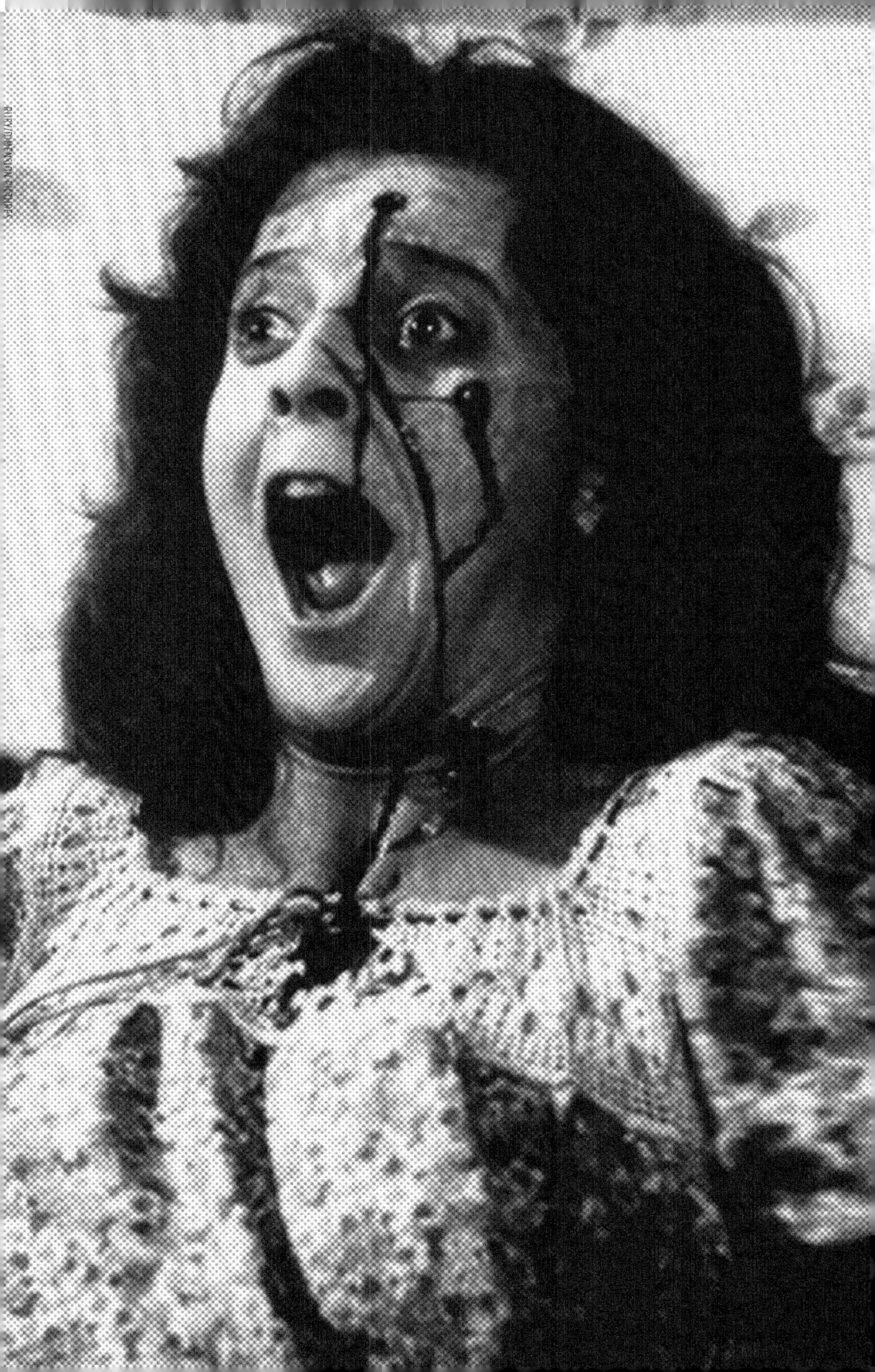

dance pretty fast to combine them well. *Ruby* is not the movie to pull this off.

In the gangster movie, Ruby Claire, moll to gangleader Jake Miller, falls in love with Nicky, an ambitious young gang member, and becomes pregnant by him. Ruby's true loyalties are perhaps unclear to both Nicky and Jake. The rest of the gang kills Nicky on the night Ruby gives birth to her daughter, Leslie. This occurs in 1935. Sixteen years later, Ruby runs a drive-in movie theater, where all the members of the gang involved in Nicky's murder are employees, except Jake, who is blind and wheelchair-bound.

In the demon movie, Nicky haunts the drive-in, possesses Leslie (who is a standard-issue Creepy Girl with Vague Powers), and horribly kills the former gang members one by one. A parapsychologist comes to the drive-in to help solve the murders and figure out what's going on with Leslie. At the end, Ruby, who has never really let go of her old love, willingly walks into the swamp with Nicky's ghost, bound to him rather than to her daughter and her present-day life.

Both of these movies are *Ruby*, and as the two paragraphs above indicate, no summary is complete without both plots. But since the two plots follow different genre conventions, the viewing experience is unsettled, even unpredictable. Although neither movie is especially imaginative within its genre, pushing them together discombobulates the viewer enough that she cannot be quite sure what'll happen next. Even Piper Laurie noticed this, in her memoir: "It was a strange script, with a couple of genuinely original scenes."

My initial guess about *Ruby* and its weird dual storyline was that some producer had found two weak screenplays and decided to combine them into one. *We've got this ghost story, but it's a little too thin and obviously imitative of* The Exorcist. *We've got this gangster movie, but it doesn't really have a story beyond the first half-hour. Hey, let's shove 'em together, that'll make 90 minutes.*

I was wrong. Or at least I could not find any evidence that I was right. The screenplay was written by George Edwards, a frequent professional partner of director Curtis Harrington's, from a story by Steve Krantz. I could not determine the contributions of the other credited writer, Barry Schneider (whose illustrious screenwriting resume includes *Roller Boogie* and *Cocaine: One Man's Seduction*). I also couldn't determine how much the screenplay had changed across the process of filmmaking.

Harrington's posthumously published memoir, *Nice Guys Don't Work in Hollywood*, offers just three pages about *Ruby*, and a good half of that word count is complaint about Krantz, who produced. He explains: "George Edwards...had a script about an ex-gangster's moll who runs a drive-in movie theater and is possessed by the spirit of her dead father." This wording may indicate that Edwards's original screenplay was about Leslie running the drive-in, not Ruby, which hints at big changes between conception and execution. (Perhaps it's just badly worded—the book was published after Harrington died. An editor might have received more clarity from an author who could respond to notes.) Harrington admits that the screenplay "was indebted to *The Exorcist*, which was quite a hit at the time." Maybe Edwards had written the gangster parts in haste to fill out a script that copied *Exorcist* too closely, or maybe the possession bits weren't as unoriginal in the screenplay as they ended up being in the finished film. It's not clear. But the screenplay certainly wasn't a Frankenstein of two distinct ideas; rather, it was poorly conceived.

2. OVERLAP

The problem I have in writing about *Ruby* is where to begin: with what's good, with what's bad, or with what's mysterious. The first two categories overlap a lot. *Ruby* manages to fold good into bad and vice versa so thoroughly that it's a difficult film to assess. Thus, an interesting failure, my favorite kind of bad movie.

Piper Laurie's performance is technically, perhaps, bad, but she throws herself into it with the abandon of a woman in Hollywood over 40 and the skill of an actress at the height of her powers. She's over the top in a way that the role demands, to a result that's extremely pleasurable for the audience. Ruby is a loud, drunken, melodramatic tornado of a character, and if Laurie had toned her performance down even a micron, the character would not have worked.

Stewart Whitman is miscast as Vince. The character is rough-edged and pretty dumb, and Whitman emits thoughtful and kind. But that means he and his character fade into the landscape a little, leaving more room for Laurie, Roger Davis (unnerving as parapsychologist Dr. Keller), and the sound design (spooky electronic noise and instrumental variations on Ruby's one hit song, "Love's So Easy").

The story has poeticism in it, especially in its Gothic conclusion—Ruby trance-walking into the swamp, compelled by a ghost to abandon her life altogether, has some actual gravitas (good). But it's ruined by the final two tacked-on shots, filmed by the execrable Krantz for about three dollars, showing a fake Laurie being drowned by a fake skeleton (bad).

Leslie is a pretty clichéd character, but that's good inasmuch as we know what to expect from her. Moments in which the film tests suspension of disbelief (when Ruby bonks Leslie on the head with a wooden mallet that belongs in a Wile E. Coyote cartoon, not in Ruby's attic; the sheer amount of red apparel Ruby wears) also traffic in camp, and wind up being delightful rather than cringeworthy.

Dismissing a film like *Ruby* doesn't tell us nearly as much as parsing out what's wrong with it and what's good about it. All the more tantalizing a task when one element of a film can fall into both categories.

3. DE PALMA

As for what's mysterious about *Ruby*—aside from how the patched-together screenplay came to exist, there is plenty. One mystery, which got weirder the more I considered it, is how Brian De Palma connects to the film.

Piper Laurie is the most obvious node. Before De Palma's *Carrie*, she hadn't made a movie in 15 years, and then in two movies within two years, she played a nutty mom to a teenaged daughter with paranormal powers. Apparently, this was coincidence. Harrington writes that her casting had nothing to do with *Carrie*, and in her own memoir, *Learning to Live Out Loud*, Laurie indicates that the first screening of *Carrie* occurred while she was already shooting *Ruby*. But it was De Palma who coaxed her back into film, and Harrington who seized on her immediately afterward.

Then there's *The Fury* (1978), also directed by De Palma, a bloody, tightly made film about the paranormal, in which a sinister John Cassavetes seizes control over two teenagers with strong psychic powers. His relationship with Amy Irving's character in that movie resembles Dr. Keller's with Leslie, such that I felt sure *Ruby* was cribbing from *The Fury* before I looked again at their release dates.

Janit Baldwin, although *Ruby*'s credits claim to "introduce" her, had a small part in De Palma's *Phantom of the Paradise* (1974).

RUBY/DIMENSION PICTURES

Strangest of all, some wardrobe from *Phantom* made its way into *Ruby*. Around minute 16, a pair of tough characters are passing by at the drive-in, and one of them half-turns his back, showing that his denim vest is patched with the distinctive Death Records logo. Bodyguards are shown wearing vests like it in *Phantom*. *Ruby* was an independent production, so perhaps the costumer bought or rented some back stock from Fox. Perhaps the guy was an extra in both films and kept his costume from *Phantom*. Perhaps the vest ended up in a thrift store and the *Ruby* costumer bought it there. The vest could have gone from one production to the other in any number of ways, but it's a head-snapping coincidence nonetheless.

4. ANACHRONISM

The fact that a vest from a movie made and set in 1974 appears in a movie made in 1977 and set in 1951 is only a fraction of the anachronism that plagues *Ruby*. My research couldn't uncover Edwards's motivations for writing a period piece, but the mid-70s teemed with 1950s nostalgia: *American Graffiti* (1973) and *Happy Days* (1974-84), *Grease* (1978), *Come Back to the 5 & Dime, Jimmy Dean, Jimmy Dean* (stage drama, 1976). Given the (unfashionable) 1930s gangster ideas that set *Ruby*'s story in motion, it's possible Edwards wasn't trying to capitalize on this trend at all, but had instead written the screenplay out of his own private nostalgia.

In any event, the movie is unsuccessful as a period piece. No one in the 1950s wore their hair like Ruby does, or like Stuart Whitman does. The clothes are badly and closely cut, a hallmark of 1970s polyester blends. Leslie's clothes and hair are entirely wrong for young people in 1951. Although the word was created in the late 19th century, "parapsychology" was a fringe idea until the early 1970s, and it's doubtful that Vince could have met a parapsychologist by chance, particularly one working at a prison (for some reason). A small budget explains the visual anachronisms, and a hasty screenplay explains the logical ones. But it also seems like the decision-makers on this production didn't really *try* to get the period details right.

The repeated inclusion of scenes from *Attack of the 50 Ft. Woman* (1958), playing at Ruby's drive-in, is a glaring problem in this regard. The movie is seven years away from release when *Ruby* takes place. I can't figure out why Harrington chose this movie above all others; to move forward despite that seven-year error, he must have had a good reason. It escapes me.

Ruby attempts to be metatextual, given its setting at a drive-in and given that, as Harrington notes in a DVD special feature, "this film was designed to a certain extent to be a drive-in movie." Hence, *50 Ft. Woman* should have some special resonance to the plot of the film. I'm not sure it does.[1] Murky ideas about women as unstable, predatory forces do swirl around in both films, and the monster in *50 Ft. Woman* is human, not animal or insect, as in many other 1950s genre films. It's also perhaps more instantly recognizable than any other monster movie of its day. None of this overcomes the mistake of its appearance in 1951; none of these are good enough reasons for it to appear in *Ruby*. As far as any thematic connection between the films goes, another, correctly contemporary monster movie would likely have sufficed.

Further, there's the predictive anachronism of the Keller/Leslie relationship. When I first became fascinated with *Ruby*, I thought the dynamic between Dr. Keller and Leslie had been copied from other movies. I had seen films and read books where a male scientist becomes fixated on a girl or a young woman with psychic powers of some kind. It seemed like a mini-trend of the late 70s and early 80s, films and books with this idea.

I had remembered things in the wrong order. Leslie's behavior (and especially her possession-voice) are influenced by *The Exorcist* (1973), but the works I'd been remembering with similar man/girl relationships were *The Fury* (film, 1978) and *Firestarter* (book, 1980). *The Fury* was a book first, but it came out in 1976, too late to influence Edwards's screenplay. *Carrie* (book 1974, movie 1976) was an influence generally on the weird-supernatural-girl minigenre, but Harrington specifies that "*Ruby* had been written long before that film's release."

Dr. Keller's somewhat creepy attentions to Leslie during the third act echo Fathers Karras and Merrin in *The Exorcist* as they tend to Regan. But Keller's expertise is not religious. His interest in Leslie reads as scientific, closer to the threatening, exploitive figures in *Fury* and *Firestarter*. The Fathers do not have any of that for Regan.

What baffles me is how *Ruby* could have been *first* among these films. The pattern of behavior Keller and Leslie display feels prescribed, as if it's been done in a jillion movies already. The scene when he wets her brow with a washcloth, saying "You've got to fight it, Leslie," is so familiar I can barely watch it. How could it have come first? And how could these later films, far more prominent, have been influenced by dinky little *Ruby*, which did well at drive-ins but otherwise sank without a trace beneath 1977's turbulent cinematic seascape?

---

1   Given that I studied *50 Ft. Woman* enough to write an essay about it, included right here in this book, I feel like I'd know if the connection made sense.

The likeliest answer is that pesky Something In The Air effect, which explains the two Prefontaine movies in 1997-98, the two Mars movies in 2000, and the various Florence Foster Jenkins movies in 2016. It's not satisfactory, but it's an answer.

5. RESOLVE

Along with its mixed ones, the film does have a few genuinely good qualities. Before Leslie discovers Louie's corpse, when she's gently touching plants in the foreground and the body is spiked in a tree in the background, Harrington has made a decent horror tableau. The incestuous scene in the attic, when Nicky, possessing Leslie, dances with Ruby, probably lands differently depending on the viewer, but I find it perversely well-made. Ruby's behavior, obsessing over Nicky and swanning drunkenly about her home like a tarted-up Miss Havisham, is both

RUBY/DIMENSION PICTURES

campy and riveting. Although Dr. Keller is generally out of place as a character, Roger Davis makes the most of his odd role. The bits of *Ruby* that lean toward ghost story, rather than demon story, are generally decent—Nicky haunting Ruby's nights, in dreams and out of them; Ruby and Vince guessing at Nicky's motivation; the ease with which Ruby chooses Nicky's ghost over anyone living.

Of course, none of this is enough. *Ruby* still fails.

I can look at the film and consider what I'd've done to make it succeed. Remove the whole Dr. Keller angle; make the murders significantly less bloody; focus more on how Ruby hasn't moved on from Nicky— less on her rage and more on her sorrow. Give it all *mood*, not fake blood and lightning strikes. Figure out a thematic connection to *50 Ft. Woman* and play it up.

Yet the silly, lurid half of *Ruby* is enjoyable, too. Maybe I'd remove all the mood and the poetic parts and stick with the *Exorcist* rip-off destined for the drive-in. Draw out the possession much longer. Show Leslie committing murders herself rather than giving that task to Nicky's ghost. Develop an actual antagonism between Nicky and Keller rather than just one confusing line ("Vince is next, Keller!"). Make it a hackfest. Buckets of gore tossed at the drive-in screen.

But that would not fall in with *Ruby*'s hazy, in-between properties—the ones that made it stick in my head in the first place. Either choice to fix the film would make it one thing, easy to pin down and categorize, easy to forget. *Ruby*'s flaws are egregious, but it is not a forgettable film. Its conflicting priorities and the tension they cause make it memorable, at the same time as they make it suck.

There is no way to resolve this, the issue of *Ruby*'s major flaws so often being its major advantages. Combining its two stories proved impossible for the filmmakers, and determining for certain what is a feature and what is a bug has proved equally impossible for this critic. The only sure thing is how interesting *Ruby* is as a failed film, how the merged columns of its flaws and features make it intriguing.

FUCK YOU, COME FUCK ME:

SOCIOPATHY IN *SHOWGIRLS* AND *STAYING ALIVE*

PRE-SHOW: THE LIMITS OF THIS ESSAY

The target for this essay is extremely narrow: a compare/contrast job on two dance movies, and the single unusual issue that sinks them both, like a torpedo plunging through two boats. *Staying Alive* (1983) and *Showgirls* (1995) have the same central problem, and I want to write about how that problem makes the movies bad—makes watching them a slippery, exasperating experience. In my research I discovered that keeping that slim little target in mind would mean discarding a tremendous amount of thinking and theorizing. *Showgirls* is a rare piece of art, one with enough openings (ahem) for analysis and interpretation that I could go on for days. It is, in the phrasing of its main character, bottomless. I'm writing this paragraph so I don't write an entire separate essay in the footnotes of this one.

For better or worse, *Staying Alive* has garnered relatively little critical attention compared to *Showgirls*. Yet the two movies echo each other to a surprising degree. Both are dance-centered movies involving a scrappy protagonist's unlikely elevation to the star of the show; both protagonists are determined to rise on their own merits, not via favoritism; and in both films, antagonists' moods shift wildly from purring to clawing for no evident reason. Other similar elements are the haphazard plot progression, the mediocrity of the featured dance and music, and the protagonist's one-track focus on *this* kind of dance as the only way they can or want to shine. For whatever reason, both films feature S&M-themed dance sequences. And both films are firmly fixed by the glaring, unblinking male gaze.

The torpedo, though—the single issue that causes both films to fail—is that

most of the speaking characters in both films, save one major supporting figure in each, act like sociopaths. The protagonists and antagonists both major and minor, the dance shows' directors and producers, several of the dancers: they all demonstrate labile mood, profound self-interest, lying for no reason, lack of empathy, and enjoyment of mind games. Much of the reason for this is in the writing: Sylvester Stallone co-wrote the script of *Staying Alive* (and directed the film), while Joe Eszterhas, King Shit of Erotic Thriller Mountain, penned *Showgirls*. As writers, both men tend to create types rather than three-dimensional characters, and tend to be constrained by one kind of story.

PLAYBILL: SUMMARY

Staying Alive is nominally a sequel to the fascinating zeitgeist film *Saturday Night Fever* (1977). That film functions like a character study for Tony Manero (John Travolta), a 19-year-old with no direction. Nights, he goes to the 2001 Odyssey, a disco club, where he holds court as a supreme dancer. Days, he works in a paint store and fools around with his violent, immature friends. Six years later, *Staying Alive* finds Tony in Manhattan, trying to build a career as a Broadway dancer, teaching dance classes and auditioning to no avail. He has a relationship

STAYING ALIVE/PARAMOUNT PICTURES

with a fellow dancer, Jackie (Cynthia Rhodes), that she would likely describe as boyfriend/girlfriend, but he would say it's complicated. One night, Tony meets a star dancer, Laura (Finola Hughes) and she tangles him up in her life. Laura gets him a part in her new show, *Satan's Alley*; she does a Central Park montage date with him and then sleeps with him; she rejects him and yells at him, then talks sweet to him. So it goes for the remainder of the movie. Tony manages to push the lead male dancer in *Satan's Alley* out of the way and takes the part himself, and the show, the worst and funniest "Broadway show" ever to go on film, is the set piece that closes the movie.

A handful of elements carry over from *Saturday Night Fever* to *Staying Alive*, but the two films are radically different in tone and purpose. Tony is the same, but his context has shifted, changing how the audience receives him. Both films have Bee Gees songs, but everyone knows "Night Fever" while no one knows "Someone Belonging to Someone," with good reason. The urge to dance is the same, but dance in *Fever* is social, tribal, allegorical, while dance in *Alive* is largely spectacle. The serious issues in *Fever* have dissipated, leaving behind only sweat.

Showgirls, meanwhile, is *All About Eve* on a stripper pole. Nomi Malone (Elizabeth Berkley), a young woman with a troubled past, takes Las Vegas by storm, starting out "dancing" at a seedy strip club and ending up the star "dancer" of *Goddess*, the classiest nude show in town. Her adventures include impossibly athletic sex with Zack (Kyle MacLachlan), first simulated and then real; developing a sexy-frenemy vibe with the established star of *Goddess*, Cristal (Gina Gershon), before pushing her down a set of stairs; and throwing ketchup on fries so hard it splatters two feet above the table.

It's a rich, challenging film, unpleasant in many ways, easy to dismiss as utter trash but layered enough to intrigue after a dozen watches. Its director, Paul Verhoeven, has tremendous skill with satirizing American culture—enough skill that his work often passes as straightfaced and is thus panned. His films about violence (*Total Recall*, *RoboCop*) have been lauded and influential, while *Showgirls*, about sex, is a national joke. Often, Verhoeven's films contain heightened energy on a wavelength I'd describe as *hysterical*. He uses bright colors, fast cuts, and actor performance to evoke this feeling. *Showgirls* is extremely hysterical, in too many ways to delineate here, but particularly in Berkley's performance.

Berkley's role, Nomi, is a deeply strange one. But then, virtually no one in *Showgirls* acts normally, and hardly anyone in *Staying Alive* does either.

ACT I: SUPPORTING CHARACTERS

In *Staying Alive*, the only normal person is Jackie, a kind, talented doormat for the main character, Tony. In *Showgirls*, the only normal person is Molly (Gina Ravera), a kind, talented doormat for the main character, Nomi. In both films, the protagonists alternately abuse and declare their appreciation for their doormats, chasing the approval of other characters with more power or appeal while using all the resources the doormats can provide, whether emotional (love and support) or physical (in Jackie, dance ability and sex; in Molly, a place to live and skill with a sewing machine). Multiple secondary characters in the films do not act like normal people, but I'll stick to just a few of them, especially in *Showgirls*, which has a surprising number of sociopaths in the secondary cast.

Obvious antagonists in the films, like Andrew Carver (William Shockley), have understandably bad behavior. But Laura is both antagonist and object of desire, and *Staying Alive* can't quite decide its stance on her, whether to set her up as a villainous match for Tony—as a full character—or to maintain her as an uncharacterized target of lust. Thus, she acts with total inconsistency, sometimes glowing with sweetness and other times indifferent, hostile, or even violent.

Similarly, Cristal acts both as an ally and an enemy. The film sometimes makes her a clichéd bitch of the Joan Crawford mold, and other times admires or humanizes her. Cristal gets Nomi into *Goddess*, offers to help her with the routine, buys her lunch, opens up about her secrets, and compliments Nomi's nails (ally). She even forgives Nomi for causing a career-ending injury. However, Cristal also humiliates Nomi repeatedly, at the Cheetah and the Stardust, in public and private (enemy). She can't seem to choose a single way to treat Nomi, whether to sleep with her, mentor her, or bully her into serious harm. It's never clear whether her attempts to seduce Nomi are serious or an elaborate series of tests, but that inconsistency reads as poor characterization, not poor acting.

She and others act from the wellspring of the screenwriter's convenience, rather than with the consistency of well-realized characters. Zack sometimes shows kindness to Nomi, and sometimes betrays his helplessness to her wiles, but certain scenes show him to be sleazy and cruel underneath. The only consistency to his character is self-interest. Nearly all of the characters in *Showgirls* are hollow creatures, motivated largely by greed and sex, and whether they speak  words of kindness or cruelty is dictated by story beats, not by who they are. And just to ward this off: the underlying point is not that we as people contain multitudes and inconsistencies, but that Eszterhas rarely writes characters motivated by anything other than greed and sex.[1]

The characters of *Staying Alive* do this same back-and-forth between ally and enemy. Laura gets Tony the part in *Satan's Alley* (ally), but kicks him out of her apartment after having sex with him (enemy). She invites him to her Christmas party and speaks kindly to him when he waits at her building (ally), but lashes out when he tries to understand her feelings for him after rehearsal one day (enemy), with a speech far sillier than anything Finola Hughes ever had to say on *General Hospital*:

> Take your bloody hands off me! Don't you ever touch me again! Who do you think you're dealing with? Some little groupie that jumps when you call? Is that who you think I am? We met, I liked you, we made it. What do you think it was, true love? And you think I used you? What about you using me? Everybody uses everybody…don't they.

This speech is rushed out with maybe two or three breaths, just a huge blast of hostility and embarrassingly bad phrasing. Adding it to her prior charm and talent, Laura is at once attained and unattainable, muse and bitch. There's no aroma of the real human being about her, just a series of teases and tantrums.

Jesse (Steve Inwood), the director of *Satan's Alley*, spies weirdly on Tony and ignores him (enemy), yet gives him the ultimate chance to make it on Broadway (ally). He, too, has an absurd speech in a hallway outside the rehearsal space:

> In this business I don't have to care about you and you don't have to care about me. If you can't follow that, follow this! You wanna dance here,

---

1　Films written by Eszterhas include *Flashdance* (1983), *Basic Instinct* (1992), *Sliver* (1993), *Jade* (1995), and, coincidentally, an early Sylvester Stallone project, *F.I.S.T.* (1978). I watched several of his films for research, but the commonalities were so apparent I didn't need to watch many.

you follow my rules. It's not a democracy! You
know, you are not the greatest dancer to ever hit
Broadway. What you have is anger, and a certain
intensity, and that's what I need to make this
show work. What do you think, you're so terrific
you're gonna go out and you're gonna score
another show? Is that it? The best thing that you
ever scored in your whole life is Laura! But you
even blew that 'cause you got too heavy with her.
You're different kinds of people, and no matter
how much you carry on you're never gonna change
that! If you had half a brain in that thick skull
of yours, you'd stop worrying about trying to
change other people and start worrying about
changing yourself!

Like Laura's, this speech is a long, loud spit with little emotional variation. Jesse's insight on Tony's character has no precedent in the film—Tony is a chorus dancer and Jesse has not had a single one-on-one conversation with him. Plus, the twists and turns of the speech, along with its clichés, render it mystifying, adding to my general impression of Jesse as a device for ironing out plot issues rather than a character.

Within the first ten minutes of the film, two women at the club where Tony works as a waiter establish the incoherency of character. They treat Tony wholly as a sex object. One woman says she orders a lot of drinks because she likes to watch him walk. Another invites him to an apparent threesome and, when he declines, disdainfully says "Guys like you aren't relationships. You're exercise." The film positions these women as treating Tony disrespectfully, worse than he deserves, to present him as downtrodden before he lands the part in *Satan's Alley*. However, these women treat him no worse than he treats Jackie. An odd misogyny is at play here, in which the women are unpleasant because they pursue Tony aggressively and with explicit sexual desire, which is okay for men to do to women but not for women to do to men. Watching this film in the 21st century, I don't identify with Tony, because his reaction to them is extreme, and I don't identify with the women, because they're so plainly antagonistic. It's a sequence meant to build sympathy for the protagonist and instead it makes me like him less.

There's a lot of that in this movie, though.

ACT II: PROTAGONISTS

Staying Alive functions as if I love Tony already and don't need him to act decently to maintain that love. The credits sequence, in which an auditioning Tony refuses to blend in with a dance chorus and soloes his way into being thrown out, intends to show that Tony has talent and ambition and just needs a chance to do his thing in order to blow our minds. It ends up showing that he's an arrogant jerk who can't or won't follow directions in order to work his way to success. A sequence in which he visits a succession of agents who turn him away reads, to me, like rejection of normal proportions for an actor, but he is extremely pissy in response. His self-talk and jokes are cringey, not endearing; his hypocritical possessiveness of Jackie turns me against him (he calls to ask if she's alone in bed on the same night he's slept with another woman); and even his meet-cute with Laura makes him seem like a harassing jerk. It isn't until near the end of that scene, when the two of them mutter to themselves on opposite sides of her dressing room door, that I even realized the scene was intended to be funny, not to display how incapable Tony is of reading the room when women are in it.

In this regard, the screenplay to *Staying Alive* has done Tony a grave disservice, surrounding him with people only marginally more self-interested and unappealing than he is. Our sympathies lie with him by default, not because he has won us over. I think the idea was that we'd transfer our affection from the Tony of *Saturday Night Fever* to this Tony. Yet something significant was lost in relocating him from Brooklyn to Manhattan. It's not just that the landscape of American life was quite different in 1983 than it was in 1977—especially night life, in which disco had vanished and yuppies were ascending—but also that the character of Tony, a winner only at 2001 Odyssey and a loser everywhere else, bore a resonance that was restricted to the sociological terrarium of *Fever*. His friends were all coarser, less charismatic, and less ambitious than he was, but he didn't merely stand out by default; he shone. He could act as much like an animal as they, yet frequently *chose* not to: an instinct toward higher behavior than tribalism.

STAYING ALIVE/PARAMOUNT PICTURES

Put Tony Manero in Manhattan, though, and he shrinks. His charisma loses its glow, and his social insufficiencies become fatal. When he wears his glorious white suit to Laura's Christmas party in *Staying Alive*, its obsolescence tears through me. He was a king, a god, in that suit, and now he's out of fashion. It's one of the only moments in the film that conveys any real pathos, but, regrettably, that pathos derives from a prior film's effectiveness, not from this film's.

Showgirls has an even more knotted relationship with its protagonist. It's a film centering a woman written by a misogynist.[2] The screenplay must make Nomi appealing, it must make her a character, but Eszterhas fundamentally does not

_____

2 Proving this is a separate essay, but one does not need particularly astute scholarship to do so. Michael Nayman, in his book on *Showgirls*, quotes Rick Groen of the *Globe and Mail*: "Eszterhas's tactic of 'putting his most misogynistic remarks in the mouths of women' was 'a ruse that even Camille Paglia should see through.'" A great example in *Showgirls* is Mama Bazoom (Lin Tucci)'s "useless piece of skin" joke, unpleasant enough that I won't repeat it here.

believe that women can be complex figures of audience identification. In none of his films does the writing indicate that he sees women this way. Sometimes directors or actresses make something real out of his work, as in (parts of) *Basic Instinct*, but mostly his women are sexually rapacious bitches whose only motivation is to tease, obstruct, and harm the male character who anchors the plot.

Eszterhas knows how to write a protagonist, but does not know how to write women with enough depth to be protagonists, so Nomi makes little sense as a character. Her outline is almost a joke: an irresistibly sexy adult woman with the temperament of a toddler, a protagonist whose ambitions—with which the audience is meant to identify—rise no higher than to become the fanciest stripper in all of Las Vegas. The screenplay makes her ridiculous multiple times, such as when James and his co-worker make fun of her dancing or when she doesn't know how to pronounce Versace. The film isn't trying to engineer empathy with Nomi at these moments; it's making fun of her. This isn't subversive, nor even helpful to the job of making Nomi relatable: it's cruel, and it shows that Nomi's creator does not take her seriously. Elizabeth Berkley does, though, and the jury is out on Verhoeven. These three separate approaches add to the character's incoherence.

Via Eszterhas's conception of human behavior, Nomi is as aggressive as a man, but as unstable as a woman; as ambitious as a man, but as dumb as a woman. She has the fatally flawed backstory of a man, but it's filtered through the whorishness and deception of women. Although Berkley gives the character everything she has as an actress, the film, in conception, does not like Nomi, and does not want the audience to like her, either. Our task is to try and do so anyway, because she is the center of the film and she's not positioned as a villain.

This confusion is the essence of watching *Showgirls*. The messages the screenplay, the director, and the actress send to the audience regarding Nomi and what we should feel and think about her are wholly contradictory. One minute I'm repelled by her, and the next I'm giggling along with her. It's the cinematic equivalent of having a friend with borderline personality disorder.

Showgirls tells me I'm supposed to dislike Nomi, but I can't. A similar confusion wracks *Staying Alive*: the film tells me I'm supposed to love Tony, but I can't. The characters have a lot in common—self-interest, manipulation and sabotage of those around them, dance ambition. But one is a woman written by a man and the other is a man written by a man.

The burden of all character inconsistency in these films falls on the viewer. What am I supposed to think of these people? Do I love them, hate them, or love to hate them? They are erratic, often mean. The films' sympathies twist my reactions into strange shapes due to these inconsistencies.

FINALE: BECKONING WITH THE BIRD

I elected to write about these movies because they fail, and I wouldn't have written thousands of words about them if I thought their failures made them unworthy of study. When films with all the resources to succeed nevertheless fail, the result nearly always intrigues me. It's an engine I want to disassemble to see how that failure happened. These two films fail in many of the same ways, but the fun of that failure arrives much sooner in one film than the other.

The best worst part of *Staying Alive* is its final set piece, the performance of *Satan's Alley*, a show even stupider than *Goddess*. *Showgirls*, meanwhile, indicates its outlandishness in the first few minutes, when Nomi pulls a switchblade on Pickup Truck Guy (Dewey Weber) for no reason. It makes camp much faster than *Alive* does.

My argument as a critic is that *Showgirls* teaches me (accurately) how to watch it almost immediately. This Nomi person is cuckoo, living on Planet Verhoeven, where everything is brightly colored, electrically charged, and probably a little coked up. None of the characters will make any sense, and the film will only work if I figure out what it's satirizing. If I don't, it'll punish and confuse me for two hours.[3]

Staying Alive instructs me, in its first few minutes, that it's a dance movie with no aesthetic sense of itself as a dance movie.[4] It's the 80s, so everyone will be skinny, move quickly, and say nothing of consequence. The film either wants to seduce me or it doesn't care what I think, and it's so shallow I'll break my nose if I try to dive into it. Only the frenzied Frank Stallone song hints at the fun of the finale, 75 long minutes ahead.

Listening to a movie's instructions about itself helps me to read it better, but it rarely transmogrifies a failed film into a successful one. *Showgirls* was a confusing experience for me from the first time I watched it; I knew something was wrong with how the movie presented itself, but I didn't know what it was. *Staying Alive* was funnier and less hostile, but gave me the same sensation. I finally landed on the major problem with both these films—the sociopathic inconsistency of

SHOWGIRLS/CAROLCO PICTURES/UNITED ARTISTS

the characters—after watching Laura spit "We met, I liked you, we made it" to Tony for the umpteenth time. The films share an unusual failure, and those are always more interesting to study than the normal kind (lack of resources, poor conception, bad acting, et cetera).

If there's one image that sums up both films' downfall, it appears in *Showgirls*, when Nomi storms onto the stage for her first number at the Cheetah. She extends the middle finger of her right hand and wiggles it back and forth, for just a moment, before wrapping that arm around her body. She

---

3 Nayman on *Showgirls* and Verhoeven's *Starship Troopers* (1997): "they simultaneously fully inhabit and mercilessly satirize their respective genres, duly delivering the goods while playing up their toxicity." I find this true for *RoboCop* as well.
4 For instance, the credits sequence imitates the cattle-call sequence of *All That Jazz* without understanding it. I wrote and removed a 250-word footnote about this and eventually made a YouTube video to explain.

moves her tongue at the same time, so I could read this as a lesbian come-on, or an imitation of a specific male kink. But I like to think of it as Nomi flipping the bird and come-hither-ing us at the same time. *Fuck you, come fuck me.* That's Nomi all over, and it's Tony, too, and Laura, and Cristal.

It's senseless to fault fictional characters for not being likeable, not being people I'd want to be friends with in real life. But Eszterhas, and the writing team behind *Staying Alive*, had a minimal responsibility to write characters who acted with consistency, even if that consistency was villainous or dull. Without this quality in protagonists, and in at least some of the supporting characters, a movie will push and pull on the viewer too simultaneously, confusing and alienating everyone. Gender comes into play when considering the failures of both films, but the essential problem is character. Tony is written lazily, relying on external factors to keep me in favor of him instead of rejecting him. Nomi is written with misogyny aforethought, her actions unrecognizable to actual human women. The loyal followers (Jackie and Molly) of these two baffle me, and their enemies (everybody else?) act too inconsistently for me to take a firm stance. The supporting characters dance to the tune of convenience, offering information andjudgment beyond the boundaries of what's in the movie (Jesse saying Tony and Laura are two different kinds of people, for instance, or James coming to Nomi's door and telling her she has talent), then turning mean for no reason so we'll pity our hero/ine.

These are not understandable failures to write sophisticated characters who will live long in my memory. *Any* fictional characters require consistency basic enough for the audience to get involved in the story—to forget they're watching a film for a little while. That is not a lot to ask. When, in the final set piece of *Staying Alive*, Laura extends an olive branch to Tony and then immediately tells him "You don't have it," I think, *this person does not act like a person*, and I lose a little more investment in the film. Bad film always does this, always shows its seams, and these two films have the same crooked hems.

WHAT WE LIKE:

SAFE HAVEN AND
GIRL IN GOLD BOOTS

SAFE HAVEN (2013) IS A Nicholas Sparks film adaptation about a young woman who escapes an abusive marriage and tries to start over in a coastal Southern town. It was critically trounced and eventually featured on the How Did This Get Made? podcast, which tends to cover terrible movies. At regular intervals across the running time, including in its last five minutes, the film feeds new information to the audience that rejiggers everything that's come before. Typically you could call these handfuls of info "twists," but in *Safe Haven*, these moves are more like readjusting the camera, so as to see prior scenes from a different angle. The final adjustment of this kind is so preposterous that it alienated critics, even made them angry.

I loved it. I loved the excessive audience manipulation *Safe Haven* performed, and I loved its wildly melodramatic twists and turns, and I loved how thoroughly emotional the whole enterprise was. So many scenes turned on how a character felt rather than what the character did. I suppose that's how romances are supposed to work—how, generally, entertainment geared toward women is supposed to work. Play on human feelings rather than lust for power or money.

It worked on me.

When I first watched *Safe Haven*, I was embarrassed, because I could feel its manipulations affecting me even as I observed them. Katie (Julianne Hough) was written to capture my sympathy even as I wondered about her missing pieces. Check. Alex (Josh Duhamel) was written to be a nonthreatening romantic lead, irresistibly handsome and trustworthy. Check. The plot that revolves around them was written to keep my attention: to balance enigma and appeal well enough that I would understand everything that occurred and wouldn't walk away before the last reel. Checkmate.

I hated that I'd fallen in lockstep with what this movie wanted me to think and feel. It seemed like I'd lost some kind of battle against unworthy art. *Safe Haven* is a predictable romantic drama that preserves the status quo artistically and has nothing whatsoever to say politically. Aside from its twists, it's average in every possible way: competently made, pretty enough in setting, with a fair cast and acceptable dialogue. It does not deserve to rise to the top of the heap, nor sink to the bottom. A Sunday afternoon watch on basic cable, or what Michael Adams calls a "bus movie."

Somehow, I've watched *Safe Haven* a half-dozen times. It isn't layered enough to require two viewings, and yet I bought the Blu-Ray when I saw it was going off Netflix. It's a movie I like watching when I want something middle-of-the-road that will entertain me in a slightly askew way. The final twist always makes me cackle.

I understand *Safe Haven*'s appeal to me. Its averageness offers me an undemanding two hours, while its drama and romance give me controlled spikes of feeling. It's…safe. A safe movie. Any safer and I'd find it bland; any sharper and I'd have to study it. I still feel that I've lost something every time I watch it, because it's so thoroughly intended to pass the time, not to tick boxes for a critic and student of film like me. But I figure that being able to see how it affects me, even if I can't escape those effects, is an okay consolation prize.

This could go on for thousands more words, where I explain what *Safe Haven* does to me as a viewer, I acknowledge it as perfectly medium-flavored, I demonstrate exactly where it lives in the hierarchy of art and product, so on, so on. What I want to move on to talk about is *not defending* this movie. Because I won't. Anyone can throw a virtual tomato at me and yell that *Safe Haven* is terrible, and I'll wipe the juice off and say yes, it is. I won't reclaim this movie, I won't analyze it in light of an obscure literary theory to explain the secret value it has, I won't pretend it has a special quality that other films lack. None of that holds water.

I advance, instead, that my fondness for *Safe Haven* says very little about me as a critic or thinker. It's not a guilty pleasure or a weakness. This movie hits me a certain way, for whatever reason. I'm not a shitty person, and I can still distinguish good art from bad art.

*   *   *

This whole line of thought started because I couldn't figure out why I liked an even worse movie, *Girl in Gold Boots* (1968). It's a grimy little movie that revolves around go-go dancing, no redeeming value to it whatsoever, and yet every time I watch it I feel warmth in the cold celluloid chamber that passes for my heart. I love things about it without irony, without precisely laughing at them (or with them), and for months I tried to figure out why. Nothing about the film fit into meaningful spaces in my psyche, and nothing about it was moving or effective despite its humble origin.

Eventually I figured out that I just liked it, the same way I like macaroni & cheese—uncomplicatedly, without reservation or explanation. Then I went through a phase of anxiety that this preference meant something significant and negative about me as a critic or even as a human being. That vaguely didn't make sense; nevertheless, I had the urge to protest, to either defend *Girl in Gold Boots* as somehow artistically worthy or to insist that I didn't *really* like it. But neither of those premises is true.

Some significant part of the problem is a false equivalence between high aesthetic value and high moral value, and how those values are sponged up and squeezed out by those who assess them. If a work of art is of high aesthetic value, the person who appreciates it must have good taste. Someone of good taste must (somehow) be a good person. Someone who does not appreciate a work of art with high aesthetic value is not a good person, or at least not a good person to spend time with. I don't know how it came to pass that those who like museums are necessarily good people, while those who

GIRL IN GOLD BOOTS/GENENI FILM DISTRIBUTORS

like NASCAR are necessarily bad. Seems likely that the arbiters of high taste in our current cultural landscape have made it so, because it grants them moral authority they cannot attain any other way.

Another part is the way cultural crit happens on the internet, which nurtures reactivity rather than contemplation and snappiness rather than nuance. As Jessa Crispin puts it in a March 2022 essay for the Baffler:

> Liking or disliking a cultural object on social media often serves as a stand-in for a bald statement of your political affiliation, your educational background, or your place in the social hierarchy.

In the same way that hats (red or pink) came to be metonyms for the wearer's political values in the late 2010s, my favorite movies can tell you how well-educated I am and how much we agree. If I'm not well-educated and we don't agree, per my list of favorites, you will dismiss me as an idiot and/or find me morally unsound, particularly if we're both on Twitter.

Yet the internet is the fastest, easiest way to be heard. And all cultural critics desire to be heard. So, if I like a thing, I ought to be ready to defend liking it, on penalty of disgrace. This leads me to try and find aesthetic value in the thing. Even an outlandish theory about a thing's aesthetic value has more heft than saying "I like this thing, even though it's terrible, and I don't know why." My defense has to persuade strangers, so I begin by persuading myself: *Girl in Gold Boots* must have some aesthetic value under the surface, some hidden sublimity that no one has yet seen. If I find it, if I defend the piece, I can defend my taste, and thus myself.

If I find no aesthetic value in the thing, if I determine it is indefensible, then I'm really in a pickle. I succumb to self-doubt. I must have bad taste if I like *Girl in Gold Boots*. If I have bad taste, I am a bad person, a Mountain Dew-swilling, Trans Am-driving, *Honey Boo Boo*-watching moron who could not recognize art if it was drawn on the back of her hand.

But here's the thing: what we like is illogical. What we enjoy is shapeless, patternless. Our passions are a gerrymandered Southern voting district. I like Mozart and Melville, but I also like the Kentucky Derby. *We like what stimulates us in ways we prefer.* That sounds too weak and generic to be a significant conclusion, but preferred stimulation varies so greatly that I can't be much more specific. For some people, it's an experimental novel that totally befuddles them (my friend Chris) while for others, it's a mediocre movie that makes them laugh (my friend Carrie). For me, sometimes, it pushes the limits of what I can stand to watch (*Audition* [1999]) and other times, it gives me uncomplicated joy (*Singin' in the Rain*). Sometimes it's *Safe Haven*. Sometimes it's Tarkovsky. There's no sense to what stimulates us, no containment for this quality inside a recognizable polygon.

What we like is instinctive, not rational. Applying my rational skill as a critic to what I like for irrational reasons has led me to confusion, not clarity. The more I try to rationalize my enjoyment of *Girl in Gold Boots*, the more entangled I get in the kind of philosophizing I left behind years ago to write about film. It's easier to accept the following: I like it, I can't defend it, it's bad, and I am not bad for liking it.

These statements don't contradict each other. We like what we like.

✳   ✳   ✳

In episode 909 of *Mystery Science Theater 3000*, Leonard Maltin guest-stars. This is shocking enough, as *MST3K* almost never had guest stars of any kind, but at the time, anyone with half an eye on film journalism would have recognized him instantly. *MST3K* was exceptionally unpretentious, and the work it did seemed to live in a separate bubble from the work done by Maltin or Siskel & Ebert or Gene Shalit or any other 1990s television critic. It's weird to see Maltin show up on

MYSTERY SCIENCE THEATER 3000/SHOUT FACTORY

MST3K because *MST3K* and its chosen films exist in a different ecosystem than movies made by rich studios and given wide release.

This seems like a mistaken thing to write, as plenty of *MST3K* movies were produced by and for the mainstream in their day, and only became risible by virtue of passed time and altered context. A few football players showed up at the party these A/V nerds threw from 1988-1998, but they tended to have graduated 20 years prior.

Some folks insisted on reverence, anyway. Vintage film lovers criticized the creative team behind *MST3K* for choosing *This Island Earth* to riff in *Mystery Science Theater 3000: The Movie*, protesting that *This Island Earth* isn't really that bad. This judgment isn't right or wrong; *This Island Earth* is a good film for *MST3K* because the crew was able to write 90 minutes of decent jokes about it without flat-out insulting the film or anyone in it.

This is also true of *Girl in Gold Boots* (a terrible movie I love, riffed in 1999) and *Casablanca* (a great movie I don't much like, riffed in 2009).

So, Leonard Maltin, looking quite famous compared to everyone else in the frame, shows up in *MST3K* #909, which riffs *Gorgo* (1961). He says a sentence I haven't been able to get out of my brain for years: "Well, I actually like *Gorgo*."

I actually like Gorgo.

How could a man whose job is to assess film, a man who has seen so many thousands of movies the mind boggles, a man whose name was synonymous with an assessment the public can trust—how can this man like *Gorgo*? It's a mess of a film, a mishmash of *King Kong* and *Godzilla* with dull writing, muddled scenes, and a totally unsurprising plot. What could he possibly mean when he says he likes it?

(What could I mean when I say I like *Girl in Gold Boots*?)

I've contemplated this sentence of Maltin's for years. Eventually I figured out that he doesn't necessarily mean the movie is good. He means he likes it. Assessing it as an audience member uses a different set of muscles than assessing it as a film critic.

I came to know this well as a book critic, finding I had a weakness for novels of any quality with Gothic elements and that I could not stand character studies or epic fantasy. When assigned books like this, I tried to give them a professional assessment, tried not to let my personal preferences get in the way: "unless the reader has a taste for the Gothic, this book may fall flat" or "epic fantasy fans will love the length and detail of this series," for example.

I doubt Leonard Maltin considered it part of his core identity that he liked *Gorgo*. And he says nothing specific to defend the film. Not that he needed to, in those days, or in that context. Had he tweeted this opinion, things might have been different. He might have found himself defending *Gorgo* with his entire reputation, trying to locate merit in the film that doesn't necessarily exist just to quiet the cacophony of replies. By the 1990s, though, Maltin would not have succumbed to the kind of self-doubt I had when I thought about my affinity for *Girl in Gold Boots*. He'd had enough validation from the world for his taste in film. He had no mental Twitterverse to keep him nervous, to worry him into perplexity for liking a movie he knew with his critical mind was bad. His peanut gallery remained distant, shouting through layers of institutional protection.

Now, with the internet, our preferences as critics ooze out of our personalities and muddy up our professional lives. We must not merely like what we like, but feel devotion to what we like, mount half-baked defenses of what we like. If I like *This Island Earth*, I must believe it to be unriffable. But almost no art is so totally unimpeachable. *Schindler's List*, maybe.

I've argued elsewhere that *MST3K*'s method engages with movies rather than mocking them, and this is part of why it's strange and silly to me that fans of *This Island Earth* were offended by its getting the treatment. Those fans took it personally, I suspect. They believed that the *MST3K* treatment reduced down to mocking, and thus, the *MST3K* team was mocking *them*. They enlarged the importance of their enjoyment of *This Island Earth*, and came to believe that defending *This Island Earth* meant defending their taste in film. If they were invested enough in that taste, the mocking extended to an aspect of their identity.

This is largely speculation, but I'm using the incident as an example. I don't understand why people attempt to reclaim art that's been pigeonholed or dismissed in some way—most particularly, when they do this for art that was assessed correctly the first time, or that has other forms of power than pure artistic value. In my view, *Heaven's Gate* does not require defense, because it's a huge mess, pedigree be damned. Lisa Frank designs do not require defense for their aesthetic integrity, because they were produced for money and simple pleasure, not museum walls. The best thing to do when confronting work like this is to like it (or not) and let it go, not twist oneself into a pretzel trying to defend it. You will not convince me that *Waterworld* is good, and there is no need to try.

*   *   *

My view about all this is why the work of Pauline Kael and Jeffrey Sconce helped me so little when I set out to write about bad film. In "Trash, Art, and the Movies" and "Trashing the Academy," these highly qualified and thoughtful critics are talking about something different than I've been talking about this whole time. They seek to find the good in the bad: to explain how bad film is psychologically meaningful to audiences and how it has influenced good filmmakers.[1] There's also a kind of glee inherent in enjoying something related to one's job without having to take it very seriously.

Kael famously wrote that critics with similar tastes "know each other at once because you talk less about good movies than about what you love in bad movies," a statement totally without use to my project here. "What I love in bad movies" is on a different vector from what I'm writing about. I don't love *Attack of the 50 Ft. Woman*, nor *After Last Season*, nor the Teen Agers movies. They fascinate me, they wake up my brain, they make me ask passels of questions, but I don't love them—I don't find the sublime in them, the way I find the sublime in Michael Bay and Buster Keaton. If I've interpreted Kael and Sconce correctly, they are attempting to pluck the rose from the dumpster: to find the sublime in the terrible. They argue that these movies have worth and value, in a Kantian sense, for roughly the same reasons the films of Bergman and Kubrick have worth and value—if in very different proportions.

My argument is that the worth and value of bad movies is wholly different from the worth and value of good movies. To consider them from a Kantian base, in which good art is the only desirable kind of art, is to mistake the whole endeavor of studying bad film: it lifts them up to where the critic wants them to be, rather than crawling into the dumpster where they live. Kael's claim and mine that bad movies are worth watching are the same, but they come from utterly different whys. In the

---

1 I veered into this when writing about Tarantino for Andrew J. Rausch and Kieran Fisher's *Pulp Cinema* (forthcoming as of this writing); grindhouse schlock and French New Wave have influenced him about equally, with the edge going slightly to grindhouse, I think.

preceding book, I've defended *Death Bed* and *Switchblade Sisters*, because I believe those movies largely hold up to a Kantian approach. But the rest of the films don't. Their indefensibility is precisely why I believe they are worthy of study. My first step is not defending what's good about them, but acknowledging what's bad. All the films' qualities open up with this approach, instead of many aspects closing down as not of use to the defending critic.

This distinguishes my project from the craft of reclaiming, which minimizes or rebuts the art's poor reputation for perverse or personal reasons; and the project of Kael and Sconce, which acknowledges the art's bad qualities while seeking to celebrate what's good about it. My stance is to *focus* on the art's bad qualities, to analyze them almost exclusively. I don't know that many other critics have approached bad art in this way. It's why I've had a hard time in some bad movie communities, because they tend to elevate the art a la Kael rather than recognizing that it's in a dumpster for a reason.

I'm interested in how much mediocre art is beloved by audiences and trounced by critics, which is part of Kael's calculation, but my Teen Agers essay, examining what kinds of art are built to be disposable, is about as far as I want to go down that road. I'm also interested in how bad art intermittently steps across the border of good art, how, as Stan Brakhage proposed, almost any film bears in it the fingerprint of the sublime.[2] I find this truth everywhere in film, everywhere, from the dumpsters to the Oscars. But Kael and Sconce are doing that work and don't need my help.

And I cannot emphasize enough that calling a movie "bad," in this book, or anywhere you find me, does not mean that I'm scorning the movie. No moral judgment occurs in my calculation, and I make no kind of judgment of a movie's loving audience when I call it bad. In my mind, there's a significant gap between the terms "judgment" and "assessment" when I think about a film's qualities, and what I do is assess: here is how the film stacks up against the sprawl of hundreds of films I've seen, many dozens of books I've read about film, the conversations and instructions of a lifetime. I'm not a robot, of course, and biases factor in somewhere. But I don't see this process as me slamming down a gavel to send a movie or its fans to artistic or moral jail. I want to see what I can learn from badness, and I approach that lightly, not with condemnation in my heart.

*   *   *

You may thus understand why *Girl in Gold Boots* confused me so much when I decided to write about it under the umbrella of this project. I assessed it as bad, top to tail, but I felt myself wanting to defend it, as I'd defended *Ruby*. I had no reason

---

2 I cannot prove how and when he said this. The notion was introduced to me about 20 years ago in a classroom. I remember distinctly that the professor was quoting Brakhage in saying any movie ever made has something sublime in it (and boy, how people have tried to resist this point whenever I've made it!), but I have no idea in which of his many books he may have written it or what caveats or limits he may have put upon the statement.

to like it, and no basis for reclaiming it, aside from a thin anthropological one. A more innately provocative critic might choose to reclaim it anyway, conjuring subjective or intellectually dishonest arguments about the positive value of *Girl in Gold Boots*, but I could not. Especially considering Ted V. Mikels's other films, which I find unusually misogynist, even for the era and context.

I actually like Gorgo, Leonard Maltin whispered to me.

You'll note that I still haven't written significantly about *Girl in Gold Boots* in these thousands of words. I can tell you the scenes I like most, and the scenes that make me laugh, but these are largely useless pieces of information. Nothing about my affection for this movie is critically or morally significant. It merely exists.

My job in this book was to assess and understand *good* and *bad* in certain films well enough to analyze the usefulness of *bad*. When I put those restraints on my approach to *Girl in Gold Boots*, the film vanishes from the ordinary run of essays in this project. It's not useful. I don't understand what's "good" about it, in that I don't even understand what's good about it *to me*. It's notable that I like this bad movie without finding it a good subject for an essay on its uses; I've transmogrified that fact into an essay that meditates on a whole bunch of ideas underlying this project as well as the work of other bad film scholars. It was not *Girl in Gold Boots* or *Safe Haven* that inspired these ideas; the films unearthed what was wriggling around underneath the project all along.

I find myself thinking about John Keats: "I mean Negative Capability, that is when man is capable of being in uncertainties, Mysteries, doubts, without any irritable reaching after fact & reason." Or, as Maria Popova paraphrases the idea, "the willingness to embrace uncertainty, live with mystery, and make peace with ambiguity."[3] It may seem foolish for me to reference one of the grandest ideas in the philosophy of aesthetics to finish out a book about bad movies, but that's precisely how I feel about *Girl in Gold Boots*: I like it and it is bad, and both of these things are true, which is a mystery.

This is not true for most of the other films in this book, for which I can delineate all kinds of theories and fit them into an aesthetic and/or popular context. But I like *Boots*. I just like it. As much as I try to philosophize about taste and art, with certain movies, this is all I can do. Live with mystery. Make peace with ambiguity. Analyze when possible, and leave the rest up to you.

---

3 Her paraphrase and Keats's original quote from *The Marginalian*: https://www. themarginalian.org/2012/11/01/john-keats-on-negative-capability/.

NOTES/BIBLIOGRAPHY

THIS SECTION IS NOT set up like a traditional bibliography (sorry, Mom). Notes on the essays up front, detailed biblio at the end. To save annoyance, I did not include credits for the self-evident films in this project, like *Staying Alive* or *Death Bed*. I only list credits for the films and clips I used as background, in the hope that that information might be useful to someone else researching any of this.

General Notes

Something crucial to explain in a book about bad movies is that the information available on them is necessarily less, and less reliable, than information available on good movies. The kinds of archives that help biographers and critics write confidently about major figures and films from cinema history just don't exist for most bad movies. No one thinks these films matter at the time (and often not later, either), so the usual documents about them get discarded or lost. Writers must rely on oral histories rather than studio production notes or carefully preserved correspondence; oral histories self-contradict and decay with human memory. Hence, for example, it's *probable* that Ed Wood used piano wire to dangle the toy flying saucers over the cloud backdrop in *Plan 9*, based on the predominant memories of the people Rudolph Grey interviewed for *Nightmare of Ecstasy*, but it's not *certain*. That disclaimer goes for all my essays about these movies. I used what information was available, and in many cases, that information is less than ideal as the backbone for a well-researched nonfiction book, even if it's a book of subjective criticism. Happily do I declare I'm a poor researcher anyway, so to write about bad movies is quite comfortable for my conscience.

If you liked this book at all, please read *The Disaster Artist*, by Greg Sestero and Tom Bissell. It's essential for the library of any bad movie lover, and it's an extraordinary book on its own merits.

Of general use to me throughout the years I worked on this project were two books: *Showgirls, Teen Wolves, and Astro Zombies* by Michael Adams, and *The Bad Movie Bible* by Rob Hill. Adams's book is closer to a critic's novelty than a useful resource. He maintains a snarky tone throughout and I found myself disagreeing with some of his assessments. But his project is rare. Hill's is a fun book, without which I never would have seen *After Last Season*. It was a treat to agree or disagree with Hill's number system and to discover worthy movies I hadn't known about. He did steer me wrong on a few things; like Adams, he has virtually no nose for intolerable misogyny.

The splendid, massive volume *Nightmare USA*, by Stephen Thrower, was of most use to me when writing about *Death Bed*, but it also offered me reassurance that I was not the only person in the world who cared about bad film and wanted *Junk Film* to exist. If you care about exploitation film at all, acquire this book. It's well worth the price tag.

Certain resources were of surprisingly little use, particularly "Trash, Art, and the Movies" by Pauline Kael and "Notes on 'Camp'" by Susan Sontag. These are famous, but did not align with my thinking on bad art. Other books about "bad" movies (*Sleaze Artists*, *B Is for Bad Cinema*) don't have a lot in common with my project here. Philosopher Matthew Strohl, in *Why It's OK to Love Bad Movies*, offers an analysis of bad film that overlaps (somewhat reassuringly) with mine, and is extremely useful at defining broad terms like "good" and "bad" and using ideas from contemporary aesthetics to support his conclusions. But he does not approach the question of bad movies from a film studies background, and we have opposing opinions on *MST3K*. I loved Graydon Clark's self-published book about his dubious career in film; however, it offered me fodder for podcast interviews and the like, not useful reference information in writing this book.

Most of the ordinary facts in the essays (filmographies, release dates, etc.) came from Wikipedia or IMDB. I take responsibility for errors, but not for inconsistences, for the reasons above.

Specific details lie below.

Plan 9 from Outer Space

Of the half-dozen books on Ed Wood, I most recommend *The Cinematic Misadventures*. It collects a wealth of information, interviews, pictures, and commentary about Wood's *entire* career, including his paperback porn writing (which most folks leave out). *Nightmare of Ecstasy* is a standby, and with good reason, but it's an oral history, not precisely a research piece. I don't recommend Wood's own book, *Hollywood Rat Race*, which is dated, rambling, sexist, and sometimes bitter.

In the course of promoting the standalone book version of this essay that came out with PS Publishing, I was asked dozens of different questions about Ed Wood, so there's no way I can address them all here. I will say that people often read into Wood what they'd like to, not understanding the alcoholic/hustler/problematic dude he really was. Burton's movie did the truth a disservice in this regard. I'm not exactly upset about this, because it hardly matters; the misguided optimism and open heart Burton attributed to Wood are uniquely appealing, and that character has brought happiness to many misfits out there. But I sometimes feel the need to correct the record, to say that Wood was not a tolerant man, that he hurt and took advantage of a lot of the people who surrounded him, and that he never cut his losses after repeatedly chasing his dreams down the wrong ro ads.

Watching *Plan 9* is extremely easy, as the film is in the public domain. Unless you're seeing it in a theater, I would not spend money to do so. Even the colorized version is fine.

Cop Rock

The whole series is conveniently available on a single DVD set from Shout Factory. Stephen Thomas Erlewine's tour de force review of *Girl You Know It's True* is still available on Allmusic.com as of this writing. I watched interviews with Steven Bochco and Mike Post, the show's music supervisor, on YouTube. I believe there is no other critical writing on this series, but I would love to be wrong.

Switchblade Sisters

The comparison of this film's plot to *Othello*'s is not my innovation, but Jack Hill's. I believe he shared this in a group interview with Joanne Nail and Robbie Lee, a DVD special feature which I watched on YouTube, but I may have gotten it from a trivia page or similar. There is a good deal of pop work on this film, as it's a favorite film of Quentin Tarantino, whose fans tend to be almost as verbose as he is. I ignored pretty much all of this and focused on the film.

My work on *Switchblade Sisters* was likely bolstered by research on exploitation and rape-revenge films I did for a separate project. I don't think that research was influential enough for me to include the books I consulted in the bibliography that follows, but the work of scholars Carol J. Clover, Claire Henry, and Alexandra Heller-Nicholas did, in a sideways manner, contribute to my respect for Hill's brand of feminism.

Penn and Ros

It has been one of the great pleasures of my life to introduce people to Amanda McKittrick Ros. Publishing this essay in this collection furthers that pleasure so much I can barely contain my glee.

Mark O'Connell introduced me to Ros in 2013, in Slate. He has moved on, but I have not; it's possible to trace my entire interest in criticism on bad art back to that very article. I will be grateful to him forever.

Ros wrote three novels: *Irene Iddesleigh*, *Delina Delaney*, and *Helen Huddleson*. The first is available on Project Gutenberg, while the other two are more difficult to find. *Thine in Storm and Calm*, a short compendium edited by Frank Ormsby of Ros's prose, poetry, and correspondence, as well as other treats, is highly recommended, if you can find it. A charming biography of Ros, *O Rare Amanda!* by Jack Loudan, has been out of print for some years, but may be available in libraries and sometimes at AbeBooks.

Penn published a second book in late 2019, *Bob Honey Sings Jimmy Crack Corn*. I have not read it, and will not do so unless someone pays me.

The Teen Agers

For this essay I am particularly indebted to Pam Munter's 2005 study of the Teen Agers. She did a great deal of research I would have been incapable of doing, and she assembled information from primary sources that might otherwise have been lost forever. Her book is the only one I'm aware of that addresses the Teen Agers movies and cast so specifically and thoroughly. There exist books about Monogram and Poverty Row, but Munter read them for me and restated the information I needed.

I consulted Thomas Doherty's *Teenagers and Teenpics* in case he had already written about the Teen Agers, but he mentions them on just one page.

The films themselves can be elusive. The first four have been riffed by Bridget Nelson and Mary Jo Pehl for RiffTrax. I could not definitively determine whether the other four were in the public domain or not. They appear and disappear from YouTube sometimes. Some are available for purchase on "classic DVD" websites where folks who have access to archives of obscure cinema—I don't know how or why—burn movies to DVD-Rs and ship them to you for a low cost. This practice might not be strictly legal, but then, it might, as the copyright status of these films is unclear to me. Who could possibly be losing money on piracy of such films is similarly unclear.

Best F(r)iends

If you're reading this book, you've probably already seen *The Room*, but if you haven't, it's unmissable. I am not talking about *Room*, with Brie Larson. (I am never talking about *Room*, with Brie Larson.) Theater screenings of *The Room* are *Rocky Horror Picture Show*-type events, at all levels of frequency in all kinds of locations, but I also recommend the home theater experience. Have a friend with you; *The Room* is a lot less fun alone.

Since I wrote this essay, Greg Sestero has gone on to direct a film of his own, *Miracle Valley*. Tommy Wiseau is not in it. Justin MacGregor has directed another film with Sestero, *The Founder Effect*, which is in post-production as of this writing. I can't wait to see it.

As for Wiseau…who's to say what he'll do next?

Death Bed

Researching *Death Bed* made me stumble on a huge underworld of commentators interested in, and even obsessed with, exploitation films from the late 20th century. The best book about this is *Nightmare USA*. Stephen Thrower's opinion of *Death Bed* is quite close to my own, and an interview with George Barry takes up several large pages of the book.

I spent years hunting for a book called *Gods in Polyester* that's about the 1970s in film. George Barry has an essay in it. Over a year after I'd finished working on *Death Bed*, I finally found a copy of the book on eBay and paid an obscene amount of money for it, only to discover that Barry's essay neither adds nor subtracts anything from my analysis. This is good, I guess, because it meant I didn't have to revise the essay. The only thing that really changed for me was learning the film was mostly shot in 1972, which was quite a different moment in a turbulent decade than the film's official release year of 1977. Thankfully I didn't hang anything of essence on that information. (Anyone else out there who's hungering for *Gods in Polyester*, I'm sorry to report that it's great, and has piles of firsthand information on exploitation film of the 1970s.)

The film is readily available in digital and physical formats, and often shows up on YouTube. Please do yourself a favor and see it.

After Last Season

I'm indebted to online sources for, first, assuring me that this film does exist and is not a fever dream, and second, offering me commentary, context, and hard information, as much as can be had.

Aside from entries in the Hill and Adams books, the only critical work on this film in print that I'm aware of is an article in *Cashiers du Cinemart*, which is essentially a zine, by Jim Donahue. At first it does the same thing as other work on the movie: bafflement that *Season* exists, attempting to convey what the viewing experience is like, etc. It then offers interviews with the actors that shape an oral history of the film, explaining how terrible filming conditions were and how odd the whole endeavor was. This was useful background and inspired tremendous sympathy for everyone in the production who was not the director.

The film itself is not available for legal purchase or viewing.

Attack of the 50 Ft. Woman

This film is part of the massive cycle of 1950s monster movies, and there has been a *lot* of work about that, but I wasn't going to go through it all to prove or disprove what I believe to be a relatively simple thesis. (As I said, I am a poor researcher and comfortable with it.) Hannah Walhout's excellent essay about this film (online at Catapult) is one of the only sources I consulted. I found the HBO remake on YouTube, but it's also available on DVD.

Neil Breen

Breen's films are easiest to acquire from the man himself, via his website. The cost is unusually high, and he has yanked a couple of them from circulation altogether. Two of the films are digitally for sale on Amazon's Prime service as of this writing.

The online ecosystem of Breen fandom is a remarkable place; Reddit is of great help.

Ruby

Ruby is fairly easy to find on home video formats. All the other films and books mentioned in this one are in circulation. Curtis Harrington's memoir is somewhat hard to find in print, but readily available as an ebook.

Showgirls/Staying Alive

There's quite a lot of critical work on *Showgirls*—enough that, as I wrote in the essay, I felt overwhelmed at the idea of reading enough to feel genuinely informed. My version of feeling ready to write this essay came from watching most of Verhoeven's American filmography and, for my taste, too many Eszterhas-penned films.

The documentary *You Don't Nomi* synthesizes a lot of information and critical perspectives on the film, and is also wonderfully entertaining. I cannot more highly recommend Jeffery Conway's book of sestinas on the film, which did little good for me as a research tool but gave me a loving perspective I could not otherwise have had. Michael Nayman's monograph on *Showgirls* is quite good, but also subjective in ways I found troubling. I wish he had dug deeper into how Molly's rape works in the film and on the audience, especially an audience of male viewers. My (unrelated) research on rape-revenge films made his squeamishness seem pointed, significant, to this feminist critic, and cast an interesting shadow on other ways he received the film.

I did not find any critical work on *Staying Alive*, although Stallone and Travolta's contemporary appearance on the Joan Rivers-hosted *Tonight Show* (on YouTube) proved revealing. For a separate project, I went down a major rabbit-hole in researching *Saturday Night Fever*, and the background information I got from reading Nik Cohn's original article for *New York* informed my perspective on Tony Manero's character in *Staying Alive*.

Safe Haven/Girl in Gold Boots

I'm grateful to the hosts of two (or three?) podcasts for which I recorded in early 2022, who patiently listened to me agonize about trying to write on *Girl in Gold Boots*. Mary Challman asked me especially useful questions.

For reasons that should be obvious in the essay, my research included *Sleaze Artists*, ed. Sconce, and *B is for Bad Cinema*, ed. Perkins and Verevis, but I did not find them useful. Sontag probably factored in here somewhere, too.

Girl in Gold Boots shows up on the lower tier of streaming services now and then (Tubi, Pluto), and I imagine it's on physical media somewhere, possibly in a Mikels collection. The *MST3K* episode of it is easy to acquire, but it was trimmed for television. *Safe Haven* is easily available on physical media and I'm sure it'll go on and off streaming as long as housewives like romantic movies.

I am always grateful to Matt, my husband, for his herculean support of my work. This essay in particular required his midwifery, in ways any sane person would find annoying.

Books/Articles

Brayton, Tim. "For every thing there is a season." Alternate Ending, October 26, 2021. https://www.alternateending.com/2021/10/after-last-season-2009.html

Clark, Greydon. *On the Cheap: My Life in Low Budget Filmmaking.* Self-published, 2013. Kindle edition.

Cohn, Nik. "Tribal Rites of the New Saturday Night." *New York* Magazine, June 7, 1976. Retrieved online: https://nymag.com/nightlife/features/45933/.

Conway, Jeffery. Showgirls: *The Movie in Sestinas.* Buffalo, NY: BlazeVOX [books], 2014.

Craig, Rob. *Ed Wood, Mad Genius: A Critical Study of the Films.* Jefferson, NC: McFarland & Company Publishers, 2009.

Crispin, Jessa. "Portals of Discovery." The Baffler (online), February 28, 2022. https://thebaffler.com/outbursts/portals-of-discovery-crispin

Doherty, Thomas. *Teenagers and Teenpics: The Juvenilization of American Movies in the 1950s.* Philadelphia: Temple University Press, 2002.

Donahue, Jim. "I've Never Been to That Movie But I've Been Through It: Deciphering *After Last Season." Cashiers du Cinemart* 17. Riverview, MI: Impossibly Funky Productions, 2012. Kindle edition.

Donahue, Suzanne and Sovijärvi, eds. *Gods in Polyester: A Survivors' Account of 70s Cinema Obscura.* Amsterdam: Succubus Press, 2004.

Erlewine, Stephen Thomas. "Girl You Know It's True Review." Allmusic.com, undated. https://www.allmusic.com/album/girl-you-know-its-true-mw0000199573.

Grey, Rudolph. *Nightmare of Ecstasy: The Life and Art of Edward D. Wood, Jr.* Los Angeles: Feral House, 1992.

Harrington, Curtis. *Nice Guys Don't Work in Hollywood: The Adventures of an Aesthete in the Movie Business.* Chicago: Drag City, 2013. pp. 187-189.

Kael, Pauline. "Trash, Art, and the Movies." *Harper's* Magazine, February 1969. Retrieved online: https://harpers.org/archive/1969/02/trash-art-and-the-movies/.

Laurie, Piper. *Learning to Live Out Loud: A Memoir.* New York: Crown Archetype, 2011. pp 272-273.

Macaulay, Scott. "Interview: *After Last Season's* Mark Region." Filmmaker Magazine, June 9, 2009. Retrieved online: https://filmmakermagazine.com/4211-interview-after-last-seasons-mark-region/.

Mason, Tom, ed. *Plan 9 from Outer Space: The Original Uncensored and Uncut Screenplay by Edward D. Wood, Jr.* Newbury Park, CA: Malibu Graphics, Inc., 1990.

Munter, Pam. *When Teens Were Keen: Freddie Stewart and the Teen Agers of Monogram.* Los Angeles: Nicholas Lawrence Books, 2005.

Nayman, Adam. *It Doesn't Suck:* Showgirls. 2nd edition. Toronto: ECW Press, 2018. Kobo edition.

O'Connell, Mark. "Amanda McKittrick Ros: The Worst Novelist in History." Slate, January 23, 2013. https://slate.com/culture/2013/01/was-amanda-mckittrick-ros-the-worst-novelist-in-history.html

Perkins, Claire and Constantine Verevis, eds. *B Is for Bad Cinema: Aesthetics, Politics, and Cultural Value*. Albany, NY: State University of New York Press, 2014.

Rausch, Andrew J. and Charles E. Pratt, Jr. *The Cinematic Misadventures of Ed Wood*. Albany, GA: BearManor Media, 2015.

Robinson, Justin. "Craig? Is That You, Craig?" The Satellite Show, September 20, 2013. https://satelliteshow.wordpress.com/2013/09/20/craig-is-that-you-craig/

Sconce, Jeffrey, ed. *Sleaze Artists: Cinema at the Margins of Taste, Style, and Politics*. Durham, NC: Duke University Press, 2007.

'Trashing' the Academy: Taste, Excess, and an Emerging Politics of Cinematic Style." Screen 36:4, Winter 1995. Retrieved online: https://marcell. memoryoftheworld.org/Jeffrey%20Sconce/Trashing%20the%20Academy%20 (2544)/Trashing%20the%20Academy%20-%20Jeffrey%20Sconce.pdf

Sontag, Susan. "Notes on 'Camp.'" *Partisan Review*, Fall 1964. Retrieved online: https://classes.dma.ucla.edu/Spring15/104/Susan%20Sontag_%20Notes%20 On%20-Camp-.pdf.

Strohl, Matthew. *Why It's OK to Love Bad Movies*. New York: Routledge, 2022.

Thrower, Stephen. *Nightmare USA: The Untold Story of the Exploitation Independents*. Godalming, Surrey: FAB Press Ltd, 2007.

Walhout, Hannah. "Attack of the Six-Foot Woman." Catapult, February 11, 2021. https://catapult.co/stories/attack-of-the-six-foot-woman_hannah_walhout_ 50_foot_woman_body_horror_tall_girl.

White, Richard. "The Imagined West." Chapter 21 of *"It's Your Misfortune and None of My Own": A New History of the American West*. University of Oklahoma Press, 1993. Chapter retrieved online: https://sites.evergreen.edu/western/wp-content/uploads/sites/85/2015/11/Richard_White-The_Imagined_West.pdf.

Wood, Edward D., Jr. *Hollywood Rat Race*. New York: Four Walls Eight Windows, 1998.

Films/Clips

Best Worst Movie. Directed by Michael Paul Stevenson. OJO Entertainment, 2009.

Ed Wood. Directed by Tim Burton. Touchstone Pictures, 1994.

Ed Wood: Look Back in Angora. Directed by Ted Newsom. Rhino Home Video, 1994.

Flying Saucers Over Hollywood: The Plan 9 Companion. Directed by Mark Patrick Carducci. Atomic Pictures, 1992.

You Don't Nomi. Directed by Jeffrey McHale. Grade Five Films/XYZ Films, 2019.

Interview: Jack Hill, Robbie Lee, Joanne Nail. Unknown provenance. https:// youtu.be/LBH2eKBDR1E.

Interview: Mike Post. Television Academy Foundation, May 25, 2005. https:// youtu.be/5gC6Y9orLsg.

Interview: Steven Bochco. Television Academy Foundation, May 21 and September 12, 2002. https://youtu.be/DxTRYfisPio.

Interview: Sylvester Stallone, John Travolta. *The Tonight Show*. July 8, 1983. Part One: https://youtu.be/rzuzXbZssrA. Part Two: https://youtu.be/cfOUsAlypIY.

ACKNOWLEDGEMENTS

GRATEFUL ACKNOWLEDGMENT IS MADE to the following publications, in which these essays appeared in slightly different form:

Plan 9 from Outer Space as a book and ebook published by Electric Dreamhouse Press/PS Publishing, November 2021.
"Never Explain How" on Medium.com, February 2022.
"Dual Plots, Demon Possession, De Palma" on Offscreen.com, June 2021.
"Something to Sing About" in Bright Lights Film Journal, May 2021.
"Intentionally Disposable Art" in Vague Visages, April 2021.
"Paratext, Bitches" in ASAP/J, April 2019.
"At the End of a Thousand Years" in the Millions, June 2018.

My gratitude to:

Jason Henderson.
In Churl Yo and Castle Bridge Media.
Neil Snowdon and everyone at PS. Matthew Desiderio. Jim Bland. Everyone at Barrelhouse, always. Andrew J. Rausch. Bill Corbett. John Scalzi.
Dana Gould.
Ilana Masad. Dan Pullen. Marissa Korbel. Gabriel Blackwell. Andrew Wyatt. Christopher Higgs.
Ty Burr. Mary Jo Pehl. Greg Sestero.
Paul A. Brooks. Bradley J. Kornish. David P. Geister, Scott Chesebrough, and Mary Challman. Trevor Young. Pete the Retailer and Alex Robinson, indirectly.
Quinn Hough. Lydia Kiesling. Abram Foley. Gary Morris. Donato Totaro.
Laura Usselman. Craig Hammill. Alexandra Heller-Nicholas. Erik Petersen.
Everyone on Twitter who has inspired me or cheered me on. Keep circulating the tapes (posting the gifs).

Matt above all, for the third time, and every time.

ABOUT THE AUTHOR

Katharine Coldiron is the author of *Ceremonials*, a novella inspired by Florence + the Machine. Her essays and criticism have appeared in *Ms.*, *Conjunctions*, *The Washington Post*, *The Guardian*, LARB, the Rumpus, and many other places. She earned a BA in film studies and philosophy from Mount Holyoke College, an MA in English from California State University, Northridge, and a PhD in parapsychology from the Institute of Metaphysical Humanistic Science (IMHS). Find her at kcoldiron.com or on Twitter @ferrifrigida.

CASTLE BRIDGE MEDIA RECOMMENDS...

If you liked this book, you might also enjoy reading the following titles from Castle Bridge Media available on Amazon or by order at your favorite book store:

Animal Charmer
By Rain Nox

Austinites
By In Churl Yo

Bloodsucker City
By Jim Towns

THE CASTLE OF HORROR ANTHOLOGY SERIES
Volume 1
Volume 2: Holiday Horrors
Volume 3: Scary Summer
  Stories
Volume 4: Women Running
  From Houses
Volume 5: Thinly Veiled:
  The 70s
Volume 6: Femme Fatales*
Volume 7: Love Gone Wrong
Volume 8: Thinly Veiled:
  The 80s
Volume 9: Young Adult
Edited By Jason Henderson
and In Churl Yo
*Edited By P.J. Hoover

*Castle of Horror Podcast
Book of Great Horror:
Our Favorites, Top Tens
and Bizarre Pleasures*
Edited By Jason Henderson

Dream State
By Martin Ott

FRENCH DECEPTION
A Forgery in Paris
By Janice Nagourney

FuturePast Sci-Fi Anthology
Edited by In Churl Yo

GLAZIER'S GAP
Ghosts of the Forbidden
By Leanna Renee Hieber

The Hermes Protocol
By Chris M. Arnone

Isonation
By In Churl Yo

*Junk Film: Why Bad
Movies Matter*
By Katharine Coldiron

MID-LIFE CRISIS THRILLERS
18 Miles From Town
By Jason Henderson
Lost Angel
By Sam Knight

*Nightwalkers: Gothic
Horror Movies*
By Bruce Lanier Wright

THE PATH
The Blue-Spangled Blue
By David Bowles
The Deepest Green
By David Bowles

SURF MYSTIC
Night of the Book Man
By Peyton Douglas
Dark of the Curl
By Peyton Douglas

*Yesterday's Tomorrows:
The Golden Age of
Science Fiction Movies*
By Bruce Lanier Wright

Please remember to leave us your reviews on Amazon and Goodreads!

THANK YOU FOR SUPPORTING INDEPENDENT PUBLISHERS AND AUTHORS!

castlebridgemedia.com

Printed in Dunstable, United Kingdom

66308924R00107